Risk-Taking in International Politics

Risk-Taking in International Politics

Prospect Theory in American Foreign Policy

ROSE MCDERMOTT

Ann Arbor

THE UNIVERSITY OF MICHIGAN PRESS

First paperback edition 2001
Copyright © by the University of Michigan 1998
All rights reserved
Published in the United States of America by
The University of Michigan Press
Manufactured in the United States of America
⊗ Printed on acid-free paper

2010   2009   2008   2007   6   5   4   3

A CIP catalog record for this book is available from the British Library.

Library of Congress Cataloging-in-Publication Data

McDermott, Rose, 1962–
    Risk-taking in international politics : prospect theory in
American foreign policy / Rose McDermott.
        p.   cm.
    Includes bibliographical references and index.
    ISBN 0-472-10867-0 (cloth : acid-free paper)
    1. United States—Foreign relations—Decision making.
2. International relations—Decision making.   3. Risk-taking
(Psychology)   I. Title.
JZ1480.M35   1998
327.73'001'9—dc21   97-21113
                                                               CIP

ISBN 0-472-08787-8 (pbk. : alk. paper)
ISBN 978-0-472-10867-1 (cloth : acid-free paper)
ISBN 978-0-472-08787-7 (pbk. : alk. paper)

For my mentors
Robert Jervis and Philip Zimbardo
with admiration, affection, and appreciation

Contents

Acknowledgments

This work would not have been possible without the sustained support and guidance of numerous friends and advisors. My most profound and overriding debts lie with my mentors, Robert Jervis and Philip Zimbardo, to whom this book is humbly dedicated. Robert Jervis's advice, insight, and support have critically informed every stage of this process. His integrity is unmatched, his loyalty unwavering, and his brilliance unsurpassed. Without his work, mine would not have been possible. Philip Zimbardo, in addition to triggering my initial interest in psychology, has been unfailing in his enthusiasm, unparalleled in his faith, and unconditional in his friendship. In addition, I owe a deep and abiding intellectual debt to the late Amos Tversky, whose ideas inspired this work, and whose training and generosity I have benefited from enormously.

I would like to thank Chip Blacker for his faith, help, and inspiration in the earliest stages of this project. I am deeply grateful to Jonathan Mercer, John Sullivan, Martin Sampson, and two anonymous reviewers for very helpful and challenging comments and criticisms on earlier versions of this manuscript. I am grateful to Lynn Eden for her consistent support and encouragement throughout this work. I express my thanks to Charles Myers, Kevin Rennells, and the University of Michigan Press for patience, skill, and responsiveness. I want to thank Margaret Padden for her help with the figures. Steve Fish, in addition to offering extremely thoughtful comments on the manuscript, has provided encouragement, solace, and support in more ways than I can count. I thank Kurt Weyland for his insistence on adequate rigor, and I congratulate him on his ultimate conversion to the light of prospect theory.

I am grateful to my mother for her endless support.

I have incurred profound debts among many friends who have provided me with unceasing love, support, and encouragement throughout this process, and I happily acknowledge their critical contributions. I want to thank Katie Greno who, in addition to originally editing the entire dissertation on which this book is based, has offered an infinite bounty of brilliance, wit, and compassion since I first met her in Lee Ross's decision-making class before I even entered graduate school. I thank Lisa Butler for good advice well received at a critical time and much nurturance through-out. I would like to thank Margaret Sullivan, Trisha Dorff and Liddy Manson for their continuous loyalty, thoughtfulness, understanding, and care. In addition, I am grateful to my cousin Tom Schuttenhelm for his artistic aesthetic and companionship over the course of the later stages of this project.

Finally, I would like to express my appreciation to two people who without being involved in political science have nonetheless helped me to function within it. I wish to thank Johanna Putnoi for teaching me through nurturance and example how to find more resources within myself. I would like to gratefully acknowledge Iris Ascher, who, without reading a word of this manuscript, did everything right to make it possible for me to both start it and complete it.

CHAPTER 1

Introduction

This book is essentially, and fundamentally, about the nature and structure of risk-taking behavior. Risk is a central feature in everyday life. We all take risks all the time, often in ways we do not even recognize. In many cases, we do not appreciate the extent of the risks we take; in others, we overestimate the risks we encounter. We usually do not think about the risks inherent in driving a car or participating in sports activities, but we actively fear the objectively low-level risks associated with food additives or flying on airplanes.

Risk is often a critical component of choice. One way to think about risk is in terms of a relative threat to values. Risk-taking behavior clearly involves dynamics of strategic interaction between factors that might threaten certain values and factors that might promote other values. Risk-taking enters the equation when we do not know, or do not care about, the impact of these factors on our options prior to our choice.

But the study of risk-taking is not just a sterile academic enterprise. Fear and greed drive risk-taking behavior. By definition, risk implies some fear of losing an important value or failing to obtain some desired goal. Assessments of risk are inherently probabilistic; outcomes may or may not occur, and they may or may not be devastating or beneficial in their effect. Indeed, in many cases, the real value of the outcome is unknown in advance, and the magnitude of its potential effect is unclear as well.

The study of risk is often more precise, however, than a vague sense of potential loss (fear) or gain (greed) would suggest. Obviously, the balance of a particular decision maker's fear and greed varies from situation to situation, just as the nature of these incentives shifts from individual to individual. The likelihood of taking chances in pursuit of certain goals or to avoid costs can be thought of as risk propensity.

Many theories of risk offer formal mathematical treatments of the distribution of outcomes and their relevant utilities and payoff matrices. Other theories are less formal in their descriptions. However, there are some basic tenets that these theories about risk have in common. First, risk is inherent in choice and can substantively affect the decision made among various prospects. Second, it is assumed that options can be ordered in some meaningful hierarchy of preferences. Last, risk is related to the distribution of the outcomes and how these outcomes are valued by the decision maker.[1]

Risk need not be a static concept; indeed, it is much more realistic to think of risk in dynamic terms. As values shift over time in response to internal or external factors, perceptions of threat, and therefore risk, are likely to shift as well. Throughout, perceptions of both value and threat remain critical to a decision maker.

In some psychological studies, risk propensity is seen as a stable personality trait of an individual that influences his or her behavior across situations and over time.[2] This is not the way risk propensity will be discussed here; rather, risk is understood as a function of the situation, seen in terms of losses (costs or fears) and gains (opportunities or greed), not as a predetermined product of an individual decision maker's personality.

Justification

This study seeks an explanation for certain irregularities in state behavior: why do nations take crazy risks, like the Iranian rescue mission; throw good money after bad, as in Vietnam; forgo easy gains, by terminating the Gulf War before reaching Baghdad; and so on? This study asks how central decision makers perceive and respond to risk in their decisions about foreign policy. Why might a president respond differently when confronting the same decision over time, as Carter did when he considered admitting the Iranian Shah into the United States for asylum? Conversely, why might a president respond similarly to different situations that take place simultaneously, as Eisenhower did by not responding militarily to either the Soviet invasion of Hungary or Nasser's nationalization of the Suez Canal? The answers to these questions all point in the same direction: issues of risk are central to understanding decision making in international politics.

The political problems raised by variations in response to risk encompass some of the central questions that have traditionally preoccupied the discipline of political science. In the arena of international relations, for example, political scientists have long sought to explain such questions as why nations go to war, how arms control treaties are negotiated, what dynamics drive weapons procurement policies, and which strategies can improve crisis management techniques.[3]

Many seemingly incomprehensible behaviors in international relations share a common element that has been virtually ignored in the existing literature within political science. The key to explaining and predicting these various phenomena lies in understanding the nature of risk-taking behavior in international politics. Many problems facing central political decision makers are united by the extent to which they involve risky choice. The underlying mechanisms of risk propensity can both explain and predict numerous political phenomena, especially those that take place under conditions of high uncertainty and incomplete information, which are precisely the circumstances which typically characterize high-stakes security decision making.

Risk is inherent in any situation where there is uncertainty, and even more so when the stakes are high or the prize is big. In a sense, any decision made under conditions of certainty is trivial almost by definition, because the outcome and its value are known in advance, or their consequences are not significant. Decisions that are easy, such as what to eat or wear, are often mandated by habit. Few significant political decisions, however, are made under such circumstances. Virtually every important decision involves some element of risk. When confronted with a problem of what to do in a given situation, a decision maker is first faced with the problem of deciding which factors should influence his choice. This assessment alone is inherently subjective and uncertain in nature from the outset.

In fact, difficult decisions are difficult precisely because they incorporate some element of risk. These decisions are not automatic (like those largely governed by habit) or inconsequential. In fact, what most people think of as "decisions" are actually break points in the decision process, representing the times when natural, automatic decision-making processes fail to operate sufficiently well to eliminate the unconscious nature of their standard operation. Decisions are the times when people are forced by the demands of time constraints, the complexity of the task, or the dimension of the stakes to stop, take conscious stock of the available options, and make a best guess as to which choice will lead to the most desired outcome.

A common example of the pervasiveness of risk and uncertainty in decision making involves political campaigning. When a politician runs for office, she must make numerous decisions about the content of her platform, which constituencies to target, how much time to spend fund-raising, and so on. All of these decisions run the risk of alienating a particular constituency or of wasting valuable time and resources. Wrong decisions could end up costing a candidate the entire election. Thus, strategic choices surrounding campaigns involve a significant element of risk in domestic political settings, just as foreign policy decisions can easily run the risk of war in international politics.

Indeed, there exists a copious literature on the problems in decision making that are associated with situations characterized by high stress, high uncertainty, and incomplete information.[4] This current work fits well within that existing paradigm of bounded rationality. Specifically, this is an investigation into the effect that specific cognitive biases concerning risk propensity have on central decision makers in the arena of international relations.

This study looks at American foreign policy decisions where the central policymaker is the president. In situations of high stress, such as those that involve acute time pressure, secrecy, or high stakes, the president is in a situation of high uncertainty where he is allowed an unparalleled element of unrestricted choice. Under such circumstances, differences in risk propensity are key to understanding the outcome of decisions.[5]

In addition, this analysis is related to, but does not derive from, well-established work on the fundamental attribution error.[6] Prospect theory presents a profoundly situationalist analysis: risk-taking behavior is based not on the individual predispositions of a particular leader, but evolves out of a cognitive response to a situation that constrains the way options are interpreted and choice is made.

Many irregularities in official behavior can be explained by systematic differences in assessing and responding to risk. This perspective holds implications for a variety of political phenomena, but is particularly relevant for problems that involve security concerns, such as ethnic conflict, crisis management, arms control, and weapons procurement.

Standard explanations may work well for standard cases, but these cases may not be the ones that are most important for understanding the nature of risk-taking in the international environment. Rather, the extreme or seemingly inexplicable cases may be the most interesting and important for future understanding and intervention. For those anomalous but significant cases, traditional explanations often are inadequate. Where conventional analysis proves unconvincing, prospect theory can offer compelling explanation.

Decision Making

The theory that is used to gain insight into the nature of risk assessment and the dynamics of risk propensity in this study is prospect theory, a psychological model developed by Amos Tversky and Daniel Kahneman.[7] The particular value of this theory is that it offers a *systematic* way to both explain and predict risk propensity, even under conditions of uncertainty. Put simply, prospect theory predicts that people tend to be cautious when they are in a good position (gains), and more likely to take risks when they are in a bad position (losses). The intuition behind this argument is offered by two simple adages: rich people vote Republican (caution in gains); and desperate people do desperate things (risk in losses). In theoretical terms, prospect theory argues that individuals tend to be risk averse in the domain of gains, and risk seeking in the domain of losses. Part of what determines whether the situation is considered to be one of "gains" or "losses" depends on how the options are "framed" or constructed prior to choice.

Before describing prospect theory in more detail in the next chapter, some definitions may prove helpful. Most decisions, as we understand them, really involve a couple of different sequential operations. The first is one of judgment, which is essentially an external assessment about the likelihood of certain events taking place in the world. Judgment often takes places under conditions of uncertainty, because people do not always know how likely a certain outcome is in advance. The second is decision making, which is fundamentally an internal evaluation of the value of various options. Decisions often take place under conditions of risk, where something of value may be at stake. Prospect theory is a theory of decision making, not one of judgment. However, decisions are based, at least in part, on judgments that are often inherently subjective in nature. As a result, decision makers are often susceptible to biases in judgment even before they encounter biases in decision making.

As noted, judgments often take place under conditions of uncertainty because they involve assessments of probabilities. In many circumstances, decision making under risk is based on judgments made under conditions of uncertainty.[8] When probabilities are unknown, the best choice becomes uncertain. Uncertainty is a basic element of the human condition. It is also a major problem in political analysis. At root, decisions are often based on uncertain judgments that may just as easily be true as false, and it may be impossible to know which is which before a decision must be made based on those uncertain judgments.

Most complex choices fall under the framework of judgment under uncertainty *and* decision making under risk because it is impossible to predict the characteristics of many different variables simultaneously in advance, especially when they may have unknown interaction effects. Even the nature of many of the critical variables may be unknown beforehand.

Thus, people are often on their own in making the necessarily intuitive and subjective assessments of their world that are required in order to function efficiently and effectively in a complex environment. Estimating the probability of uncertain events necessarily involves a large, basically subjective element because in many situations such judgments are all people have in order to make guesses about future events. This is especially true in cases where nothing like the uncertain event has happened before, and thus averages of past outcomes can not be used as a basis for prediction, as might normatively be indicated. In the case of such unknown events, like a nuclear war or global warming, there is no real precedent and so estimates must rely on highly subjective or speculative assessments of the likelihood of events. Indeed, much controversy is generated solely on the basis of experts' disagreements concerning probability assessments about whether certain events, such as global warming, will occur and what effects will result.[9]

Decisions often depend on judgments that fall prey to heuristic biases that are common under such conditions of uncertainty. Heuristic biases are cognitive shortcuts that help people to understand and process information about the world more efficiently; they are judgmental rules of thumb. As noted, decisions, as opposed to judgments, take place under conditions of risk. Risk is about the chance of loss. Thus, risk involves two components, the chance and the loss. Chance is fundamentally about probability, in terms of likelihood or frequency. In this way, assessments of chance can be biased by the judgments on which they are based. Loss is critically a function of magnitude. Thus, risk is about how much of what is lost. When this is related to how much something is valued, it is often expressed in terms of utility. Thus, any investigation into risk must examine both components: the likelihood of outcomes, as well as their relative value.

Judgmental Heuristics

Because decisions are often based on judgments about options that take place prior to choice, biases in these judgmental processes can play an important role in understanding the constructions of the options that are available for decision. In prospect theory, decisions are influenced by how options are first "framed." In this way, uncertainty in judgment prior to choice plays a crucial role in framing options for subsequent evaluation, or decision making. Framing tasks fall prey to systematic judgmental biases that are often labeled "judgmental heuristics." Such biases in judgment can thus substantially affect how options come to be framed.

As noted, people are susceptible to errors in the judgmental processes; these errors are *systematic* in nature. Three of these heuristic biases are representativeness, availability, and anchoring.[10] Each will be discussed briefly in turn.

Representativeness refers to judgments where the probability that one object or event belongs to a particular category is based on their similarity. For example, someone might mention that she went to a talk on arms control that had three-quarters academics and one-quarter artists in attendance. She then describes a questioner who was dressed entirely in black, listened to a Walkman, and wore an earring in one ear and a beret on his head. The listener is then asked to guess if the questioner was an academic or an artist. Many people might respond "artist" because the *image* of the questioner provides a closer fit with the prototypical image of an artist than that of an academic. While this judgment may be accurate, it fails to take account of the fact that there are many more academics than artists in attendance at an arms control seminar. Thus, any given individual at the talk is more likely to be an academic than an artist, regardless of conformity of appearance to stereotype. In this way, representativeness, while often helpful in facilitating efficient judgment, fails to incorporate adequately the normatively useful base rate, or statistical likelihood in the total population, into judgments of probability. The use of a historical analogy, such as Vietnam, Pearl Harbor, or Munich, being applied to a current situation serves as a good example of this bias operating in a political arena.

A second judgmental heuristic is availability. *Availability* refers to inferences about the frequency of events, where such frequency is judged according to the associations triggered in memory or imagination. So, for example, people often judge homicides to be more frequent than suicides, even though the reverse is true, because examples of homicides are more available in memory due to their disproportionate prominence in the news media. People fail to recognize that perceptual salience may not always provide an accurate reflection of actual frequency.[11]

The third judgmental heuristic is anchoring. *Anchoring* relates to predictions that are based on initial values, or anchors, that may or may not be adequately adjusted before a judgment is made of a second, possibly unrelated, object or event. For example, an experimenter might give a subject a piece of paper with the number 1,000 on it. She tells her subject that the number should have *no* effect on the following task. She then asks her subjects to estimate the number of hospitals in the United States. Subjects are likely to be unduly influenced by the original number, even if they are *consciously* aware that the number is irrelevant to the task at hand. This effect is particularly dramatic if other people are given the same task with an initial number of 1,000,000. In this case, most of those with the initial value of 1,000 make estimates relatively close to this estimate, while the majority of those with 1,000,000 as their initial number make judgments much closer to this figure. In this example, it is obvious that each group insufficiently *adjusts* from the original anchor in guessing the number of hospitals in the United States.[12]

As noted, these judgmental heuristics can influence the framing of options prior to choice. Framing is a particularly powerful aspect of prospect theory because of its implications for manipulation as well as intervention. If advisors are aware that others are substantively affected by the manner and order in which options and messages are presented, they might easily manipulate information in such as way as to elicit from others the choices they themselves favor, for possibly irrelevant, malicious, or self-interested reasons. Advocates might do this by adding additional alternatives that favor their perspective, and so on.[13] In this way, advisors might be able to entice leaders to behave in whatever way is preferred by the advisor, without ever arousing the decision maker's attention or suspicion. Aside from the profound ethical implications the possibility of manipulation raises, recognition of this bias also offers the opportunity for positive intervention. Such an intervention strategy might demand that options be presented to leaders in as many different formats at the same time as possible so that framing effects become more transparent and less insidious in their effects on choice. Options chosen in a situation where framing effects are obvious are more likely to capture true preferences.

Prospect Theory

Prospect theory is a descriptive, empirically valid model of choice. It was originally developed in explicit opposition to normative models of choice, such as those represented by subjective expected utility models. The evidence supporting prospect theory is almost exclusively derived from classroom experimentation, which has also shown the inadequacy of normative models for capturing actual human decision-making behavior.[14] Prospect theory was originally developed in response to overwhelmingly robust findings that demonstrated the profound and pervasive way in which many people systematically violate the most basic axioms of rational decision-making models in their actual choice behavior.

Part of the inherent theoretical value of the experiments on which prospect theory is based is the way in which they empirically invalidate the assumptions upon which subjective expected utility and other rational decision-making models rely.[15] These normative axioms are often systematically violated in actual decision-making behavior, but they are accounted for by the functions of prospect theory. Moreover, prospect theory holds predictive as well as explanatory force, which makes it particularly useful for understanding political decisions made under circumstances of high uncertainty, uniqueness, and complexity. This predictive power also makes prospect theory a serious alternative to more static rational choice models, which fail in their descriptive accuracy and explanatory elegance.

The original studies that demonstrated the descriptive accuracy of prospect theory possessed high degrees of internal validity. The goal of a study such as this is to extend the test of prospect theory's accuracy and external validity through empirical case-study work from archival sources. This study is designed as part of an effort to establish and demonstrate the empirical validity of prospect theory *outside* the confines of the classroom.

The relevance of this model for political decision making is clear. If the model proves to be an accurate representation of individual political decision making, it then becomes possible to predict risk propensity in certain situations. In other words, once the domain of the situation is classified as one of gains or losses, it then becomes possible to predict individual choice based on that classification, according to the dictates of prospect theory. In this way, the conditions under which risk-averse or risk-acceptant behavior is seen become clear and predictable, no matter how uncertain the surrounding events, how unique the situation, or how complex the environment.

To reiterate, prospect theory can show how domain, in terms of gains or losses, can produce systematic, predictable tendencies in risk propensity. This dynamic can then be used to *explain* the causal mechanisms behind particular choices in the realm of international relations, including issues surrounding bargaining, conflict negotiation, and crisis management. In addition, prospect theory can *predict* risk propensity given prior determination of domain.

Prospect theory is more than a mere transfer of individual psychology into the realm of political behavior. Political decisions are by their very nature highly uncertain, ambiguous, and dynamic. High-risk situations are precisely the conditions under which political decision making most commonly takes place. Prospect theory offers unique explanatory and predictive insight into complex, uncertain decision making under conditions of risk.

Application

Methodologically, this work falls within the scope of what Theda Skocpol and Margaret Somers have called a "parallel demonstration of theory."[16] The goal of this methodology is to explicate a particular theoretical proposition and then repeatedly demonstrate its utility when applied to a group of historical cases. In this way, historical cases are used to show the applicability of the theory to multiple instances where it should be able to make sense of the relevant data if it is indeed valid. This methodology allows an analyst to demonstrate both the applicability of the theory across a variety of cases and how relevant variables are operationalized and manifested in specific instances. In this case, prospect theory is delineated and then used to order the evidence in a compelling way for four disparate cases: the decision to launch the rescue mission of the hostages in Iran in 1980; the decision concerning the entry of the Iranian Shah into America; the U-2 affair; and the Suez crisis. All these cases are similar in the ability of prospect theory to illuminate and illustrate the relevant impact of domain on risk propensity.

The parallel demonstration of theory does not only allow for a demonstration of the virtues and applicability of a theory; it also allows the analyst to refine and develop the theory as well. Thus, this study is explicitly designed as such a parallel demonstration of theory and *not* as a contrast of contests or as a macrocausal analysis.

In seeking to apply prospect theory to decisions in the international environment, the United States offers the perfect country for investigation because of its hegemonic status in the immediate post–World War II period. After 1945, the predominant power of the United States led it to confront particularly complex and important foreign policy decisions. Hegemonic status is precisely the condition under which cognitive biases in decision makers would most likely surface and be able to have an impact on choice, because there is less constraint forced by the dynamics of the system itself.

The empirical testing of this model in the international environment presents some interesting challenges. This study focuses on the president's decision-making process. The goal is to test the same president under each domain, both gains and losses, to see if there are any differences in his risk propensity, especially in the direction predicted by the theory. When risk propensity conforms to the predictions of the theory, the results offer support for the applicability of the theory to decisions in international relations. When no differences are found, the lack of correlation between risk propensity and the predictions of the theory provides evidence against the theory and its suitability for, or applicability to, questions of decision making in international politics. When such a failure occurs, it also demonstrates the falsifiability of the theory itself.

The independent variable in this study is domain, which is operationalized in terms of gains or losses. The dependent variable is risk propensity, coded as either averse or seeking. Domain and risk were each measured independently to avoid risk of tautological reasoning.

Domain is classified as one of gains or one of losses. Domain is determined according to a number of different variables that helped define a decision maker's subjective sense of situation. These sources include memoirs, interviews, public opinion polls, number of congressional overrides, and other salient international events. In many cases, domain is a subjective assessment and can be difficult to ascertain. However, in many circumstances, the situation was so obvious as to offer a fairly clear categorization. A good analogy here is one of a thermometer. If it is a hundred degrees outside, you do not need to know a whole lot about a particular individual to assume that he is probably hot.[17] While domain may remain a crude assessment, in many cases it offers an accurate descriptor of the national and international environment that a particular president confronted.

The relative riskiness of a given option was evaluated relative to the variance presented by each choice. In other words, an option with a high potential for either gain or loss constitutes a more risk-seeking choice than an option with more constrained outcome probabilities. In high-risk instances, both the costs and benefits of the outcome values are higher; where more opportunities exist for greed and fear to motivate, more risk becomes possible. This is true even if the more cautious choice does not offer outcomes either as positive or as negative overall as a more risk-seeking choice. In practice, it is often difficult to determine what the outcome possibilities might be or what value each option possesses; such judgments are even more challenging in retrospective reconstruction.

Empirical testing of this model examines Presidents Eisenhower and Carter to determine risk-taking propensity across variations in the independent variable, as coded in terms of gains and losses. Carter offers two almost paradigmatic cases. One of the best illustrations of the theory is provided by the failed rescue mission of the hostages in Iran in 1980. This was clearly a decision taken in the domain of losses. Indeed, the mission itself appears to offer an almost classic example of a gamble with a high chance of failure and a low probability of success taken in the hope of recouping even larger losses.

Carter's decision to exclude the Shah of Iran from the United States between January and October 1979 was a choice made in the domain of relative gains. By the time the Shah was admitted to the country for medical treatment in October, Carter's domain had shifted into one of relative loss, and he then made a riskier decision and let the Shah in. In this case, the shift in relative domain is mirrored by the subsequent shifts in administration policy.

In the U-2 incident, negative press concerning the Soviet downing of the American reconnaissance aircraft placed President Eisenhower in a domain of losses. In this state, he took a risk and publicly lied about the origins and purpose of the aircraft. Severe recriminations, including the cancelling of a carefully crafted summit conference, followed in the wake of the revelation that he had lied.

In the Suez crisis, Eisenhower behaved cautiously while in a domain of gains. In this case, Eisenhower took a sure gain in public opinion in the

Third World over a risky gamble, which offered the possibility of strengthening the Western alliance and intimidating potential aggressors, but also risked instigating a world war with the Soviet Union.

By examining two presidents, each making a decision in both domains, the applicability of prospect theory to explain and predict risk-taking behavior in the international environment is demonstrated through parallel demonstration of theory. By illuminating the kinds of tendencies that pervade central decision-making processes under conditions of complexity, stress, uncertainty, and risk, it becomes easier to design intervention strategies that can be invoked to reduce the more counternormative implications of these findings.

Normative Issues

The empirical nature of prospect theory raises some normative questions. Normative theories developed through the efforts of eighteenth-century French noblemen who wanted to calculate how to gamble most efficiently in order to garner the highest winnings. As a result, they pestered the court mathematicians about probabilities and outcomes, and certain normative ideas grew out of these compulsive gamblers' trials and errors.

Normative approaches look at the best way to make a decision given some specific goal and some particular environment; the goal is thus to maximize the payoff while minimizing the cost. These theories are prescriptive, formal, and deductive; they are based on logic, probability, and statistics, and they are not empirical in nature. Normative theories can be tested, but not derived, empirically.

Descriptive theories, which are based on empirical evidence, look at how people actually do make decisions. These approaches use empirical evidence, often derived from experimental manipulations, to arrive at their conclusions. Historically, formal, normative work preceded descriptive formulations.

The problem with normative approaches is that many problems present no clearly dominant solution; that is why certain concerns become problems. In many cases, the optimal decision depends on the goals, values, and capabilities of the relevant actors; choices can be affected by the various conceptions that different players hold of the situations or options available. The failure of a decision does not necessarily render it wrong or unwise, especially once emotional values, such as regret, are taken into account.[18]

On the other hand, descriptive models are not necessarily normative in their implications. This normative discrepancy raises the most important distinction between rational choice models, such as subjective expected utility theory and prospect theory. Subjective expected utility theory is a normative theory; prospect theory is a descriptive one. Normative theories describe what people ought to do; in doing so, normative theories can function prescriptively. Descriptive theories refer to what people actually are doing; thus, no normative implications can be drawn from descriptive theories. What people do can be right or wrong; telling them it is better not to act that way does not help change what they actually do. An analyst might argue that normative silence constitutes an inherent weakness of descriptive theories, such as prospect theory. However, normative silence offers greater possibilities for freedom of expression and accuracy of explanation.

In an attempt to reconcile normative and empirical approaches, classical decision theorists have tried to relax some of the basic axioms of normative theory by incorporating various descriptive elements in ways that make subjective expected utility models less rigid and more descriptively adequate. These adjustments are rationalized as offering a broader interpretation of the goals and information available to a decision maker in a choice situation. However, even under these relaxed and minimal guidelines, people fail to adequately conform to normative principles. In this way, it is difficult to conceive of a descriptively accurate theory that would also remain normatively valid in even the most basic and minimal ways.

Indeed, Tversky and Kahneman argue that a complete reconciliation between normative and descriptive theory is not possible given the consistent and fundamental ways in which people violate normative rules.[19] After all, it is not obvious that people *should* make decisions in line with the predictions of prospect theory; it is only clear that they do make decisions this way.

Summary

Prospect theory can both explain and predict risk propensity in the international environment. Prospect theory argues that risk aversion is more likely in the domain of gains and that risk-seeking behavior will tend to occur in the domain of losses. This study seeks to explain variations in foreign policy behavior in terms of the way situational factors interact with cognitive biases. It is precisely those political decisions that take place under conditions of extreme uncertainty and complexity, and that affect the most closely cherished values, that are often most difficult to explain and predict using conventional explanations. However, these are the conditions under which prospect theory proves most illustrative and convincing. Through the methodology of parallel demonstration of theory, prospect theory will be shown to provide a valuable approach to any analysis of risk-taking in international politics.

In addition, prospect theory potentially constitutes a frontal assault on the dominance of rational choice models for understanding and predicting risk-taking behavior in the international environment. There is no rational choice model that is both descriptively accurate and normatively valid. Prospect theory makes no claim to normative imprimatur, but it provides a descriptively accurate, empirically valid, and predictively powerful instrument of analysis with regard to risk-taking behavior. Any rational choice theorist who wishes to lay claim to the superiority of his paradigm must necessarily come to terms with prospect theory's devastating criticisms of rational choice's descriptive inaccuracies. Even if rational choice models claim robust predictive power, prospect theory can match that power and add descriptive accuracy and explanatory insight to the equation as well. In the end, the superiority of prospect theory renders rational choice models descriptively vacuous, empirically static, and normatively bankrupt with respect to understanding risk-taking in international politics.

CHAPTER 2

Prospect Theory

Prospect theory is a theory of decision making under conditions of risk. Decisions are based on judgments. Judgments are assessments about the external state of the world. They are made especially challenging under conditions of uncertainty, where it is difficult to foresee the consequences or outcomes of events with clarity. Decisions involve internal conflict over value trade-offs. They are made difficult when choices promote contradictory values and goals. Prospect theory directly addresses how these choices are framed and evaluated in the decision-making process.

This chapter provides the theoretical basis for the empirical casework that follows. First of all, there is a brief reference to rational choices theories in terms of the historical foundations from which prospect theory emerged. These theories are mentioned here because rational choice theories constitute a better known approach in political science and often represent the dominant alternative model for explaining the behavior under investigation here. The rational choice discussion is brief and simple because rational choice models are not the main concern of this work. The objective is not to test the predictions of prospect theory against those of rational choice models. Rather, this outline is provided as a basis of comparison to examine the explanatory and predictive value afforded by prospect theory. Second, prospect theory itself is then discussed in detail in order to place the theory in its appropriate psychological and political context. Last, the applicability of prospect theory to international politics is discussed, and some definitions, issues of operationalization, and a brief outline of the case studies that follow are offered.

Historical Context

Expected value was one of the first theories of decision making under risk. The expected value of an outcome is equal to its payoff times its probability. This model failed in predicting outcomes in many instances because it was obvious that the value that a particular payoff held for someone was not always directly related to its precise monetary worth.

Daniel Bernoulli was the first to see this contradiction and propose a modification to the expected value notion in 1738.[1] In fact, Bernoulli was the first to introduce the concept of systematic bias in decision making based on a "psychophysical" model.[2] Specifically, Bernoulli used a coin toss game known as the St. Petersburg paradox to demonstrate the limitations of expected value as a normative decision rule. While the specifics of the game are complex and irrelevant to this study, Bernoulli's analysis of the dynamics of the St. Petersburg paradox led him to appreciate that the subjective value, or utility, that a payoff has for an individual is not always directly related to the absolute amount of that payoff, or expected value. Rather, the value a person attaches to an outcome can be influenced by such factors as the likelihood of winning, or probability, among other things. In this way, Bernoulli showed that people would not always bet solely on the basis of the expected value of a game.

Out of his analysis, Bernoulli proposed a "utility function" to explain people's choice behavior. Bernoulli assumed that people tried to maximize their utility, and not their expected value. Bernoulli's function proposed that utility was not merely a linear function of wealth, but rather a subjective, concave, evaluation of outcome. The concave shape of the function introduced the notion of decreasing marginal utility, whereby changes farther away from the starting point have less impact than those which are closer to it. For example, Bernoulli's utility function argues that $1 is a lot compared with nothing; people will therefore be reluctant to part with this dollar. However, $101 is not significantly different to most people than $100. Thus, people are more willing to part with their hundred-and-first dollar than with their only one.

Because Bernoulli's concave utility function assumed that increments in utility decreased with increasing wealth, the expected utility model implicitly assumed risk aversion. Specifically, Bernoulli argued that a person would prefer a sure outcome over a gamble with an equal expected value. In other words, people would prefer $100 for sure over a gamble that paid $200 or nothing on the toss of a fair coin.

Bernoulli's model was the beginning of utility theory. As such, it combined a mixture of descriptive and normative elements. The description seemed sensible, and the normative implications merely represented the idea that caution constituted the better part of prudence. To the extent that Bernoulli assumed that people are typically risk averse, he explained this behavior in terms of people's attitudes toward the value of the payoff, rather than in terms of the phenomenon of risk-taking behavior itself. People's attitudes toward risk were posited as a by-product of their attitude toward value.

Two centuries later, von Neumann and Morgenstern revolutionized Bernoulli's expected utility theory by advancing the notion of "revealed preferences."[3] In developing an axiomatic theory of utility, von Neumann and Morgenstern turned Bernoulli's suppositions upside down and used preferences to derive utility. In Bernoulli's model, utility was used to define preference, because people were assumed to prefer the option that presented the highest utility. In the von Neumann and Morgenstern model, utility describes preferences; knowing the utility of an option informs an observer of a player's preferences. Von Neumann and Morgenstern's axioms do not determine an individual's preference ordering, but they do impose certain constraints on the possible relationships between the individual's preferences. In von Neumann and Morgenstern's theory, as long as the relationship between an individual's preferences satisfies certain axioms such as consistency and coherence, it became possible to construct an *individual* utility function for that person; such a function could then be used to demonstrate a person's pursuit of his maximum subjective utility. This shift in utility theory toward revealed preferences allowed room now for different people to have different preference orderings.[4]

In von Neumann and Morgenstern's model of subjective expected utility, there is no clear distinction between normative and descriptive aspects. As mentioned, Bernoulli combined these elements, because risk aversion was assumed to offer prudent counsel. In von Neumann and Morgenstern's model, it was assumed that axiomatic subjective expected utility is not only the way rational people should behave, but do behave. People seek to maximize their subjective expected utility; one person may not share the same utility curve as another, but each follows the same normative axioms in striving toward their individually defined maximum subjective expected utility.

The crucial axioms in subjective expected utility models are transitivity, dominance, and invariance. Transitivity assumes that if option A is preferred to option B, and B is preferred to C, then A is preferred to C as well.[5] Dominance argues that if one option is better on at least one aspect, and at least as good on all other aspects, it will be preferred to lesser options. Invariance posits that a preference should remain unchanged regardless of order or method of presentation. All three of these axioms are basic to almost any rational model of decision making. All of these assumptions seem logically correct, and yet people demonstrate systematic violations of all of them in actual choice behavior. This is one of Tversky and Kahneman's crucial findings.[6]

Prospect Theory

Tversky and Kahneman have demonstrated in numerous highly controlled experiments that most people systematically violate all of the basic axioms of subjective expected utility theory in their actual decision-making behavior at least some of the time.[7] These findings run contrary to the normative implications inherent within classical subjective expected utility theories. In response to their findings, Tversky and Kahneman provided an alternative, empirically supported, theory of choice, one that accurately describes how people actually go about making their decisions. This model is called prospect theory.[8] In short, prospect theory predicts that individuals tend to be risk averse in a domain of gains, or when things are going well, and relatively risk seeking in a domain of losses, as when a leader is in the midst of a crisis.

Prospect theory is based on psychophysical models, such as those that originally inspired Bernoulli's expected value proposition. Traditionally, psychophysics investigates the precise relationship, usually mathematically expressed, between the physical and the psychological worlds. The goal is to determine the point at which a change in the physical stimulus is psychologically perceived as a sensory change by the subject. Most research in the sensory domain, for example, has determined that physical stimulus must increase geometrically for psychological experience to increase arithmetically; this produces a concave curve, much like Bernoulli's risk-averse utility curve.[9]

Tversky and Kahneman applied psychophysical principles to investigate judgment and decision making. Just as people are not aware of the processing the brain engages in to translate vision into sight, they are not aware of the kinds of computations the brain makes in editing and evaluating choice. People make decisions according to how their brains process and understand information and not solely on the basis of the inherent utility that a certain option possesses for a decision maker.

Much of Tversky and Kahneman's work is designed to show that descriptive and normative theories cannot be combined into a single, adequate model of choice, as von Neumann and Morgenstern attempted to do with their axiomatic subjective expected utility model; rather, the behavioral violations of expected utility in which people systematically engage are too basic to allow for integration within the axioms demanded by normative models. In short, theories that are empirically accurate in description fail to meet even the most basic normative prescriptions. Thus, Tversky and Kahneman ultimately argue that normative theories need to be abandoned altogether in analyzing judgment and decision making because they fail to offer an adequate understanding of actual decision behavior.[10]

Prospect theory shares certain characteristics with previous notions of expected utility. Like Bernoulli, the value function of prospect theory assumes that the *shape* of the curve is similar for everybody. Like von Neumann and Morgenstern, prospect theory recognizes that the curve is not a straight line and that the *utility* of that curve can differ between individuals. Despite these similarities, however, prospect theory is not merely a descendant of earlier utility models.

In classical decision models, utility is understood to exist independent of probability. In games of chance, subjective utility is typically defined as the point of indifference between a sure thing and a hard lottery. For example, a given player's subjective utility might lie at the point where he has no discernible preference between receiving $50 for sure and a gamble with a 50 percent chance of winning $200 and a 50 percent chance of winning nothing. As a result, subjective utility might differ across individuals for the same payoff matrixes. Subjective utility is used to "find out" the worth of any given objective outcome to a particular individual. In short, utility is the value an individual places on a given outcome. In this way, calculations of subjective expected utility serve to define "revealed preferences."

What does this mean in practical terms? How do these decision strategies play out in real life questions? An example might be illustrative. Imagine a classical decision analyst who wants to find out how much an industry would have to "pay" (in taxes, improved safety standards, and so on) in order to increase pollution in an area by a factor estimated to be one additional death per year from cancer, on average. The first thing such an analyst might do is seek to determine how much life is worth to people in that area. In this example, a classical decision analyst undertaking such a task might ask someone to place an objective value on the relevant outcome, their life. So, the analyst might ask the subject, "what is your life worth to you, in monetary terms?" An individual asked such a question would most likely balk at even attempting to think about the value of his life in terms of money unless he was an advocate of such classical decision models beforehand. Even a naive subject who wished to be cooperative might have a hard time figuring out how to think about even beginning to translate the value of his life into monetary terms. If such a person asked the analyst for help in making this transition, the decision analyst might say, attempting to be helpful: "How did you get here today? Did you drive? Don't you realize that you risked your life by approximately 1 in 50,000 per year by driving here in your car today? If you are willing to risk your life for mere transport, what is so difficult about translating that value into monetary terms?" At this point, the subject may be less confused, but will certainly be more depressed and probably angry at the decision analyst as well for making him think about his life so callously. Thus, even in this simple example, it is possible to see some of the difficulties that naive subjects might encounter in determining utility. Yet some of these same obstacles are frequently present for many analysts who attempt to accurately apply classical decision models to difficult, personal, or otherwise highly evocative and important questions. Even under more mundane circumstances, people still find it fairly complex to assess utility at all, challenging to understand its implications for everyday behavior, and even more difficult to translate these values into monetary, or similarly objective, terms.

Thus, it is possible to see that people often fail in the most basic requirements of subjective expected utility theory, namely providing accurate and reliable assessments of utility. Because it is so very difficult for people to assess utilities, analysis rests on a much stronger foundation when it redefines utilities on the basis of psychological theory and experimentation, such as that provided by prospect theory.

In this way, prospect theory advances the notion of utility in a useful and accurate direction. Prospect theory adds the insight that utility curves differ in domains of gain from those in domains of loss. Moreover, the shape of prospect theory's value curves are similar across individuals. As a result, an analyst need not know an individual decision maker's particular utility in each case; once the domain is clear, predictions of risk propensity become possible regardless of the individual decision maker's particular utility. Thus, while prospect theory may appear to be less analytically rigorous and precise than expected utility models, it is in fact sufficiently precise to allow for prediction on the basis of whether a decision takes place in the domain of gains or losses. Analytically, prospect theory is also more adaptable than a subjective expected utility model that would require greater information about the *individual* utility curve before prediction would become possible.[11]

Prospect theory is designed to explain a common pattern of choice. It is descriptive and empirical in nature. Prospect theory looks at two parts of decision making: the editing, or framing, phase, and the evaluation phase. The editing phase encompasses what are widely known as framing effects. The evaluation phase involves the decision process of choosing among options; this decision is influenced by two processes, one related to subjective value, the other to perceptual likelihood. The following section looks at these three processes in more depth.

Framing Effects

Framing, or editing, is the first phase of prospect theory. This initial phase leads to a representation of the acts, outcomes, and contingencies that are associated with a particular choice problem. Framing involves a number of basic operations that simplify and provide a context for choice.

Framing effects refer to the way in which a choice, or an option, can be affected by the order or manner in which it is presented to a decision maker. This is a crucial concept for a number of reasons. In many situations, a decision maker does not know the relevant options that are available to her. She must construct and figure out what the options are or have this done for her prior to choice. In some sense, this activity of determining and constructing the available options constitutes the heart of creative decision making.

Choice can be affected by relatively trivial manipulations in the construction of available options. Most rational decision makers would argue that seemingly innocuous transformations, such as the order in which options are presented, should *not* substantively affect their choice decisions. The paradox is that framing effects are often embedded in decision problems in such a way that few decision makers realize the disproportionate impact that these framing effects have on them. Decision makers frequently remain unaware of these framing effects and resort to intuitive assessments of predetermined options because it is often impossible for them to recognize the way in which more rational procedures are being violated in the original determination of these preframed options. Thus, any descriptively adequate model of choice must be sensitive to these framing effects.

A couple of examples serve to illustrate the impact of framing on choice. In most of the experiments that demonstrate these phenomena, money, in the form of payoffs, bets, and gambles, is used to demonstrate the findings. However, in the case of framing, it has been shown that decisions about life and death are affected as readily and as profoundly as decisions about money. Two experiments serve to demonstrate these findings.

The first experiment asked people to pretend that they were responsible for making public policy in the face of a major flu epidemic that was expected to kill 600 people. They were asked to decide between two different programs that were each designed to contain this epidemic. The choices were presented to the first group as follows: policy A will save 200 people; policy B has a one-third chance that 600 people will be saved, and a two-thirds chance that no one will be saved. In this case, 72 percent chose the *first* option. The second group was presented with these choices: policy A will cause 400 people to die; policy B has a one-third chance that no one will die; and a two-thirds chance that 600 people will die. In this case, 78 percent chose the *second* option. When these two option sets are compared, it is obvious that they present the exact same "net" outcome; the only difference lies in the framing of the options. Clearly, the discrepancy in results can only be attributed to framing effects, since there was no change in the expected value between the options presented.[12]

In another example, physicians were asked whether they would treat lung cancer with radiation or surgery. In one condition, doctors were told that surgery carried a 90 percent immediate survival rate, and a 34 percent 5-year survival rate. In this experiment, subjects were told that all patients survived radiation, and that 22 percent remained alive after 5 years. In a second condition, respondents were told that 10 percent of patients die during surgery and 66 percent die by the end of 5 years. With radiation, no one dies during the therapy, but 78 percent die within 5 years. Once again, the two choice sets differ only in the way the problem is presented, or framed, to decision makers. Again, the results are strikingly different across options. In the first, "survival," frame, 18 percent chose radiation; in the second, "mortality," frame, 49 percent chose radiation.[13] This example is particularly striking because it involves real choices concerning life and death outcomes. Moreover, when the options are presented side by side, it is obvious that an individual attempting to maximize his or her long-term expected value is best served by surgery. What is also noticeable in both examples is that in each case, when the alternatives are placed side by side at the same time, the optimal choice is rendered transparent.

What does framing consist of and how does it operate? Tversky and Kahneman write, "Framing is controlled by the manner in which the choice problem is presented as well as by the norms, habits, and expectancies of the decision maker."[14] These norms and habits can be quite idiosyncratic to the particular decision maker, and his expectancies can be significantly affected by many cognitive biases. However, framing operations concerning the *manner* in which choice problems are presented can be described systematically.[15]

The purpose behind framing, or editing, various options, is to simplify the evaluation of choices that are available to a decision maker. This editing is done through the use of several kinds of procedures, the most important of which are acceptance and segregation, but also including such mechanisms as coding, combination, and cancellation.

In recent expositions of prospect theory, Tversky and Kahneman have further distilled the essence of framing effects to two basic functions: segregation and acceptance.[16] Acceptance argues that once a decision maker is presented with a reasonable construction of a choice problem, she is not likely to recast it. In other words, a decision maker is most likely to accept whatever framing of options is presented as the most appropriate formulation of the given decision and not be prone to second-guess the presentation of choices. There are a few exceptions to this rule, as when there is a particularly familiar way to construct an option. For example, it is customary to discuss "unemployment" figures, not "employment" ones. Nonetheless, these familiar presentations become less common as the choice becomes more novel in nature. Note the opportunity such acceptance offers for a manipulative political advisor or rival to obtain personal gains through the mere control of the choice options that are presented as viable.

Segregation is best captured by the idea that when people make choices, they tend to focus on the factors at hand that seem most relevant to the immediate problem; decision makers do not tend to adequately account for related factors that may have an actual impact on the outcome but do not appear to be directly relevant to the specific choice at hand. With the flu experiment, for example, not many decision makers faced with such a choice would first ask about the overall probability that this flu might not take hold in this population at all. While seemingly irrelevant to the decision about what to do if it does arrive, the overall probability of how likely it is that the flu will hit is not inconsequential in determining how much should be spent to combat it before an epidemic occurs.

Coding refers to people's tendency to categorize outcomes in terms of gains and losses, rather than in terms of final absolute states of wealth or welfare. This is intuitive to any fan of competitive sports. Your team's final score is irrelevant without knowing whether it is higher or lower than the opponent's score. In this case, the opponent's score serves as the reference point by which to evaluate your team's performance. In the end, it doesn't matter whether it was your team's highest score ever, if the total is still less than the other team's score.[17]

Combination is an editing strategy that refers to the tendency of people to add together the likelihood of choices that present identical outcomes. For example, if a person lives in a part of the country with a 10 percent chance of dying in an earthquake and a 10 percent chance of dying in a fire in a given year, that person will evaluate potential moves to a part of the country with a 10 percent likelihood of dying in a tornado assuming a 20 percent chance of dying in an earthquake or fire by staying in the same place.

Cancellation refers to the discounting involved in evaluating choices that carry similar outcomes. If one part of an option is the same across choice sets, that aspect tends to be ignored in evaluating prospects. For example: one route home carries a 1 percent chance of being injured in a car crash and a 10 percent chance of being killed by a gunman; another route home carries a 10 percent chance of being killed by a gunman and a 20 percent chance of being mugged. The likelihood of being killed by a gunman is then ignored, in essence, because it is the same across cases, and the decision then becomes one between a 1 percent chance of injury in a car accident and a 20 percent chance of being held up. The similar option is canceled out for purposes of choice between options.

Other editing operations include simplification and detection of dominance. Simplification refers not only to mathematical rounding of probabilities but discarding very unlikely alternatives as well. Detection of dominance reflects the almost unconscious habit of dismissing alternatives that provide a less valuable outcome on each dimension than other alternatives that are available.

Because editing makes decision making more efficient, it occurs frequently. However, the order in which these various operations take place can differ, and the sequence of processing itself might easily affect the outcome of the evaluation process. Once an option is canceled, it may not reappear later to be coded as a gain or loss, even if the context changes to make the canceled option viable once again. For example, if a person makes a decision not to pursue a graduate education because he doesn't have enough money, coming into a subsequent financial windfall in the wake of a wealthy relative's death may not prompt an immediate reevaluation of the earlier education option, because this prospect had been previously canceled from consideration. In this way, sequencing of framing processes can affect final options by altering the initial context in which the choices are presented.

These editing operations, which constitute the framing of a problem, are important because of the way in which they can affect choice. Coding alone can determine the relevant reference point and help to define the outcomes, acts, and contingencies associated with a choice. Merely by including some and excluding other options from consideration, the process of framing itself creates the very choices that are understood to be available to a decision maker at a given time.

While the implications of framing for risk perception and assessment will be examined in greater detail below, a couple of examples at this point prove illustrative. People engage in unconscious coding and framing all the time. Advertising, in some sense, is little more than structuring the presentation of a product within a context designed to highlight its superiority over competitive options in the most memorable and salient way. To do this, the advertiser must frame his product within an image that will be readily invoked in a purchase context and that will remind the consumer why this particular product is better than the competition, because of price, status, quality, or whatever aspect is considered advantageous, given market research. In a more personal domain, people constantly frame information they receive and persuasions they attempt, often without even being aware of it. Oftentimes, gossip people hear is framed in terms of its source, because the source may have something to gain by harming the reputation of the person being discussed.

What are the political implications of framing? Choice can be manipulated by the order and presentation of the options available, without changing the substantive content of the information. In this way, framing becomes a powerful mechanism by which influential advisors can structure the choices, and thus influence the decisions, of decision makers.[18] Manipulation of framing can have profound effects on outcome, and therefore sophisticated practitioners can invoke these effects to their strategic advantage.[19] In this way, framing can bias decisions in systematic and predictable ways. For example, it may be possible to frame a favored option in the most positive terms, or to position a preferred option against much less desirable choices without including more attractive options for consideration. This can be done in simple and subtle ways: favored options are enhanced by easy comparison; nonfavored options are helped by complicated comparison; additional options hurt similar choices more than different ones; and so on.[20]

Framing demonstrates the process by which certain prospects become labeled as potential options while others are disregarded from consideration. Indeed, there may be a systematic bias in the kinds of prospects that are elevated to the status of seriously considered options; if this is so, such additional biases in the decision-making process become worthy of attention and possibly intervention.

Why is it that framing effects are considered to be counternormative? The primary reason is that frame changes can elicit changes in preference that violate rational choice theories requiring axioms of invariance to operate. With framing effects, people will make different choices based *solely* on the order of presentation. In other words, the same decision can elicit different choices depending on how the question is framed;[21] this finding is in total contradiction to any normative theory of decision making. What is more, if people are shown that they were influenced by framing effects, they agree that they should not have been so affected by them.

From the perspective of normative decision making, these findings are disturbing. As Tversky and Kahneman write:

> [D]ecisionmakers are not normally aware of the potential effects of different decision frames on their preference . . . Individuals who face a decision problem and have a definite preference (i) might have a different preference in a different framing of the same problem, (ii) are normally unaware of alternative frames and of their potential effects on the relative attractiveness of options, (iii) would wish their preferences to be independent of frame, but (iv) are often uncertain how to resolve undetected inconsistencies . . .

> Further complexities arise in the normative analysis, because the framing of an action sometimes affects the actual experience of its outcomes . . . The framing of acts and outcomes can also reflect the

acceptance or rejection of responsibility for particular consequences, and the deliberate manipulation of framing is commonly used as an instrument of self-control. When framing influences the experience of consequences, the adoption of a decision frame is an ethically significant act.[22]

In short, although people believe that their decisions should not be affected by simply changing the frame of the decision problem, they are manipulated by framing effects nonetheless.[23]

Two important points should be emphasized. One is that framing can be a purely cognitive constraint. Once people recognize their failure of invariance, they often agree that their decisions *should have* been made independent of the framing of the problem. So framing is not necessarily a motivated phenomenon, but can be a purely cognitive occurrence. In other words, it is a psychophysical property of choice.[24]

Second, from the perspective of intervention designed to reduce or prevent such undesired framing effects, choice should be presented to others, or to oneself, from a variety of frames simultaneously in order to help determine the most accurate and consistent preferences.[25] If the same problem is presented at the same time, framed in a couple of different ways, it is possible to recognize the impact of framing effects in a more transparent way. This was noticeable in the experimental findings, presented earlier, about choosing between radiation and surgery in the treatment of lung cancer.[26] Once the choices were presented side by side, in both survival and mortality terms, the better long-term survival strategy of surgery became obvious. Such a strategy of simultaneous presentation might render framing effects more transparent and thus reduce the extent to which a decision maker is influenced by them, without knowledge or desire.

One of the methodological quandaries in attempting to document the impact of framing effects on choice is the difficulty of predicting how people will choose to frame any given issue or choice, given the myriad of possible alternatives. Fischhoff experimented with predicting frames by arguing that "in order to predict behavior in less controlled situations, one must be able to anticipate how problems will be represented and what frames people will use to represent them."[27] Fischhoff's experiment met with little success outside the robust finding that "people do not readily adapt to absorbing losses."

Fischhoff explains his difficulty in predicting frames by noting individuals' inability to introspect accurately about what factors affect their choices and decisions. Much experimental evidence demonstrates that although people may be able to generate reasons after the event for why they behaved in a particular way, they may not recognize the real factors that control their behavior while they are in the situation itself.[28] Simple introspection confirms the intuition that it is more difficult for people to predict than explain their own, or others', behavior. However, once a person generates an explanation for his behavior, he is very likely to then believe that the explanation is an accurate one.[29]

Fischhoff argues that his experiment failed to elicit the desired result because the research methodology he used was not the most effective way of predicting frames. While his findings are discouraging from a predictive standpoint, it may be that more substantive knowledge about a particular decision maker's history or goals might help to predict frames more accurately. In the cases that follow, it becomes clear that historical analogies play an important role in determining the framing of an issue for many decision makers. Information on the particular historical analogies that are invoked by a leader in explaining behavior can often provide clues as to how the issue is being framed by that person.

Cases that analysts are most interested in *explaining* are also the ones that are most difficult to *predict* in general, regardless of whether one is using a psychological or a rational choice model.[30] The surprise with which almost every analyst greeted the demise of the Soviet Union and the end of the cold war is proof enough of the difficulty of predicting even very large scale and terribly important occurrences. While it may be possible to explain such events post hoc, it appears more challenging to predict behavior beforehand, regardless of the model that is used to generate such predictions.

Framing is important not only because of its direct influence on the choices available, but also because of its indirect effect on choice, through the value and weighting functions of prospect theory. These functions are part of the second, evaluation, phase of prospect theory.

Value Function

Once prospects are edited, or framed, the decision maker evaluates these options and makes a choice among them. The evaluation phase of prospect theory encompasses two parts, the value function and the weighting function. The proposed value function is illustrated in figure 1.

This value function has three crucial characteristics. The first is that it is defined in terms of gains and losses relative to the reference point, not in terms of final absolute wealth or welfare. This is quite different than expected utility theory, which assumes that the final asset position is definitive in calculating subjective utility and predicting choice. Emphasis on change from the reference point in prospect theory is in keeping with

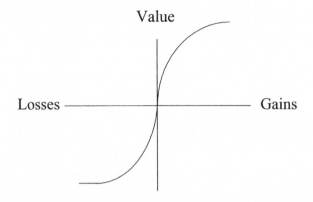

Fig. 1. A hypothetical value function. (Reprinted from Daniel Kahneman and Amos Tversky, "Choices, Values, and Frames," *American Psychologist* 39 (1984). Copyright © 1984 by the American Psychological Association. Reprinted with permission.)

basic human perceptual processes, which tend to notice shifts more than resting states. In prospect theory, value is a function of this change, in a positive or negative direction, rather than a result of absolute welfare, as is the case with subjective expected utility theory. This focus on change emphasizes the importance of the starting point, which in prospect theory is referred to as the reference point. Change is evaluated relative to that position, but value itself derives from the difference between that starting, or reference, point and the amount of any positive or negative shift away from it; again, this differs from expected utility theory, which considers value to derive exclusively from final states, and not the magnitude or direction of change from the status quo.[31] Recall the psychophysical analogue for the evaluation of change in prospect theory. Just as perception of sound or light is more sensitive to change than static intensity, so are assessments of welfare more reactive to change than absolute outcome in prospect theory.

The second important aspect of an S-shaped value curve is that it *is* S-shaped; that is, it is convex below the reference point and concave above it. In practical terms, the status quo typically serves as the operative reference point.[32] To be clear, the right-hand side of the graph refers to the domain of gains; the left-hand side of the graph represents the domain of losses. The slope measures the sensitivity to change; the curve is maximally sensitive to change nearest the origin and progressively less sensitive as it moves away from this reference point. Thus, for any given change, there is more impact closer to the starting point than farther away from it.

This finding is intuitively confirmed by the observation that the difference between $10 and $20 has more psychological impact than the same ten-dollar increase from $1,110 to $1,120. This decreasing marginal utility reflects a general psychophysical principle concerning the evaluation of outcomes, whereby comparable changes have a greater impact closer to the steady state of adaptation than farther away from it.

In theoretical terms, the S-shaped curve means that people tend to be risk averse in the domain of gains and risk seeking in the domain of losses; this is the crux of prospect theory. In short, prospect theory predicts that domain affects risk propensity.

The third aspect of the value function is the asymmetric nature of the value curve; it is steeper in the domain of losses than in that of gains. This implies relative loss aversion. In other words, losing hurts more than a comparable gain pleases. For example, losing ten dollars hurts more than finding ten dollars gratifies. In fact, loss aversion is intimately related to research on the phenomenology of happiness.[33] Individuals are understood to adapt to the steady state, or status quo, relatively rapidly. They are typically relatively satisfied with it, as well as averse to losing any component part of their present position. Loss aversion is exemplified by the endowment effect, whereby people value what they possess to a greater degree than they value an equally attractive alternative. This endowment bias makes equal trade unattractive. It also presents a bias toward the status quo in almost any negotiating context. This phenomenon holds interesting implications for political battles that involve such things as negotiations over territorial possession rights or weapons in arms control talks.[34]

Weighting Function

The second component of the evaluation phase of prospect theory is the weighting function. It is graphically represented in figure 2. In this second part of the evaluation phase of prospect theory, each outcome is given a decision weight. This weight does not correspond directly to traditional notions of probability.

In making a decision, a decision maker multiplies the value of each outcome by its decision weight, just as expected utility maximizers multiply utility by subjective probability. However, decision weights in prospect theory differ from those in subjective expected utility theory because decision weights do not obey any of the rational choice probability maxims. Decision weights do not serve solely as measures of the perceived likelihood of an outcome, as probability does in subjective expected utility theory. Rather, decision weights represent an empirically derived assessment of how people actually arrive at their sense of likelihood, rather than a normative standard about how they should derive probability, as subjective expected utility theories advocate. However, decision weights can be

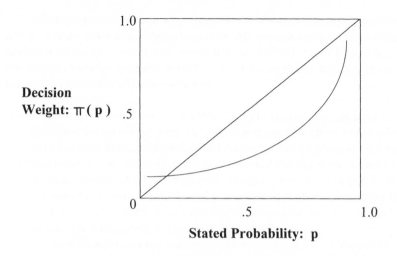

Fig. 2. A hypothetical weighting function. (Reprinted from Daniel Kahneman and Amos Tversky, "Choices, Values, and Frames," *American Psychologist* 39 (1984). Copyright © 1984 by the American Psychological Association. Reprinted with permission.)

affected by factors, such as ambiguity, that impact probability assessments in rational choice theories as well.[35]

The weighting function in prospect theory has several important features. First, the function does not operate consistently near the endpoints, which can be thought of as absolute certainty on the one end and absolute impossibility on the other. Thus, the function is defined as (1) = 1 and (0) = 0. In other words, people have difficulty with probability at extreme ranges: sometimes people may treat highly likely but uncertain events as certain; on other occasions, people may treat highly unlikely events as impossible.

More specifically, events that are judged to be either certain or impossible receive much heavier *psychological* weights than other events. The most dramatic illustration of this is provided by a study that showed that individuals would pay a great deal more money to remove the last bullet from a gun in a game of Russian roulette than to remove the fourth bullet, even though each removal reduced the risk by the same percentage, one-sixth. Regardless, eliminating the risk to 0 percent *feels* more important than merely diminishing it to 50 percent, even if the percentage of reduction is the same in both cases; indeed, this response is not wrong from an emotional perspective, only from a rational one.[36] This example illustrates that people have a hard time comprehending and evaluating the meaning of probability with extremely improbable or almost certain events; in effect, there is a limit to the decision weight that people can effectively attach to either the most or the least likely events. The result is that the evaluation of the likelihood of these extreme events becomes more biased than that of events that are only somewhat likely. Both the surgery and flu experiments illustrate this argument nicely as well.

This is where editing can come into play, as highly unlikely events are simply treated as though they were impossible and are thus ignored, and highly likely events are treated as if they offered certain outcomes.[37] The problem with this strategy lies in both directions; very unlikely events do occur occasionally, and very likely events do not happen every so often. An example of an extremely unlikely event that actually did happen can be seen in the tragic explosion of the space shuttle Challenger, where the combination of many highly effective systems created a situation where failure was more likely than it appeared; a hundred systems with a one in a hundred chance of failure results in almost certain disaster of the system over time.[38]

The flip side of this problem occurs when almost certain events sometimes do not actually take place. This occurrence was artfully captured in the famous photograph of Truman holding the newspaper that read, "Dewey beats Truman." Anyone who has bought or sold a house knows that even when everything appears to be progressing as planned, and all the agents consider the sale to be a "done deal," something can happen with the financing and the whole agreement can evaporate in the final stages.

The second important aspect of the weighting function is that low probabilities are overweighted while high and medium probabilities are subjectively underweighted. In other words, events that are not judged to be very likely are given more importance than they deserve. This happens, for example, when people place high risk assessments on an environmental toxin that has a very low probability of causing harm to any given individual. Similarly, occurrences that are estimated to be "somewhat likely" to "almost certain" are treated with less importance than they merit in the decision-making process. An example of this is seen when people were asked whether there are more homicides than suicides in the country every year: most people will say that homicides kill more people than suicides when in fact the opposite is true. Or they may claim that airplanes kill more people than what is actually true.[39] This is because low probability events, especially when they provide vivid and salient representations (airplanes, homicides), are overweighted, and high probability events (suicide, car accidents) are relatively underweighted.

This means that something that is perceived to be unlikely has more impact on decision making than it normatively should. The classic examples of this are lotteries and insurance. In lotteries, people are willing to take a sure loss, however small, for the essentially nonexistent chance of a huge gain. In this way, people can be risk seeking in gains when the probability of gain is low. In insurance, people are willing to take a sure loss in the present to prevent the small likelihood of a larger loss in the future. In this situation, people can be risk averse in losses when the probability of loss is small. In both these situations, expected utility models might not consider such behavior to be normative. However, prospect theory accounts for these discrepancies by noting the extreme (over)weight and attention that individuals give to small probabilities that potentially involve either huge gains (winning the lottery) or huge losses (losing your house in a fire). This phenomenon helps account for worst-case scenario planning.

Simultaneously, events that are, in actuality, quite likely have less influence on decision making than they normatively ought. This helps explain why many policies, such as gun control, are not pursued until after a salient example of its failure is made public. For example, it was not until James Brady, President Reagan's Press Secretary, was shot in 1981, thus becoming the active conservative poster image for the gun control lobby, that the issue started to be taken seriously in Congress. Although Brady's injury did not increase the overall risk of handguns in society, the salience of the issue was increased because of Brady's position and visibility.

In most cases, the weighting function contributes greatly to the risk propensity dictated by the S-shaped value function. As Kahneman and Tversky write:

> Underweighting of moderate and high probabilities relative to sure things contributes to risk aversion in gains by reducing the attractiveness of positive gambles. The same effect also contributes to risk seeking in losses by attenuating the aversiveness of negative gambles. Low probabilities, however, are overweighted, and very low probabilities are either overweighted quite grossly or neglected altogether . . . The overweighting of low probabilities reverses the pattern described above: It enhances the value of long shots and amplifies the aversiveness of a small chance of a severe loss. Consequently, people are often risk seeking in dealing with improbable gains and risk averse in dealing with unlikely losses. Thus, the characteristics of decision weights contribute to the attractiveness of both lottery tickets and insurance policies.[40]

One of the consequences of the weighting function is that probabilistic changes in the midranges are undervalued relative to equal changes that manage to transform an event from merely probable into one that is either certain or impossible. This has been called the certainty effect. In other words, reducing a 50 percent risk in half does not have the same impact as eliminating a 25 percent risk, as demonstrated by the example of removing bullets in a game of Russian roulette. Obviously, in policy-making decisions, any change in likelihood that makes an outcome either impossible or certain promises to have the greatest impact.

The pseudocertainty effect is another important aspect of prospect theory, whereby "an event that is actually uncertain is weighted as if it were certain."[41] Again, this phenomenon contributes to the predilection many decision makers have for worst-case-scenario planning. This tendency can be particularly problematic in political situations where weighting effects are exacerbated by the use of representative analogies. If a leader believes that another is *certainly* like, say, Hitler, then many subsequent assessments and decisions will be based on assumptions flowing from such a characterization, which may not, in fact, prove accurate. This was the case, for example, with the European leaders who believed that Nasser was a latter-day Hitler during the Suez crisis, and yet this prophecy was not borne out by subsequent history. Note that this bias can serve to make someone appear to be *either* more or less malicious than he may be in reality.

Application to International Politics

One of the central benefits of invoking psychological theories for understanding political events is the superior descriptive power that psychological theories offer. Psychological models do not require an analyst to pretend that people will, or should, act in a certain way that is counterintuitive. Rather, psychological models rest on empirical testing of how people actually make the decisions and choices they do in all kinds of situations. The value of theory developed on such empirical testing lies in its validity, accuracy, and authenticity.

Now that the substance of prospect theory has been discussed, it is appropriate to turn to the question of its applicability to political issues in the international arena. As noted in the introduction, this study sets out to conduct a parallel demonstration of theory, to illustrate that prospect theory can order evidence in a compelling way across cases and over time. This method is more appropriate to this study than in-depth case study methodology because establishing patterns across cases is more convincing and persuasive in demonstrating the fruitfulness of applying prospect theory to international relations. In addition, this study also seeks to test the external validity of prospect theory to the real world. In this way, the goal of this work is to determine whether or not prospect theory presents the accurate and powerful predictive and explanatory tool for understanding decision making under conditions of risk in international contexts that it does in a psychological laboratory.

Needless to say, there are several limitations to utilizing a psychological theory to illuminate political decision making. Not the least of these considerations is the extent to which political demands can compound psychological biases. Prospect theory is relatively new; although it has been applied extensively in economic models, it has not really been well tested in explicitly political arenas. Indeed, one of the challenges of this work is to demonstrate the applicability of prospect theory outside experimental conditions.

There is no technical or theoretical reason why the theory can not be applied well beyond the monetary gambles that defined its characteristics. The theory can be applied to decisions where the probabilities are not known, unlike monetary gambles where probabilities are determined in advance of play. Analysts must remember, however, that decision weights, although tied to subjective probabilities, are not technically the same as such probability estimates, and they fall prey to many biases that do not enter into consideration when all the probabilities are known in advance.[42] In applying prospect theory beyond the realm of monetary gambles, the goal is to show that the expectations remain the same: outcomes are evaluated in terms of gains or losses relative to the status quo reference point; and this domain, in turn, affects risk propensity in systematic and predictable ways.

There is clear empirical support for prospect theory at an individual level in the laboratory. Although many people are intrinsically suspicious of classroom findings, the mirror of introspection seems to support intuitively the validity of the experimental findings in this particular case. Decision makers are *not* immune to the effects of psychological tendencies merely by virtue of their roles. Indeed, there is an extensive literature investigating the impact of expertise on the ability to overcome some of the biases under discussion. While greater exposure to certain information can occasionally help an expert to greater accuracy than a novice in judgments of frequency,[43] other findings show no difference in the way that experts and novices are affected by framing or in how they respond to incomplete information.[44] In most cases, experts are found to display essentially the same biases in judgment and decision making as college students.[45] Susan Fiske and her colleagues have argued that experts have better organized knowledge and thus may have more space in memory for inconsistent information.[46] However, there is empirical evidence that elite beliefs are remarkably resistant to change, even in the face of dramatic changes in the international environment.[47] While there may be some difference between expert and novice inferential strategies, they are not significant enough to warrant excluding experts from the biases under discussion in this study by virtue of their position. In fact, experts are more similar to than different from novices in the way in which cognitive biases affect their judgment and decision-making abilities.

Prospect theory does not require that individual differences have *no* impact or importance. Rather, prospect theory reintroduces the importance of the situation into the analysis of decision making. Prospect theory relies on experimental evidence of mean differences between groups with regard to the impact of domain on risk propensity to point to significant preferences in choice above and beyond that which might be accounted for by individual differences.[48]

If the relative riskiness of response in international relations is affected by the perceived domain of action (gains or losses), this finding has important implications for the way in which political questions should be framed and presented to decision makers; this is particularly crucial if normatively unacceptable biases need to be minimized in order to avoid suboptimal decisions, and thus potentially hazardous outcomes. This is certainly the case if a simple linguistic manipulation of the available options early on might prevent a counternormative choice later. For this reason, it is worthwhile to investigate the extent to which a decision maker's cognitive biases might affect his choices, and subsequently even his state's behavior, in systematic and predictable ways.

Applying prospect theory to the international environment is an attempt to conceptualize the nature of risk in a more productive manner. If the predictions of prospect theory hold true in international settings, it might then be possible to introduce procedural or institutional mechanisms designed to compensate partially for such counternormative tendencies as framing effects. These kinds of changes could have a very positive influence on the decision-making process. For example, as discussed previously, it may be useful to present a decision maker with the same options framed in several different ways simultaneously, so as to make framing effects more transparent and thus less unconsciously influential on the substance of decision making.

Operationalization

In seeking to apply prospect theory to international relations, this study concentrates on the security arena, where decision making often takes place under conditions of greatest risk. The goal is to see whether decision makers manifest systematic differences in risk propensity as a result of differences in the perceived domain of action. This study will look at the president's risk-taking in the domain of gains and in the domain of losses.

This work focuses on postwar American foreign policy behavior. For purposes of this study, domain, coded as gains or losses relative to a reference point, is the "independent variable." Risk propensity, categorized as being either risk seeking or risk averse, is the "dependent variable." Domain causes risk propensity. If the theory holds, actors will be risk averse if facing potential gains, and risk seeking when confronted with potential losses.

Needless to say, it is challenging to determine domain and risk in ways that are not only independent of one another, but not tautological either. In most cases, a decision maker's behavior (words) offers the best evidence for perceived domain; however, an actor's assessment of domain is often subjective, or suppressed for political reasons, and this constraint must simply be admitted. However, when a public consensus concerning domain is present, it increases the likelihood that such a consensus is shared by the central decision maker, especially if he is sensitive to polls; such consensus enhances confidence in the accurate characterization of a given domain.

In some sense, the problems faced by prospect theory in this matter are no greater than those faced by scholars who prefer rational choice modeling, which starts from a position of "revealed preferences." Prospect theory may appear to be less precise than rational choice theories claim to be, but, in reality, prospect theory proves to be more analytically malleable. This is because, with rational choice theories, utilities are notoriously difficult to assess, and basic supporting axioms are frequently violated in individual behavior. Assessments of information are often subjective and open to debate; merely applying mathematical formulas, letters, and numbers to certain variables does not render those variables, or their outcomes, any more "objective." Most importantly, rational choice models require an unwieldy amount of information, detail, and precision and may not be useful for this reason. Prospect theory requires only knowledge of domain in order to predict risk propensity. Moreover, rational choice models are vulnerable to different analysts structuring the same problem in contradictory ways. In contrast, prospect theory builds on experimental findings concerning human judgment and decision-making behavior. In fact, it is worth remembering that *experimental* findings are one of the few ways to definitely establish *causal* links.[49] Psychological accuracy makes prospect theory a more realistic and manageable model. Rational actor models, after all, invoke rationality assumptions that are without question empirically invalid; prospect theory is not nearly so wanton in its starting assumptions. As a result, prospect theory is sufficiently rigorous to test in the international environment, and it is not as intractable in assessing utility as are many rational choice models.

Domain

Domain refers to whether an action takes place in the perceived realm of gains or of losses. Domain can be relatively objective or subjective. For purposes of prospect theory, framing in domain is restricted to a sense of whether the actor perceives himself to be acting from a position of gains or losses. Gains or losses can be defined by objective criteria, such as public opinion polls. Domain can also be ascertained by subjective assessments derived from memoirs, interviews, and archival materials. The problem in international relations is that it is often impossible to tell the difference between the objective and the subjective framing of domain. Polls are examples of data that are often difficult to characterize; results may be considered "objective," but how they are interpreted must clearly be regarded as "subjective." As a result, there can be confusion as to the appropriate domain of action. This is especially important when the objective and subjective domains do not match. When this occurs, both types will be noted, and differences in assessment will be highlighted.

An additional complication in determining domain derives from the fact that different people may use different criteria in order to define their domain of action. For example, some presidents may consider their domestic political support to be the crucial variable; international public opinion may be irrelevant as long as the politician is certain that he can win reelection at home. Positive international public opinion may be irrelevant to a president who has lost his domestic support; Richard Nixon may have been held in high esteem by the leadership of the Soviet Union and China in 1974, but this did not prevent him from being forced to resign in the wake of the Watergate debacle. Different actors may look to different appraisals in order to determine whether or not they are acting in a realm of gains or losses. Obviously, this assessment can change over time, as the situation changes, as decision makers use different measures of success in different issue areas, or as leaders come to rely on certain indicators as being more valid in certain situations or at different times than others. In some cases, the judgment may be overwhelming, as when all indicators show the person to be in deep trouble, as Johnson was during Vietnam, or Nixon was during Watergate. However, in many other situations, the judgment is less clear and will depend on the best guess concerning the criterion of most value to the actor. As always, the central concern must focus on whether the decision maker is operating in a relative state of gains or losses.

As a result of the inherently subjective nature of perception, domain, like risk propensity and reference point, must be defined case-by-case and actor-by-actor. To assess a decision maker's domain accurately, an analyst needs to distinguish among the various criteria that different actors may use to determine perceived domains of action. In many cases, the analyst may be aided in this task by information about the relevant historical analogy that the decision maker is invoking in responding to the current situation. The perception that counts in this regard is that of the particular decision maker under investigation. In most cases in the postwar security arena, this individual will be the president. More specifically, the relevant objective sources may include: the content of speeches; archival material; public opinion polls; congressional indicators, such as the number of overrides on vetoes; economic indicators, such as the stock market index and inflation or unemployment rates; newspaper editorials; and world public opinion as manifested through diplomatic channels. Sources of subjective assessments of domain might come from interviews, private memoirs, archival letters, diaries, transcripts, and foreign relations documents. The danger in using these personal, historical sources is that they run the risk of being informed by retrospective bias, whereby leaders may selectively remember factors that show them off in the best light. From this perspective, it is easiest and best to trust information from a memoir that makes a leader look bad; he is very unlikely to have a good reason for portraying himself in a negative light unless it is the truth. The most relevant or informative of these indicators can be used to assess how the decision maker felt about the environment he faced and whether or not his assessment matched the objective criteria. In this way, different evidence will be used for different cases.

Clearly, there may be some technical problems with this approach. However, real-life decision making rarely mimics the precision of an experimental laboratory, where all variables can be controlled. Rather, it is only possible to work with the information that is available and make the best judgments possible. Prospect theory's value lies in the variables that the theory points to as significant for analysis and discussion. To the extent that these variables differ from those investigated under more traditional paradigms, it offers the possibility of shedding light on previously ignored, but potentially important, factors in decision making, such as domain.

Risk

Risk is an even more difficult variable to operationalize than domain. The central concern is fear of tautological definition; risk cannot be determined by domain, on the one hand, or by outcome, on the other. In operationalizing risk in an independent fashion, an economic definition of risk will be invoked; risk will be analyzed in terms of relative variance in outcome. A choice is relatively risk seeking if it has greater outcome variance in promoted values than alternative options. For example, if one option presents a 50 percent chance of winning $5 and a 50 percent chance of losing $10, it is less risky than a gamble which offers a 50 percent prospect of winning $50 and a 50 percent chance of losing $100. In this case, neither the positive nor the negative outcome of the first gamble is as extreme as that offered by the second; it is thus a riskier choice to play the second bet, regardless of outcome and independent of domain.

The difficulty is that choices vary in both probability and desirability. Another problem is that political decision makers *never* present their options in cardinal form, with concrete subjective probability assessments attached to each choice as decision analysts would prefer.

Most of the time, all that political decision makers offer is the fact that one policy option is preferable to another in a particular issue area. Yet military risks can conflict with political ones and so on. It can be difficult to separate out these factors, but one way to compare across policies that offer different "expected" values across issue areas is through the use of ordinal comparisons. For example, let's say a policymaker is trying to decide between policies A and B. Policy A generates the best outcome if it works, and the worst outcome if it doesn't. Policy B, on the other hand, does not offer as good an outcome as A if it works, but the outcome of B is not as bad as the outcome in A if B fails. So, an analysis of these options might proceed as follows. First of all, B is a less risky choice than A because there is less variance in the outcome: the best of B is not as good as the best of A, but the worst of B is not as bad as the worst of A. A graphic hierarchy of these options might appear as illustrated below:

Best-A
Best-B
Worst-B
Worst-A

Second, using this method of analysis, it becomes possible to compare across policies that offer different expected values by comparing the ordinal ranking on the issue area of major concern. For example, if policies B and W are compared, and all possible outcomes for B are superior to all possible outcomes for W, then B is clearly the risk-averse and obviously better, more "rational" choice. A graphic depiction of the hierarchy of such an option set might look similar to the one presented below:

Best-B
Worst-B
Best-W
Worst-W

Clearly, B is the superior choice in rational terms. This is because B maximizes all outcomes in a way W is not able to accomplish. The worst outcome from B will always prove superior to the best outcome from W. Using this strategy, it becomes possible to compare policies in terms of variance in outcome values without having to precisely determine a decision maker's subjective probabilities, and without having to risk tautology in the definition of risk.[50] This perspective also acknowledges that different policies possess different "expected values" in their outcomes. In many circumstances, choices are made precisely because they promote the greatest expected value, and not for any other reason. In these instances, prospect theory may provide no additional insight over standard political analysis, as when a decision maker picks an option with the greatest expected value while acting cautiously in a domain of gains.

Given this method of determining risky choice, relative risk propensity in this study will be categorized in terms of risk-seeking and risk-averse behavior. The riskiness of the option chosen will be assessed relative to that of the other options perceived to be available at the time in terms of the variance in outcome just described.

The second benefit of this definition is that it takes into account the other options that are considered. This is important in order to see if the framing of options appears to have an effect on the substance of the decisions that are made. In this way, it may be possible to demonstrate that risk assessment changes as the frame changes. By looking at risk propensity in terms of the other options that are considered at the time, framing effects may be thrown into illuminating relief.

Reference Point

The reference point is a critical concept in assessing gains and losses; thus, it is central to the notions of domain and risk. The reference point is usually the current steady state, or status quo, to which a person has become accustomed. This status quo point can be influenced by a number of different factors, including cultural norms and expectations. Moreover, it might be affected by such variables as personal levels of aspiration. These considerations may or may not be realistic in nature.[51] Some expectations, though unrealistic, may still have an impact on the choices an individual makes. For example, however unrealistic it may be to expect to obtain an academic job in a bad market, many individuals still pursue graduate degrees. In this case, it is up to the analyst to sort out whether the student is irrational, grandiose, or merely risk seeking in a domain of losses, as prospect theory would predict.

The definition of the reference point is crucial to the determination of domain. Most importantly, shifts in reference point can affect definitions of domain. As Kahneman and Tversky write:

> There are situations in which gains and losses are coded relative to an expectation or aspiration level that differs from the status quo . . . A change of reference point alters the preference order for prospects. In particular, the present theory implies that a negative translation of a choice problem, such as arises from incomplete adaptation to recent losses, increases risk seeking in some situations . . . This analysis suggests that a person who has not made peace with his losses is likely to accept gambles that would be unacceptable to him otherwise . . . a failure to adapt to losses or to attain an expected gain induces risk seeking.[52]

At this point, an example may be helpful to illustrate the impact of expectation or aspiration on the assessment of reference point. A junior faculty member can survive on "promise" for a few years after being hired. During this time, the young professor need not have a long publication list in order to be in a domain of gains. However, by the time the tenure clock ticks away, promise is no longer an adequate measure of success. While the objective reality of the publications record may not have changed at all (indeed, that is the cause of concern for the tenure committee), the reference point has shifted. Time slowly but surely affects the way "promise" translates into "disappointment" by continually shifting the reference point from the realm of reality into that of aspiration.

In this way, level of aspiration can affect the assessment of reference point, just as social norms and cultural values might as well. Nonetheless, in most circumstances, the default reference point is typically the current status quo.

However, prospect theory itself is theoretically silent about the issue of temporal change. Gains and losses are always evaluated relative to the reference point. That is, the theory makes no comment on how the direction of change in the status quo affects the assessment of the reference point. However, normal psychological theory would predict that the reference point would tend to gravitate, with time, to an adaptation point, which would correspond to the new status quo. The issue then becomes the period of lag time. During that time, things are still evaluated relative to the old status quo. This old status quo remains the reference point until adaptation takes place. Moreover, loss aversion suggests that the lag will last longer in adjusting to losses than to gains.[53]

As with domain, the relevant reference point will have to be determined on a case-by-case basis; the reference point will have to be defined independently for each actor at each decision point, since each person may have a different idea of the relevant status quo, even in the same objective situation for reasons of expectation, as discussed previously. For example, Eisenhower held a very different notion of the status quo during the Suez crisis than did British and French leaders. By and large, however, the reference point will be defined in relation to the central decision maker, which in these cases is the president.

Loss Aversion

Because losses loom larger than gains in prospect theory, it is expected that there will be greater focus and attention on real or feared losses than on prospective or forgone gains. This phenomenon is predicted by the steep convex shape of the value curve in the domain of losses. The impact of such loss aversion is heightened by the fact that political punishment for losses is generally greater than for failure to make gains.

Loss aversion also suggests that it is much more difficult for people to adjust to losses than to gains.[54] As a result, more energy will be spent trying to avoid or recoup losses than will be devoted to consolidating, or obtaining, new gains.

Loss aversion induces a preference for the status quo in most situations. This property is particularly noticeable in negotiating and bargaining contexts, such as arms control, but is certainly not limited in its effect to those issue areas. The phenomenon of loss aversion is exacerbated by other psychological tendencies as well. First, the differences between options will seem more important if they are *framed* in terms of losses or negative aspects rather than if they are *framed* in terms of positive aspects or gains. Second, adding a loss to a particular choice will hurt it more than adding an advantage will help it. In this way, it can be shown that sabotaging an undesired alternative becomes a much easier maneuver than enhancing a favorable one. Lastly, a beneficial policy that is hindered by even one small disadvantage may appear less attractive than another policy that boasts two much smaller positive qualities, but carries no possibility of a negative outcome.[55]

Loss aversion raises an additional important point concerning frame change and ambiguity effects. In many situations the status quo is unclear, and in addition it may incorporate other subjective assessments, such as expectations, as previously discussed. The real status quo might be up for perceptual grabs, just as is the reference point upon which it is based. Relevant definitions of gains, losses, status quo, and reference point are ambiguous and dynamic; they change from actor to actor and situation to situation. The best effort to clarify these conceptions will be made on a case-by-case basis, but all these definitions are affected by framing effects and subjective assessments that are not always clear or available.

Case Outline

The casework that follows constitutes an empirical investigation applying prospect theory to international politics. Four examples are examined in substance in the following chapters: two decisions from the Eisenhower administration and two from the Carter administration. Both presidents led the United States in the nuclear age, so it is possible to control for differences in decision making that might result from the development of such weapons of mass destruction. These presidents also come from different political parties, so the effect of affiliation or, more broadly, ideology on risk propensity can be roughly controlled for in these cases as well.

These cases were chosen to differ along the lines of the independent variable: one case from the domain of losses, and one from the domain of gains, for each president. In the domain of losses, the cases are: Carter's decision to go ahead with the failed rescue mission of the hostages in Iran in April 1980; and Eisenhower's cover-up following the Soviet downing of the U-2 American reconnaissance aircraft in May 1960. In the domain of gains, the cases are: Carter's decision to exclude the Shah of Iran from entry into the country until October 1979; and Eisenhower's decision to resist his French and English allies in their military venture against Egyptian President Nasser in the Suez crisis of 1956.

The goal of this investigation is to analyze these domain-specific cases to determine whether the dependent variable, risk-taking behavior, differs in accordance with the predictions of prospect theory along the independent variable, domain. A graphic display of the central hypotheses might appear as follows:

	Risk Seeking	Risk Averse
Gains		PT predicts
Losses	PT predicts	

As delineated, prospect theory expects risk seeking in the domain of losses and risk aversion in the domain of gains.[56] The cases were of interest initially because the president's behavior appeared to be anomalous and not easily explicable from within the context of alternative analytic paradigms.

The application of prospect theory to each case that follows proceeds in four parts. First, each chapter begins with an examination of the relevant domain of action, either gains or losses. Next, each chapter looks at the options that were considered at the time. In this part, the particular framing of the relevant issues and questions to the president by his principal advisors will be investigated at a substantive level. In this way, it is possible to examine differences in the political emphases and goals of various players. The third step consists of the evaluation of the specific risk propensity of the action taken, risk seeking or risk averse. The actual decision is then examined and a comparison is made between the predictions of the theory and the actual decisions reached. The last part briefly describes the outcome of each particular event. The crucial aspect of these analyses lies in the relationship between domain and risk, and not in the success or failure of the actual decision or policy. Thus, the decision-making process is not judged by the success or failure of the outcome.

The claim is not that prospect theory explains everything. Rather, the purpose of the case studies is to document that domain and framing can have a profound and predictable, though often subtle, effect on the substance and content of decision making under conditions of risk. Through a parallel demonstration of theory, it is possible to show that prospect theory can illuminate a variety of important cases in postwar American foreign policy and thus offers useful insight into risk propensity in international politics.

Prospect theory can help explain the choice of an option that does not in fact promote the greatest expected value. Prospect theory helps explain how choice decisions are evaluated when the options available do not differ significantly in their expected value or where optimal choice is not evident. Prospect theory helps explain why nonoptimal choices are often made, especially in the case of loss aversion. Finally, prospect theory addresses those cases where decisions require choices among options that promote conflicting values. By examining how these options are compared and evaluated in terms of gains and losses in each issue area and not only in terms of absolute outcome, it becomes possible to shed new light on critical but previously unrecognized aspects of important decisions.

Prospect theory offers a wealth of knowledge that can be fruitfully applied to problems in the international environment. The following chapters will apply prospect theory to events in the international arena that explicitly involve judgment under uncertainty and decision making under risk. In this way, it is hoped that prospect theory will provide a more theoretically sophisticated understanding of the nature of risk propensity.

CHAPTER 3

The Iranian Hostage Rescue Mission

After exhausting all diplomatic channels to achieve the release of 53 Americans held hostage in Iran for over six months, President Carter undertook a dramatic military rescue attempt in April 1980. Carter's action was not only completely contrary to his explicit commitment to human rights and to seeking nonmilitary solutions to foreign policy crises in world politics, but it was a highly risky prospect from a military standpoint as well.

How is it possible to understand the nature of the risks Carter was willing to run, both militarily and politically, in order to force the release of the hostages from Iranian control? The flashlight of prospect theory illuminates a case that might otherwise prove inexplicable.

Background

The most dramatic events of the Carter administration revolved around the Iranian hostage crisis. The November hostage crisis had been foreshadowed by an earlier seizure of the U.S. Embassy by militant students in February 1979. At that earlier time, the Iranian government stepped in and served as a successful intermediary in facilitating the release of the hostages. In 1979, there were about 70,000 Americans in Iran.[1] After the hostage seizure in February, the United States took many precautions to secure personal safety for the embassy personnel and to encourage other Americans to leave Iran. In a memo explaining these precautions, National Security Council Staff Advisor for Iran, Gary Sick, wrote:

> Our thinking on protection took off from the fact that, during the February 14 takeover, the Foreign Minister himself came to the Embassy compound to take charge of American personnel and to clear the compound. At that time, assurances of protection for our remaining people were given . . .
>
> On the security side, we proceeded on the basis of the following strategy: Since our protection ultimately depends on the willingness of the host government to provide protection, we would harden the

Embassy to enable our people to take refuge safely for a period of
time until help could come . . .

There were approximately 15 police on duty when the Embassy was
attacked on November 4 and they were unable to resist the large
crowd which invaded the Embassy.

When we learned of the Shah's medical condition and decided to
admit him to the U.S., we informed the Foreign Minister and in the
same meeting asked for his assurance that our Embassy people would
be protected. He provided that assurance then and on two following
occasions.

When we learned of the massive demonstrations scheduled for
Thursday, November 1, our Chargé again approached the Iranian
authorities and received a further reconfirmation that the embassy
would be protected.[2]

Shortly before the hostages were taken prisoner at the American Embassy,
the U.S. government showed increased concern about the security of
American civilians in Iran, as noted in this internal memo to the president:
"The security of the building has been greatly reinforced since February
and is nearly impregnable short of a heavy weapons attack. The Iranian
police have promised to provide security for the compound."[3]

Because of these extensive precautions and the assurances provided
by Iranian governmental officials, few in the American government anticipated that the embassy and its personnel would be so seriously threatened
in the November demonstrations.

The events that followed were quite a surprise to the Carter administration. On November 4, 1979, in the context of a broader Islamic revolution, as many as 3,000 Iranian students seized the U.S. embassy in Tehran,
taking 66 Americans hostage in the process. The students themselves
undertook this attack as a symbolic gesture and expected the takeover to
last only a matter of days; they were almost as surprised as the Carter
administration when they received the vociferous blessings and benedic-
tions of the Imam, Khomeini, and thus they proceeded to settle in for a
longer episode than originally anticipated.[4] Fifty-three[5] hostages were
kept for 444 days, until their negotiated release was completed on January
20, 1981, about two minutes into the Reagan presidency.[6]

The Carter administration consistently sought to negotiate diplomat-
ically for the release of the hostages, although they simultaneously developed contingency plans for military action beginning on November 4.[7]
The rescue attempt took place at the very nadir of the crisis, following the
collapse of negotiations with Western-educated Iranian revolutionaries,
such as President Abolhassan Bani-Sadr, through French legal intermedi-

aries. The actual rescue mission attempt took place on April 24, 1980. This mission resulted in the deaths of eight American soldiers, caused four additional American injuries, and failed to bring about the release of any of the hostages.

Domain

Carter was clearly operating in a domain of losses at the time of his decision to proceed with the rescue mission. Carter confronted a situation where things were bad, and they were clearly continuing to get worse as time went by and the hostages remained in captivity. This is obvious from every external indicator Carter confronted: a revolutionary Islamic power held 53 Americans hostage and refused to negotiate directly with him; a tough reelection campaign in the face of an increasingly frustrated and hostile American public; a growing sense of desperation about the safety and a clamoring for the release of the hostages among numerous members of Congress, other governmental officials, and the American public; and declining international prestige and credibility for the U.S. government in the wake of the hostage crisis. Carter could only have seen himself operating in a domain of losses, both domestically and internationally.

On the domestic front, Carter's popularity was declining rapidly. Even before the hostage crisis began, one poll taken in June 1979 reported that only 20 percent of the population approved of Carter's foreign policy.[8] Immediately following the seizing of the hostages by the Iranian militants, public reaction followed the standard rally-round-the-flag phenomenon. Public opinion was strongly supportive of Carter, but also strongly hostile to Iran. As one indicator, 97 percent of telephone calls to the White House supported imposing economic sanctions on Iran, pursuing action against Iranian nationals in the United States, and taking military action in Iran. Moreover, 89 percent of the calls supported cutting off oil imports from Iran and 51 percent advocated deporting the Shah in order to end the crisis. More to the point, 421 calls in a six-hour period on November 21 responded positively to a White House hint of military action against Iran.[9] Thus, the vocal public strongly supported strident action against the Iranians. Carter's failure to take such action over the subsequent five months cost him greatly in public opinion polls over that time and pushed Congress to place greater pressure on the administration to do something to resolve the hostage crisis.

Immediately after the hostages were taken captive, Congress, while supporting the president's policy broadly, consistently agitated for more action by the U.S. government against the Iranian militants. On November 8, Advisor Bob Beckel told White House Chief of Staff Hamilton Jordan that "there is an extraordinary amount of hostility running through the Congress toward the Iranian students in the United States . . . There is a demand that we do *something* about the students."[10] Congressional aggravation continued to mount against the Iranians throughout the following month. By December, a memo on foreign policy issues commented to the president:

> In the most troubling move, Representative Stratton introduced a resolution which calls upon you to set a deadline for the release of the hostages. If the deadline is not met, 'selective military action' is recommended. As of mid-day November 29, the Stratton resolution had over sixty co-sponsors.[11]

The public polls in early December reflected the administration's ambivalence toward resorting to military action to resolve the crisis. A Roper poll conducted between December 1 and 8, 1979, summarized U.S. public opinion concerning this issue as follows:

> By a two to one margin the public rejects a military raid into Tehran to free the hostages—at present at least. Three out of four feel such a raid would fail which may—or may not—be the reason for their opposition to such a raid.[12]

However, as the hostage drama dragged on without any prospect of negotiated resolution, the American public grew increasingly impatient with Carter and his diplomacy-based foreign policy toward Iran. By the end of January, the popular sentiment began to show increasing frustration with the hostage stalemate. According to a Louis Harris poll conducted in January,

> A 53–27 percent majority now feels that if 'in three weeks, the hostages are still held by Iran and it does not appear that any real progress has been made in getting the release,' then President Carter's policy on the Iran crisis has been a failure. If the statement continues on for another three months, then an even higher 74–12 percent majority would then view the President's efforts as a failure . . . It is now clear from these ABC-Harris Survey results that . . . people have simply run out of patience and will accept nearly any condition in order to get the hostages back alive.[13]

The results of these polls demonstrate that not only was Carter in a negative position in terms of public opinion and popularity, but his status was decreasing with every passing day that the hostages remained in captivity. In other words, President Carter was in a bad place, and things were clearly getting worse. An additional irony of the Harris poll is that the rescue mission was conducted just about three months after the poll was taken, by which point the poll indicated that tolerance for a strategy of extended patience would have retained the support of less than 12 percent of the public.

By the time that the military preparations and weather conditions were conducive to the execution of the rescue mission, Carter's support had declined substantially from what it had been in January. According to a *Time* poll conducted during the last two weeks of March, 60 percent of the American public felt that Carter was too soft on Iran.[14]

Carter's reelection campaign, moreover, was going badly. During the last week of March, a month prior to the rescue mission, Carter had sustained two large losses in the New York and Connecticut Democratic primaries to Senator Edward Kennedy. Although he won the Wisconsin primary on April 1, there were widespread press reports that he used the hostage crisis to manipulate that victory by prematurely announcing false good news about their impending release.[15]

In addition, just prior to the decision to proceed with the rescue mission attempt, Carter slipped below his Republican opponent, Ronald Reagan, in the election polls for the first time; Carter had held a two to one lead over Reagan in December 1979. By March, however, almost half of the people who supported Carter did so "without enthusiasm." Moreover, 81 percent of the population said they felt that America was in serious trouble, and about 70 percent said they thought it was time for a change in the presidency.[16]

Carter's relationship with Congress was deteriorating as well. Presidential victories on votes in Congress declined from 81.4 to 73.3 percent in the Senate alone between 1979 and 1980. Moreover, Republican support in the Senate for Carter's positions fell below 50 percent.[17]

Pierre Salinger, who covered the hostage crisis for ABC News, provides a good summary of the situation:

> Other factors were weighing on the President. Better than anyone, Carter knew how the hostage crisis had paralyzed his administration's efforts in other fields, if only because it diverted his own attention and energies so greatly. Politically, therefore, he was twice wounded—first by the crisis, and again by its impact on his programs. His campaign for reelection registered the frustrations of the American public. While his political fortunes had risen after the taking of the hostages, he was beginning to slip in the polls and had lost a key

primary in New York to Senator Edward Kennedy. Jimmy Carter was now in the midst of a fight for his life, and it looked as if he was losing. A military option that freed the hostages would dramatically alter the odds.[18]

It is significant that Salinger notes here that a military option that freed the hostages might somehow rectify all the losses and perhaps even restore or improve the previous status quo. In other words, it appeared that things would continue to get worse unless something dramatic, such as the rescue mission, was attempted proactively in order to rectify the situation.

The view from inside the administration was equally bleak, as White House aide for Iran Gary Sick commented:

> The image of U.S. weakness generated by months of humiliating setbacks and frustrations was not healthy for relations with allies or adversaries. In domestic politics, continued passivity not only condemned the President to self-immolation in the polls but it risked generating a popular backlash in favor of forces who opposed everything Vance and Carter represented.[19]

The relationship between the international and domestic political pressures were interactive; as the international situation worsened, domestic tension increased. Secretary of State Cyrus Vance had had great difficulty encouraging the allies to cooperate with the United States by joining with America in enforcing economic sanctions against Iran.[20] In a State Department telegram sent to Canada and Italy on March 26, allies were warned that "without . . . support from our close friends, the U.S. will have little choice but to undertake further and more severe unilateral actions."[21] Yet, in spite of allied fears of American military action against Iran, and the possibility that such action might endanger critical oil shipments, allied response was moderate at best. In the month before the rescue mission attempt,

> U.S. allies in Europe, in a move given lukewarm approval by U.S. officials who wanted stronger action, decided to reduce their diplomatic staffs in Iran and promise to impose economic sanctions if no 'decisive progress' is made in the hostage crisis by May 17.[22]

International channels of conflict negotiation proved no more useful to the United States in fighting Iranian actions against America than the allies were individually. A United Nations Security Council measure against Iran had been vetoed by the Soviet government earlier in the year.[23] Grievances brought against Iran by the U.S. in the World Court were slow to reach fruition and lacking in any enforcement mechanism upon conviction.[24] Moreover, Carter had been warned by President Anwar Sadat of Egypt that America's "international standing" was being damaged by "excessive passivity."[25]

Thus, Carter was a man who had sustained tremendous losses to personal popularity, national honor, and international prestige when the hostages were taken. By the time of the rescue mission, Carter was desperate to redress his losses. If the hostages could be released, Carter could have reasonably expected that national pride and international honor would be restored, and his political fortune might turn upward. Carter was not willing to accept the new status quo, one that absorbed the loss associated with the hostages having been taken captive. The new status quo was not an acceptable reference point for Carter. In terms of prospect theory, Carter was a man operating in the domain of losses because he had not renormalized to a new status quo that incorporated a serious loss. Carter's operative reference point throughout the crisis remained one that refused to recognize the seizure of the hostages as an acceptable loss.

The Options Considered

Prospect theory suggests that relatively subtle manipulations in coding and framing can have a profound influence on choice. In this way, the presentation of the status quo and the options available can impact heavily on the judgments and decisions that are made.

Each central decision maker held a unique perspective concerning the situation that he was confronting. Prospect theory tells us little about how individuals construct the frames that they espouse.[26] However, once these frames are developed and expressed, prospect theory can predict and explain risk propensity based on the subjective structuring of domain. The following discussion is designed to help establish the relevant frames within which specific decision makers saw themselves acting. In this case, as in others, it is clear that historical analogies were very powerful forces in establishing relevant frames for central decision makers. For example, throughout the crisis, Vance invoked two previous World War II hostage crises involving Agnus Ward and the USS Pueblo as relevant analogies, where American hostages were released safely in the absence of American military action.[27] Brzezinski, on the other hand, was working off the Bay of Pigs analogy and saw the rescue mission as the American equivalent of the successful Israeli raid at Entebbe.[28] Carter shared Brzezinski's Bay of Pigs analogy, as ironically demonstrated by his request for Kennedy's speech following the Bay of Pigs debacle to prepare his own speech after the rescue mission failed.[29] In this way, historical analogies can provide powerful references for the development of frames that can then help explain the relative domains in which each actor perceived himself to be operating.

According to Gary Sick, there was a consensus within the administration on the hierarchy of risk presented by the various available options. The main disagreement among advisors and decision makers surrounded which level of risk was the optimal one for the United States to take. In terms of decision analysis, the question is which option holds the greatest chance of achieving the most positive outcome. The problem, of course, is when the most desirable outcome is offered by an option that also possesses a high probability of failure. Recall that for purposes of this study risk is assessed in terms of variance in outcome. The option that presents the greatest variance in outcome is considered the most risky.

From the outset, there were five basic options that were seriously considered to bring about the release of the hostages.[30] From the lowest to the highest level of subjective risk assessment, these options were: to do nothing; to engage in minimal political and diplomatic sanctions; to undertake a rescue mission; to mine the harbors; and to engage in an all-out military strike.[31]

The first option was to do nothing and wait for the internal situation in Iran to stabilize and hope that the crisis would resolve by itself over time. This was the option that Vance supported.[32] The strategy here was to continue with political pressure, but not to offer new initiatives until after the Iranians had formulated their political system into a coherent new structure. The benefit of this strategy was that it did not risk antagonizing the Iranians any further. In Vance's view, this approach was most likely to protect the hostages from further harm.[33]

As might be obvious, the variance in potential outcomes with this option is low. While doing nothing would certainly be unlikely to provoke a bad response from the Iranians, neither was it likely to precipitate the release of the hostages. However, doing nothing carried with it some domestic political risks given the public demand for action to be taken. The political risk was not greater with this option, however, than the political risk of triggering broader armed conflict with Iran as might result from either mining the harbors or engaging in an all-out military strike. In this way, the variance in outcome from doing nothing was actually less than with other options, which offered greater risk of conflict but also offered greater potential for resolution.

The political risks of this policy from a domestic perspective are obvious. Carter would be charged with ineffectiveness and be accused of being pushed around by the Ayatollah. Within the administration, the personal sense of anger at the Iranians was running very high at this time.[34] Thus, while the military risks of doing nothing were relatively low, the domestic political risks were high. From the perspective of central decision makers, it was virtually impossible to conceive of accepting deliberate international humiliation in the face of such abominable Iranian action without doing something in response. In short, there was a universal sense that the situation was intolerable and doing nothing about it was unacceptable. Emotional motivations like deep anger and frustration added to the cognitive belief that there was no strategic or political reason why the United States should allow itself to be pushed around by a lesser power in the Middle East.[35]

The second option was to up the ante slightly, but only through diplomatic means. In practical terms, this meant breaking political and economic relations with Iran, placing an embargo on shipments of military and other sales, expelling Iranian citizens from the United States and so on. Everyone assumed that these things would be done, and all of these options were eventually executed.[36]

These economic and political sanctions were both serious and extensive. Beginning on November 12, 1979, the president placed an embargo on all Iranian oil products; at the time, this amounted to imports of 750,000 barrels a day, which represented about 4 percent of the American daily supply.[37] On November 14, the president declared a State of National Emergency in order to invoke various powers under the Internal Emergency Economic Powers Act that allowed the U.S. government to freeze Iranian assets held in the United States.[38] This act was renewed one year later, as required by law, to prevent automatic expiration.[39] On April 7, 1980, the United States broke diplomatic relations with Iran.[40] On April 17, 1980, five more serious financial and travel restrictions were imposed against Iran by the U.S. government.[41] Additional punitive, though non-military, measures were taken by the U.S. government against Iran throughout the crisis. These sanctions included: expelling Iranian diplomats and students from the United States; embargoing all imports, amounting to about $1,000,000 a month; prohibiting all exports, including food and medicine and weapons paid for by the Shah; prohibiting travel; freezing all Iranian assets and prohibiting any financial transactions; blocking telecommunications; and closing Iranian air, travel, and financial institutions in the United States.[42]

These sanctions were not regarded as particularly risky from either a political or a military standpoint. In other words, these options possessed a low *variance* in outcome value. Although sanctions were not likely to produce a worse outcome for the hostages, neither were they terribly likely to produce an optimal one either, at least not immediately.

This is where the notion of weighting comes into play. Recall that when probabilities are estimated to be low, they are overweighted in terms of their impact on decision making. In other words, when an outcome is judged to be of low probability, that outcome receives more consideration than it might normatively deserve. In this case, because the likelihood of the success of sanctions was assumed to be so low, that option may have been given too much weight, and thus more emphasis may have been placed on sanctions in American decision-making strategy about the crisis than was normatively warranted given the psychological overweighting of its low probability of success.

One important goal in pursuing these political and economic actions was to bring pressure on the Europeans to join in the sanctions against Iran. This policy amounted to a balancing act between pursuing American interests in Iran and protecting U.S. relationships with reluctant European allies. Political and economic measures were undertaken and were somewhat successful in gaining European cooperation, but only because of the implicit threat of U.S. military force if such endorsement was not forthcoming.[43] Soviet bloc countries were advocating caution as well. East German leader Erich Honecker wrote to President Carter on December 31, expressing his hope that "all parties will exercise extreme restraint and will do nothing that might lead to an aggravation of the situation. A peaceful resolution of the conflict will be in the interest of all people."[44] After the rescue mission took place, the Europeans felt betrayed by the action, especially in light of their earlier begrudging cooperation. In fact, diplomatic initiatives did serve as a good cover for the rescue mission preparations, as the Europeans charged.

The third option that was seriously considered was the rescue mission itself. This was really an intermediate option in terms of *political* riskiness. However, it was the riskiest option that could be taken militarily without engaging in an outright act of war. The mission was intended to work by stealth. The goal was to minimize casualties and bring about the release of the hostages directly. Everyone involved in the planning considered it to be a clever and carefully thought out plan. Even those who now have the benefit of hindsight, such as Sick and Brzezinski,[45] consider the plan to have been subtle, sophisticated, and likely to have succeeded if so many of the helicopters had not malfunctioned.

According to Sick, all the decision makers understood the serious military risks involved in undertaking the mission, but believed it still offered the only real possibility of rescuing most of the hostages alive. The planners knew that the possibility of success was not certain. The risks here were seen as being more about the probability of *military* success, rather than the amorphous *political* costs associated with doing nothing or failing at such an endeavor.[46]

The key factor here is that the rescue mission was perceived by the Carter administration as the best balance of political and military risk. If the mission succeeded, the hostages would be freed, Carter would be a hero, and America's international credibility would be salvaged. Theoretically, a success would have amounted not only to a return to the status quo ante as the reference point, but an additional advance into a domain of gains as well if America effectively demonstrated its unparalleled military prowess before the world.

In the Carter administration almost all attention was placed on the return of the hostages rather than on punitive action for its own sake.[47] Everyone agreed that the military risks of a rescue mission were admittedly high, and the probability of complete success relatively low. But any possibility of retrieving the hostages directly was considered paramount for personal, political, and international reasons.

Because the mission was known to be risky from the outset, the planning was designed to minimize the military risks to the greatest extent possible. The strategy was to enter Iran on a holiday weekend; the rescuers were to hit hard and quickly, under cover of darkness. The American Embassy in Tehran was surrounded by large grounds, and no one expected enough noise would travel outside the compound to arouse suspicion, especially with the use of silencers on all weapons. The rescuers knew where the hostages were being held within the building in advance, and they expected the captors to be unprepared and unskilled for combat.[48] There was every expectation, however dismissed, that large numbers of Iranian captors would be killed in the course of the mission. However unrealistic the assessment, the risks to American soldiers and hostages were expected to be more limited and designed to be minimized. In light of such careful planning, the rescue mission seemed to be a particularly attractive option when the alternatives were perceived to amount to either letting the situation continue to fester without resolution or proceed to all-out war.

The fourth option was to mine Iranian harbors or to otherwise interrupt commerce. This was seen to be quite politically risky because it constituted the equivalent of an act of war. The United States had no intention of declaring war, but wanted to have a significant negative effect on Iran's ability to export and import goods without having to set up a blockade.[49] Mines would constitute a passive sea blockade, and if it was well publicized, most ships would not try to run the risk of entering the mined area.

Mining the harbors was viewed as a sharp escalation. Mining was seen as a significant, but not an overwhelming, international risk. Using mines with automatic self-destruct mechanisms would allow some flexibility, and this option was seriously considered. However, there was a military risk of repeatedly losing non-Iranian planes and ships in such an action. Political risks caused by inflaming the region were seen to be quite high. The fear was that the Iranians would invite the Soviet Union into the region to help with minesweeping and that this offer would provide the Soviet government with a political and military opening in the region that the United States wanted to prevent.

From the administration's perspective, the problem with the mining option was that it would do nothing directly to further the primary goal of releasing the hostages.[50] If the hostages were judged to be important as symbols, punitive military action designed to demonstrate the credibility of American deterrence would appear to be a reasonable response, particularly if the goal was to show the world in general, and Iran in particular, that the United States could not and would not be manipulated by a lesser power. But if they were viewed to be important as individuals, as in fact they were, then the goal became to rescue them and return them to their families for personal as well as political reasons. A mining strategy might have threatened the lives of the hostages, and the Carter administration was never seriously willing to entertain any option that threatened to antagonize the hostages' captors.[51]

The last available option was an all-out military attack. This was judged to be extremely risky from both political and military standpoints and was never seriously considered. As with the previous option, the main reason this option was abandoned was because it did nothing to guarantee the release of the hostages. War would have inflamed the entire Islamic region and escalated the crisis without doing anything directly to bring about the return of the hostages. Basically, this option was rejected all along because the potential adverse consequences were judged to be too great, and the risks were too high, both politically and militarily, domestically and internationally. Everyone in the administration felt that war would come at too high a cost to justify any conceivable benefit.[52]

In testimony before Congress in December, Carter explained his reasoning as follows:

> [What is] crucial to us, is for us to be right and for our actions to be defensible, and I believe that if we took preemptory action that would cause bloodshed that we would lose the support of the world and we would lose the lives of our hostages, although that is my natural inclination is to strike back, but I get absolutely furious.[53]

Despite Carter's personal frustrations with the situation, options that were perceived to be riskier than the rescue mission, but did not offer the chance of returning the situation to the status quo ante by bringing about the release of the hostages, were not seriously considered. In other words, war may have been militarily more risky than the rescue mission, just as limiting the response to economic sanctions would have politically riskier than the rescue mission. However, neither option directly promoted the primary goal of freeing the hostages.

The collapse of the administration's only chance for negotiations through Bani-Sadr on April 1 led to Carter's actual decision to undertake the rescue mission.[54] The administration had been involved in complex and sophisticated negotiations with the Iranians through the United Nations to bring about the release of the hostages. Iranian leaders indicated to UN Secretary-General Kurt Waldheim that the hostages would be transferred to Iranian government control and then released, in exchange for certain public statements on the part of the Carter administration and the establishment of a Commission of Inquiry into the crimes of the former Shah. The timing of the transfer and release was supposed to occur in concert with Waldheim's previously scheduled visit to Iran. The early stages proceeded without incident, but, at the last minute, the Iranians reneged on their promise, and the deal failed to go through as planned.[55]

At this point, after numerous, varied, and extended attempts at negotiating release of the hostages, the administration reached the limits of its patience with the Iranian government. Originally, the possibility of undertaking a military option in response to the hostage crisis had been raised a couple of days after the embassy was taken in November 1979. At that time, under the instigation of National Security Advisor Brzezinski, through Secretary of Defense Harold Brown, the Joint Chiefs of Staff put together a Joint Task Force and began planning for a rescue attempt. The timing of the mission in April was closely related to weather conditions. There was only a brief period of time when the weather remained cool enough and the nights long enough to provide maximum security and efficiency.[56] This military window of opportunity happened to coincide well with the failure of negotiations.

Framing

Prospect theory argues that choice can often be substantively affected by seemingly trivial manipulations in the framing and construction of available options. For example, the status quo helps define the reference point, and the presentation and construction of options defines the universe of contingencies that are considered.

As mentioned, the main decision makers agreed on the choices that were available and the relative levels of military and political risk that each option posed. However, each advisor operated from a different worldview, and each of these perspectives differentially affected how he formulated issues for the president to address. As a result, each advisor framed his arguments to Carter in quite different ways.

The main perspectives that will be examined here are those of the advisors whose opinions most strongly influenced President Carter, namely Secretary of State Cyrus Vance, National Security Advisor Zbigniew Brzezinski, and White House Chief of Staff Hamilton Jordan.[57]

From the beginning, Secretary of State Vance was stridently opposed to the rescue mission and saw it as being too risky from both military and political standpoints. In the end, Secretary of State Cyrus Vance resigned over this episode, because he believed that the mission could not work and should not be pursued because it was too dangerous. The final decision to attempt the rescue mission was made by Carter on April 11 in a meeting that took place without Secretary Vance's presence.[58] Upon his return from what everyone involved described as a "well-earned" vacation, Vance expressed shock and concern that such a momentous decision had been made without his input. As a result, another meeting of the principals was called on April 15, at which time Secretary Vance outlined his objections. At that meeting, Vance argued:

> I pointed out that we had made substantial progress in gaining allied support for effective sanctions . . . [I] pointed out further that the formation of the Majlis, to which Khomeini had given jurisdiction over the hostage crisis, could be a major step toward a functioning government with whom we could negotiate in Iran . . . Even if the raid were technically successful, the mission was almost certain to lead to a number of deaths among the hostages, not to mention the Iranians. The only justification in my mind for a rescue attempt was that the danger to the hostages was so great that it outweighed the risks of a military option. I did not believe that to be the case.
>
> I reminded the group that even if the rescue mission did free some of the embassy staff, the Iranians could simply take more hostages from among the American journalists still in Tehran. We would then be worse off than before, and the whole region would be severely inflamed by our action. Our national interests in the whole region would be severely injured, and we might face an Islamic–Western war. Finally, I said there was a real chance that we would force the Iranians into the arms of the Soviets.[59]

In spite of Vance's objections, the decision to go ahead with the mission was reaffirmed. At that time, Secretary Vance tendered his resignation to President Carter. Vance justified his action to the president by reference to his opposition to the rescue mission:

> I know how deeply you have pondered your decision on Iran. I wish I could support you in it. But for the reasons we have discussed I cannot.
>
> You would not be well served in the coming weeks and months by a Secretary of State who could not offer you the public backing you need on an issue and decision of such extraordinary importance.[60]

Carter waited to announce Vance's decision until after the rescue mission had taken place so as not to arouse the suspicions of the Iranians.

Secretary Vance argued throughout the hostage crisis that the United States should use patience and negotiation in order to gain the release of the hostages safely. As noted, the historical analogies that he most closely identified with this crisis were peacefully and successfully resolved without the use of force. His overriding concern was the lives and safety of the hostages, and in the contemplation of the rescue mission, the lives of the American soldiers as well. He framed options in terms of mortality, and everything was evaluated in terms of the likelihood that a particular action would lead to the death of a human being. He also appeared to be more concerned about gaining and keeping the support of the European allies than were the other advisors.[61]

In terms of the options presented earlier, Vance's threshold for risk was really at the first stage. More specifically, he wanted to do nothing and wait for the internal situation in Iran to settle down.[62] He believed that once this happened, the Iranians would no longer have use for the American hostages and would release them of their own accord, without requiring additional pressure from the United States. From Vance's perspective, anything that America might do to bring about the hostages' release in the meantime could only serve to further antagonize the Iranians, thus risking the ultimate safety of the hostages. He also thought that military action would alienate the European allies he had worked so hard to assure. He thus saw a rescue mission as unacceptably risky from both a political as well as a military standpoint.

Vance believed that the hostages would remain safe and be released unharmed as long as the United States was patient, restrained in action, and willing to negotiate.[63] In other words, Vance thought that the new status quo, while not optimal, was nonetheless acceptable as long as no one was killed. Death was the one loss he was not willing to consider tolerating. He feared that American military action would lead to the loss of life, and thus it was not an advisable course of action.

In terms of prospect theory, Vance did not see himself as being so obviously in the domain of losses as Carter. Vance did not think that things would get drastically worse unless America took positive steps that might cause additional problems. He believed that as long as the United States was patient and did not use force, things would resolve themselves over time in America's best interest. Vance did not see the international political situation as rapidly deteriorating. Thus, while Vance knew things were worse than they had been before the hostages were taken, he seemed to have accepted, indeed "renormalized," the hostage situation as a new status quo "reference point" in a way that Brzezinski, Jordan, and Carter were not so readily able to accommodate. This may have been because Vance framed things in terms of lives lost, and since no lives had been lost prior to the rescue mission, he saw the situation as still being in a domain of gains.

President Carter's override of Secretary Vance's objections to launching the rescue mission was rendered all the more significant by the fact that Secretary Vance had traditionally been the advisor closest to President Carter, both personally and ideologically.[64]

Vance held sway in most of the early foreign policy decisions of the Carter administration. However, Vance was not the only senior member of the decision-making team; Brzezinski was equally important. There is little doubt that Brzezinski's opinion was taken quite seriously by Carter. Indeed, Gary Sick characterizes his importance to the president in quite a fascinating fashion:

> Brzezinski was the very antithesis of Cyrus Vance . . .
> This restless energy and persistent pursuit of fresh approaches made Brzezinski a natural alter ego to Jimmy Carter's activism. Although the two men were psychologically very different and never really became personally close, they complemented each other in very special ways. Carter was dissatisfied with things as they were and was determined to use his Presidency to generate change. Brzezinski sparked new ideas at a dazzling rate and refused to be constrained by the status quo in devising his strategies. Although Carter probably rejected more of Brzezinski's ideas than he accepted, he obviously valued the irreverent inventiveness that Brzezinski brought to any subject.[65]

According to Gary Sick, the real shift in Carter's policy allegiance from Vance to Brzezinski came after the Soviet invasion of Afghanistan in late

1979. It is clear from Carter's much-publicized statements that he was deeply shocked and personally offended by the Soviet action. Indeed, it was only after the Soviet invasion of Afghanistan that Vance announced that he would not stay in office beyond the 1980 election. It was following this event that Carter's policy changed from one emphasizing patience and negotiation to one based more on confrontation and competition. Indeed, a change in frame at this time from gains to losses resulted in a noticeable change in general foreign policy preference from negotiation to deterrence. This shift was mirrored by a change in the relative power positions held by Vance and Brzezinski within the White House policy advising circles.[66] It was within this context that the decision about the rescue mission was made.[67]

Brzezinski was a powerful force in the decision to proceed with the mission. Brzezinski promoted quite a different agenda than Vance. Brzezinski's frame encompassed national power and prestige as well as the hostages' welfare. Brzezinski's operative analogy was the failed Bay of Pigs incident, where he believed that America had been humiliated by a lesser power. The difference between the two advisors was that Brzezinski was more willing to accept mortality risks than Vance and saw them as more unavoidable.[68] As Brzezinski wrote:

> In effect, I felt that the question of the lives of the hostages should not be our only focus but that we should examine as well what needed to be done to protect our vital interests. I was painfully aware that at some point perhaps a choice between the two might even have to be made.[69]

Brzezinski's threshold of acceptable risk on the list of options was the highest of the central decision makers. Indeed, he went so far as to support a punitive military raid against Iran, in the face of universal opposition. As Harold Saunders, Assistant Secretary of State for Near East and South Asia, notes, "Zbig Brzezinski was more concerned with national interest and honor, while Cy Vance emphasized human values."[70] In ideological terms, Vance was an idealist, Brzezinski, a realist.

Brzezinski favored some kind of military rescue mission from the very outset. Brzezinski wanted to accomplish what the Israelis had achieved at Entebbe. Not surprisingly, it was Brzezinski who phoned Brown on November 6 to get the JCS to begin work on a rescue mission. Brzezinski, like Vance, recognized that military risks were involved in the rescue mission: "My view was that casualties in the rescue mission would be unavoidable; but we also had to face the possibility that the attempt might fail altogether."[71]

Brzezinski was the one who questioned whether the mission should not go ahead with five helicopters after the crucial sixth malfunctioned during the course of the rescue mission itself. Indeed, his commentary on this event provides singular insight into the conscious manipulation of framing to persuade a decision maker:

> I stood in front to his desk with my mind racing: Should I press the president to go ahead with only five helicopters? Here I was, alone with the President. Perhaps I could convince him to abandon military prudence, to go in a daring single stroke for the big prize, to take the historic chance. And at the same time, a contrary thought flashed through my mind: Would I not be abusing my office by pressing this man into such a quick decision after months of meticulous planning? Would I not be giving in to a romantic idea?
>
> I had decided to urge going ahead with five only if Colonel Beckwith was prepared to do it, but not to press for it without the field commander's concurrence.[72]

Brzezinski was also the one who began to plan for a second rescue mission, two days after the first mission failed.[73] In fact, Brzezinski had a great impact on Carter's thinking with regard to the hostage rescue mission. In the memo he wrote to the president the day before Carter approved the mission, Brzezinski argued:

> In short, unless something is done to change the nature of the game, we must resign ourselves to the continued imprisonment of the hostages throughout the summer or even later. However, we have to think beyond the fate of the fifty Americans and consider the deleterious effects of a protracted stalemate, growing public frustration, and international humiliation of the U.S.[74]

Brzezinski started from a set of assumptions that prioritized America's international credibility. It is not that Brzezinski was not exposed to respected alternative perspectives on the matter. Vance provided such a function within the administration. From Harvard, Brzezinski's highly esteemed and respected colleague, John Kenneth Galbraith, wrote to express his opposition to invasion late in November:

> I write to urge the absolute disaster for our interests that would follow any military action or reprisal, however seemingly justified or pressed by our own policies. The Islamic world is not strong or even emotionally secure. But its pride, sense of assailed dignity, sense of com-

munity and tendency to fierce, unfearing reaction—death in Islam as the Prophet urged is not the occasion for tears—are both powerful and universal. Military action against Iran, however our own people and others attempt to vindicate it, would and literally [*sic*] lose us all this world . . . And the explosion that it would precipitate would easily cost us the lives of hundreds of thousands of our people. The economic (and military) consequences I need not stress. And I promise that this is not an alarmist estimate.[75]

In spite of such a thoughtful and heartfelt analysis, Brzezinski believed that things would get worse in Iran unless America took drastic action. At the meeting to decide about the mission, Brzezinski argued that:

> We ought to attempt the rescue as early as possible because the nights are getting shorter; that we should consider taking prisoners back with us, so that we would have bargaining leverage in the event that the Iranians seized other Americans as hostages; and that we should consider a simultaneous retaliatory strike in the event the rescue failed.[76]

Brzezinski saw an entirely different situation than Vance. He clearly saw himself in the realm of serious losses. He framed things in terms of threats to national prestige and honor, rather than in terms of lives lost. From the perspective of international stature, the United States was certainly in a worse situation than it had been before the hostages were taken captive.

In a classic case of loss aversion, Brzezinski did not assimilate his losses quickly or easily. Rather, he was prepared to take great risks in order to return to the status quo ante and to increase America's international standing by bringing about the release of the hostages. He believed that the situation was bound to get significantly worse unless America took drastic action to prevent further deterioration right away. As a result, Brzezinski argued against Vance's preferences. Brzezinski argued that the mission was likely to succeed, albeit with casualties:

> A very comprehensive review of the rescue plan by Brown, Jones, and myself in mid-March led me to the conclusions that the plan had a reasonably good chance of success, though there would probably be casualties . . .
>
> [W]e could undertake the admittedly risky but increasingly feasible rescue mission . . .
>
> With the passage of time, we were all becoming more confident that

possible kinks were being worked out of the rescue plan and that the
probability of success was increasing . . .[77]

White House Chief of Staff Hamilton Jordan provided a third
influence upon Carter's decision-making process concerning the hostage
rescue mission, at least partly because of his emphasis on domestic political considerations.[78]

Jordan tended to frame options in terms of their impact on the reelection campaign. He made arguments based on how particular actions
would affect the president's domestic appeal and popularity. Jordan's perspective is interesting in light of Brzezinski's argument that domestic considerations were irrelevant to Carter during this time. Brzezinski argued:

> Perhaps surprisingly, there was never any explicit discussion of the
> relationship between what we might do in Iran and domestic politics:
> neither the President nor his political advisor ever discussed with me
> the question of whether one or another of our Iranian options would
> have a better or worse domestic political effect.[79]

Nonetheless, in spite of Brzezinski's claim, it is clear from Jordan's memoirs and Carter's comments at the time that the reelection campaign was a
far from insignificant concern during this time period, particularly given
Carter's pledge not to campaign on the road during the crisis.[80]

Jordan presents his political hopes concerning the rescue mission as
follows:

> As I listened to General Pustay's presentation [on March 24, 1980],
> I began to be convinced that maybe it would work. After months of
> waiting and hoping, negotiating and failing, here was a way to go in
> and snatch our people up and have the whole damned thing over! Not
> to mention what it would do for the President and the nation. It
> would prove to the columnists and our political opponents that
> Carter was not an indecisive Chief Executive who failed to act. It
> would bolster a world community that was increasingly skeptical
> about American power. A daring mission would right the great wrong
> done to our country and its citizens.[81]

Jordan's sentiments are particularly notable for their emphasis on
righting a wrong, returning to normal, or otherwise restoring the status
quo ante as the appropriate reference point. Once again, the prospect of
recouping all of the personal, national, and international losses in one
great daring gamble emerges as a highly appealing option, from both a

political as well as a psychological standpoint. This is exactly what prospect theory would predict in a domain of loss.

Riskiness of Chosen Option

The variance in outcome values across options indicates the relative riskiness of the various choices available. The first option, to do nothing, had a very low variance; it was unlikely either to accelerate the release of the hostages or to increase the likelihood of the hostages being tried or killed by their Iranian captors. This option presented very low utility, but it also offered the lowest risk.

The second option, using economic and political sanctions, poses a somewhat wider variance in outcome values. The positive outcomes are more attractive and more likely to succeed than doing nothing, but the likelihood remained that sanctions would take a long time to produce a positive effect, if they ever worked at all. Negative outcomes were unlikely, but not impossible, if the Iranians decided to retaliate by harming the hostages. Thus, the second option was riskier than the first.

The third option, the rescue mission, was the riskiest combination of military and political options, since the variance in possible outcome was widest. More specifically, a successful payoff from this option would present the most positive outcome offered by *any* of the choices considered: the hostages would be released, American military prowess would be demonstrated, American credibility and prestige would be restored in the international community, and Carter's popularity would increase. The reason that this option does not present the highest expected value, in spite of possessing such high utility, is because the probability of actually achieving such a positive outcome was very low. In addition, the negative outcome, which was much more likely, could result in quite negative payoffs: the Iranians might harm the hostages in retaliation; America would appear militarily impotent before the world; Islamic fundamentalists in the region might be inflamed by American "imperialism"; the Soviet Union might be encouraged to intervene; and Carter might look foolish and possibly even lose the election. Although not all these negative outcomes took place, many of them occurred in the wake of the failed rescue mission. Thus, this option was riskiest because its variance in outcome was widest. That is, this gamble presented the most extreme positive as well as the most extreme negative payoff possibilities of the options considered.

The fourth option, mining or blockading the seas, offered positive payoffs similar to those offered by sanctions: mining might facilitate the release of the hostages, but it would take time. However, the possible negative outcomes would be much worse than those presented by sanctions:

an act of war might necessitate diplomatic, political, and military escalation. Such action might also inflame the fundamentalists in the region and risk Soviet involvement. In addition, it was unlikely to offer a more positive outcome than sanctions. Because the variance in outcome was greater, mining was a riskier strategy than sanctions. Mining offered no superior outcomes, yet presented worse negative ones. However, mining was not as risky as the rescue mission because it did not advance as positive an outcome, by not being able to force the release of the hostages directly, although the negative possibilities were roughly equivalent to those that could result from the rescue mission. Thus, again, the risk of blockade was not as great as the rescue mission because the variance in outcome possibilities was smaller, even if only in the positive region.

The final option, an all-out punitive military strike, again offered some positive outcome possibilities. More than any other option, it responded appropriately to the emotional anger and frustration felt by Americans against the Iranians. However, this was rarely considered to be a justifiable reason for military action. War posed the same negative risks as installing a blockade, but offered fewer positive outcomes than sanctions.[82] In addition, the probability of the negative outcomes was much higher than the likelihood of positive results.

Thus, the rescue mission was the riskiest choice because it presented the widest variance in possible outcomes. However, the rescue mission did *not* offer the greatest expected value because the probability of positive outcome was lower with the rescue mission than with sanctions, for example. The problem with sanctions, again, was that it was estimated to take a long time to produce an uncertain positive effect and was not directly related to securing the release of the hostages.

What factors led to Carter's decision to take a chance on the rescue mission succeeding? By April, almost all political, economic, and diplomatic sanctions possible had been unilaterally imposed on the Iranian government by the U.S. government.

From the start, Carter believed that military options should be pursued only if there was an immediate threat to the hostages' lives: if, for example, the Iranians put them on trial and condemned them, as threatened, or if all negotiating channels failed. This failure of negotiation is in fact what occurred in April 1980.

At that time, the rescue mission was the option that offered the greatest prospect of recouping all previous losses and returning to the status quo that existed before the hostages had been taken in November. Everyone believed that a successful mission could redeem all losses. Moreover, the political risk of a failed mission was difficult to assess in advance, especially when no one wanted to believe that the mission would fail. Unfortunately, the outcome of events proved just how politically risky a failed mission could be: the hostages were dispersed all over Iran and not released for another nine months; America's international stature diminished even further; and Carter eventually lost his bid for reelection.

The Decision

The most important decision maker throughout the crisis was President Carter himself. Carter's memoirs are not remarkable for their level of cognitive or emotional introspection. It is painfully evident throughout, however, that Carter was a man who deeply experienced the personal burden of his global responsibilities. Carter spoke movingly of his experience of these obligations in his testimony to Congress:

> It is a constantly—it is constantly a burden on my mind, no matter what I am thinking about. If I am worrying about an announcement that I am going to be a candidate for president or if I am worrying about the windfall profits tax or if I am worrying about anything else, I am always concerned about the hostages.
>
> It is just as though my wife was in the hospital on the point of death and I had my duties to carry out and I didn't know whether she was going to live or die. I worry just as much about those hostages, and I feel like they are all my own family.[83]

In reading through the documents of the time, Carter emerges as a sincerely moral, genuinely kind and caring man whose leadership abilities were seriously challenged by the enormity of the crises he faced; this is not surprising, given the complexity and seriousness of the problems he confronted.

Given the challenge Carter faced and the diversity of the opinions that he was presented, it may appear somewhat difficult to determine exactly how he weighed the options he considered. In making his decision, Carter attempted to assimilate and integrate the opinions that had been offered to him by his advisors. He may not have been aware, however, of the way in which this advice was skewed by each advisor's different framing of the appropriate choice set and perceived domain of action.

This situation offers a nice opportunity to see one of the subtle and less obvious predictions of prospect theory in action. Ordinarily, an observer would expect Carter to be more closely in line with Vance than Brzezinski in making decisions; they were closer both personally and ideologically. There would be no reason to expect or predict a different alignment in this case, and yet Carter sided with Brzezinski at the cost of his professional relationship with Vance. Why? In this instance, Carter sided with Brzezinski because they shared the same domain, one of losses, which differed from Vance's domain, based at least partly on the invocation of differing historical frames. With the insight of prospect theory, Carter's alignment is not only explicable, but predictable as well.

Following a framing analysis it is possible to take a brief look at how options were assimilated by Carter. Carter faced a situation that clearly augured against the impact of a deleterious groupthink-type effect;[84] the president's mindset can be examined in light of the different frames that his advisors presented. His perspective is assumed to include his own perception of broader domestic and geopolitical considerations as well.

Prospect theory would predict that, in the domain of losses, Carter would opt for a risky gamble that might return the situation to the status quo ante if it worked. Once again, the notion of variance may be helpful. The rescue mission may have had the highest outcome value if it succeeded, but it also had one of the lowest outcome values if it failed. Relative risk is demonstrated in this situation because the probability of success is lower than that offered by other options, but the utility of a successful outcome is higher.

On the one hand, if the rescue mission had been a success, Carter would have presumably gained the release of the hostages, the respect of his allies and adversaries, and the votes of his constituency. In other words, he could have recouped all his losses and made some gains as well. *No other option available offered this possibility.* On the other hand, if the mission failed, it promised to confirm Carter's domestic image as incompetent and ineffective, and add foolish and reckless to the equation; enrage the Iranians, possibly leading to a humiliating trial or even murder of the hostages; possibly prompt the instigation of guerrilla retribution or war in the region; entice the Soviets into the region under the ostensible justification of trying to ensure peace in the area; and render the ongoing negotiations with the Europeans about sanctions moot.

What is curious, given the lively debate among his advisors, was Carter's confidence in the likelihood of the rescue plan's success. Even after the mission failed, he insisted on its viability in the April 24–25 diary entry:

> The cancellation of our mission was caused by a strange series of mishaps—almost completely unpredictable. The operation itself was well planned. The men were well trained. We had every possibility of success, because no Iranian alarm was raised until two or three hours after our people left Iran.[85]

Carter's confidence is surprising because of the complexity and enormity of the task as well as the low estimates of success offered by the JCS and others prior to the mission. Carter's confidence is a central issue because it clearly helped to promote his decision to go ahead with the mission.[86] He understood the risk, but, possibly as a result of wishful thinking, had confidence that the risk was worth taking because of the possibility, however small, that this prospect might restore status quo ante.

The military fully acknowledged the high risks involved in planning such a rescue mission. Indeed, the JCS report on the mission states explicitly that "the rescue mission was a high risk operation. People and equipment were called on to perform at the upper limits of human capacity and equipment capability."[87]

General Jones of the Joint Chiefs of Staff queried Charles Beckwith, the man who eventually led the mission, at the outset of planning concerning the associated risks. Upon being asked the probability of success and the risks involved, Beckwith responded, "'Sir,' I said, 'the probability of success is zero and the risks are high.'"[88]

Intelligence estimates of success were lower than may have been appreciated by the military planners. Pierre Salinger describes an alleged CIA report given to Stansfield Turner on March 16 that evaluated the prospects for the success of the rescue mission as follows:

6. The estimated percent of loss among the Amembassy hostages during each of the five major phases was:
   (a) Entry/Staging: 0 percent
       Assumes no loss of cover
   (b) Initial assault: 20 percent
       Assumes . . . immediate loss of those under State FSR and FSS cover and others
   (c) Location/Identification: 25 percent
       Loss of State personnel before full suppression of resistance
       Problem accentuated since Amembassy hostage not collocated
   (d) Evacuation to RH-53D's: 15 percent
       Assumes loss from snipers, inside and outside Amembassy compound, and from AT and Apers mines.
   (e) Transfer-RH-53s to C-130s: 0 percent
       Assumes maintenance of site security
7. The estimate of loss rate of 60 percent for the Amembassy hostages represents the best estimate.
8. It is presumed to be equally likely that the Amembassy rescue

attempt would be a complete success (100 percent of the Amembassy hostages rescued), as it would be a complete failure (0 percent of the Amembassy hostages rescued)

9. Of special note is the fact that no analogous large-scale rescue attempts have been mounted in heavily populated urban areas within hostile territory during the past 15 years. The only roughly similar attempts (Son Toy-Nov. 1970; Mayaguez-May 1975; Entebbe-July 1976) were all made in lightly populated rural areas of hostile territory.[89]

The story of this supposedly secret report was originally leaked to George Wilson at the *Washington Post* in August 1980 but was denied by Frank Carlucci, then Deputy Director of the CIA. According to Jody Powell, Carlucci's response to Wilson was as follows: "I have been unable to find anything in the alleged CIA document that is either accurate or which approximates any memorandum we prepared." Wilson refused to print the story, but a similar one was published by Jack Anderson several months later.[90]

However, a *Time* report the week after the rescue mission stated:

Pentagon officials have adamantly denied reports in Washington of a CIA estimate that 60 percent of the 53 hostages would probably have been killed in the rescue attempt. But *Time* has learned that initial casualty estimates once ran as high as 200 fatalities, including both hostages and rescuers. The final plan did, indeed, envision the possibility of losing from 15 to 20 hostages.[91]

Whether or not Carter was aware of such dismal estimates of success, he ultimately decided that the mission was worth the risk of failure. Indeed, in response to Vance's objections on April 15, Carter replied:

I understand and am not unconcerned about their welfare. But my obligation is to those hostages, who represent me, you, and our country! . . .

I disagree with your assessment of the reaction to the rescue mission. If it works, our friends all over the world will breathe a sigh of relief that it's over and that they won't have to impose further sanctions. The Moslem countries may make a few public statements for the sake of Islamic unity, but you know as well as I do that they despise and fear Khomeini and will be snickering at him behind his back.[92]

Carter described his goal for the rescue mission in a diary entry of November 10:

> We want it to be quick, incisive, surgical, no loss of American lives, not involve any other country, minimal suffering of the Iranian people themselves, to increase their reliance on imports, sure of success and unpredictable.[93]

Carter kept these as his basic goals throughout the crisis. Carter's explicit goal was to bring the hostages home, not to punish the Iranians. The possibility of catalyzing the release of the hostages is at least part of the reason why the rescue mission, even though more risky in terms of its variance in outcome and probability of success, was chosen over the other militarily risky options, such as mining the harbor or launching a punitive strike. Carter felt tremendous personal and political pressure to do something to free the hostages. Yet he could not bring himself to engage in an act of war such as mining the harbors, especially if it would do little directly to bring about his primary goal of releasing the hostages.

So, on April 11, Carter decided to proceed with a rescue mission he believed would succeed in releasing the hostages without alienating allies, inflaming the Islamic world, pushing Iran into the Soviet camp, or resulting in the seizure of additional American hostages. In other words, Carter took a gamble he understood to be militarily risky in order to seize a chance at recouping previous losses and reestablishing the earlier status quo. He took this risk over the option of pursuing sanctions, which represented as close to a sure thing as the real world offered.

The Iranian Rescue Mission

The actual outcome of the decision to attempt a rescue of the hostages in Iran highlights the *reality,* as opposed to the feasibility, of the military risk that was involved in the undertaking. Indeed, the overwhelming complexity of such a plan is a critical part of any assessment of the risk involved prior to making the decision to proceed.

The rescue attempt, code-named Operation Eagle Claw (the planning phase was called Rice Bowl), was a highly complex undertaking.[94] The plan was for eight RH-53D helicopters to be launched off the aircraft carrier Nimitz, stationed in the Arabian sea, and fly 600 miles to a landing field within Iran, designated as Desert One, near a town called Tabas. These helicopters had to fly under total radio silence at a low altitude to avoid Iranian radar detection, using only visual navigation and very limited inertial guidance. At the designated site, the helicopters were to meet with six C-130 transport planes that were to fly in from Masirah Island, off the coast of Oman. Three C-130s carried the assault force of about 120 men; the other three carried fuel for the helicopters.

After meeting, the C-130s were to refuel and transfer their special operations men to the helicopters and return to base. The helicopters were then to fly on to another location in the hills about 100 miles southeast of Tehran, called Desert Two, where the men were going to hide out during the day until they attacked the embassy by surprise as planned the following night. Local sympathizers had arranged ground transportation to the embassy at that time. After the ground attack on the embassy, the helicopters were going to pick up the soldiers and the hostages at a stadium across the street from the embassy compound, fly them to a nearby abandoned airfield at Manzariyeh, and fly them out of the country on C-141s that were to meet them there. Each phase was timed to coincide.

Every stage of the plan was acknowledged to be risky, both in terms of its low probability of success as well as its high likelihood of lives and material lost. The initial phase of inserting the aircraft into the country without detection was considered to be the most difficult aspect of the plan by the members of the rescue team.[95] However, the subsequent stages of the plan never came to fruition because the mission was aborted at Desert One due to an insufficient number of operational helicopters required. Planners judged that the mission required a minimum of six helicopters in order to complete the task; eight helicopters were considered by all planners to be sufficiently redundant for the success of the mission. However, the mission was aborted because only five operational helicopters reached Desert One.[96]

Following the decision to abort the mission, the accident that resulted in the American casualties occurred. A helicopter that was refueling for the return flight kicked up a blinding amount of sand, accidentally flew into the nose of a transport plane, and instantly exploded. Eight men were killed, four were badly burned, and the rest were quickly evacuated, leaving six helicopters, three with sensitive classified material, on the ground for the Iranians to find.[97]

Even in the wake of the rescue mission debacle, administration officials continued to defend the decision in the press conferences that followed. National Security Advisor Brzezinski was willing to openly acknowledge, and justify, the risks that were taken in pursuit of liberating the hostages by force in a television appearance with correspondent Sam Donaldson:

We undertook the rescue mission, knowing full well that it was risky.

We calculated very precisely its chances of success. We felt they were sufficiently high to warrant this activity, because we had a moral obligation to help our people. We have a political obligation to try to bring this problem to an end, if the Iranians, themselves, are not capable of reaching the requisite decision . . .

Everyone recognized that the operation was risky. We also know from history that there are moments in which a certain amount of risk has to be taken. We calculated very closely what the risks were. We knew that we were undertaking something which involved risk.

We also knew that the stakes were very high. After the full weighting of this . . . in which all the President's advisors took part, the President took the right decision, took the courageous decision.[98]

Conclusion

The failure of the rescue mission in Iran in April 1980 was a tragedy whose failure weighed heavily on the principal decision makers involved in its planning and execution. On April 25, 1980, the president issued a statement that read, in part, "The President accepts full responsibility for the decision to attempt the rescue."[99] In a statement made to the American people later in the day, Carter elaborated on this explanation in a statement that read:

Our rescue team knew, and I knew, that the operation was certain to be difficult and it was certain to be dangerous. We were all convinced that if and when the rescue operation had been commenced that it had an excellent chance of success . . . They knew then what hopes of mine and of all Americans they carried with them.[100]

In a separate statement made to Congress, Carter once against focused on the primary importance that he attached to the release of the individual hostages:

The sole objective of the operation that actually occurred was to position the rescue team for the subsequent effort to withdraw the American hostages. The rescue team was under my overall command and control and required my approval before executing the subsequent phases of the operation designed to effect the rescue itself. No such approval was requested or given because . . . the mission was aborted.[101]

   The failure of the rescue mission made things even worse for Carter. Aside from some initial rally-round-the-flag support, the failure cost Carter valuable political capital.[102] He was criticized in the press for inadequate planning, as well as for not making a stronger military move from the start. Moreover, the failure of the mission made any subsequent attempt to facilitate the hostages' release even more difficult. In short, Carter's plan failed to release the hostages and reaffirmed his growing domestic image of impotence. From a more personal perspective, the death of the eight American soldiers was especially difficult for President Carter.

   The decision to undertake the rescue mission in Iran was made during a time of extreme difficulty for the Carter administration. There is no question that it took place during a domain of loss for the administration in general and for Carter in particular. This was true on both a domestic as well as on an international level. The taking of the hostages was a severe blow to American power, prestige, and credibility on the international scene. The lack of allied and UN support for sanctions was considered an insult. Moreover, Carter was facing an increasingly arduous reelection campaign at home. In fact, had the mission succeeded, history might look quite different, because it is easily conceivable that Carter could have won reelection on the crest of popularity that would certainly have followed such a courageous rescue, successfully completed.

   The choice of the rescue mission was indeed the riskiest option considered in terms of the potential variance in outcome values. Other military options were unequivocally rejected by Carter because they offered little probability of securing the release of the hostages. In spite of these military limitations, Carter felt that he had to facilitate the release of the hostages.

   In retrospect, an analyst can see that the option that eventually led to the release of the hostages was offered early in the crisis by Secretary Vance. The hostages were released essentially unharmed by the Iranians when they no longer served any internal political function. Once the Iranian revolutionary government had stabilized, the hostages were allowed to leave, although there may have been some other political factors involved in releasing them only a few minutes after Carter was no longer officially the president of the United States.[103] In some sense, Carter received the "right" advice, to do nothing, from Vance; he chose to ignore it, however, and took the more risky military option, which offered the chance, however small, of recouping all his previous losses. Carter chose the military gamble over the slow-but-sure option offered by political and economic sanctions.

   Throughout the crisis, it was difficult for many participants to assess the balance of political and military risks. This was especially true because national and international political risks were often as inversely related as were political and military risks. Nonetheless, Carter made a relatively risk-seeking choice. He had other choices that were both militarily less risky, like mining the harbors, or politically less risky, like seeking additional indirect diplomatic negotiating channels. However, he took the one gamble that offered a chance of recouping all the losses he had previously sustained in order to regain the status quo ante. Had he succeeded, the payoff would certainly have been great. But the probability of success was low, and the mission failed. While other options may not have offered the same potential for immediate positive payoff that the rescue mission promised, less risky options, such as imposing sanctions, proved more likely and more effective in the end.

To reiterate, the rescue mission option did not possess the highest expected value. The highest expected value was the option that offered the lower variance in outcome value as well as the higher probability of success. This option was the one that pursued economic and political sanctions as well as negotiations. This strategy did bring about the eventual release of the hostages.[104]

This outcome is perfectly consistent with, and even predictable from, prospect theory. Carter saw himself in a domain of losses. He took a seemingly irrational gamble over the real world equivalent of a sure thing, as represented by continued sanctions. In order to recoup his losses and regain the previous status quo, Carter engaged in risk-seeking decision making. Thus, the failed rescue mission of the hostages in Iran provides a superb illustration of risk-seeking behavior in the domain of losses and the operation of prospect theory in international politics.

CHAPTER 4

The Decisions about Admitting the Shah

The decisions surrounding the admittance of the Iranian Shah, Moham-mad Reza Pahlavi, into the United States are illustrative of both the benefits and limitations of the application of prospect theory to cases in the international environment. The Carter administration showed itself to be fickle in its official approach to the Shah's request for asylum. The administration's vacillation concerning admitting the Shah, in combina-tion with the extended time period involved, provides a series of decisions that are as close to a controlled experiment as the real world offers. The same decision makers faced the same problem, but as the domain shifted from one of gains into one of losses, they reached different conclusions over time. As a result, changes in policy can be compared to shifts in the conception of domain.

The operative domain for President Carter changed significantly between the time of the Shah's departure from Iran on January 16, 1979, to the time of the Shah's death in Egypt in July 1980. Initially, Carter was in a domain of gains. By October, however, conditions had deteriorated significantly, both domestically and internationally, and Carter entered a domain of loss.

As he entered the domain of loss, Carter increasingly took risks, finally allowing the Shah into New York for medical treatment on October 23, 1979, in response to mounting criticism of his administration's policy from the domestic right wing. Admitting the Shah was the ostensible justification offered by the Iranian students for their seizure of the Ameri-can hostages in Tehran on November 4. In the wake of the student seizure of the American Embassy, Carter and his administration were plummeted even further into the domain of losses. In response, Carter was prompted to take even further risks, forcing the still-sick Shah back out of the coun-try in hopes of facilitating the release of the hostages. Over the following months, Carter continued to refuse re-admittance to the Shah, even for essential surgery to remove his spleen.

This case demonstrates that as Carter's assessment of the environ-ment he faced shifted from one of relative gains to one of losses, it resulted in a change of his position regarding the Shah over time. In January,

Carter made a cautious choice by refusing the Shah's request to seek asylum in the United States. By October, the Shah's condition had deteriorated significantly. Carter received new information concerning the Shah's medical condition that helped him change his mind and decide to admit the Shah, still knowing full well that this decision could lead to retaliation against Americans in Iran.[1] After the American hostages were taken captive in Iran, Carter once again reversed his decision and all but forced the Shah to leave the country. The Shah was thereafter refused re-admittance.

The decisions surrounding the Shah's entrance into the United States provide an opportunity to examine the dynamics of prospect theory over time; as domain shifted, so did risk propensity. The first decision surrounds the refusal to admit the Shah during the early days of his exile; the second decision involves the shift that allowed the Shah to enter the United States for medical care in October of 1979; and the remainder of the decisions refer to the administration's effort to force the Shah back out of the country after his hospitalization in New York and refusing his readmittance after December.

Why did key decision makers make the choices they did concerning the Shah? More importantly, what factors were responsible for the tremendous shifts in U.S. policy toward the same problem over time? Prospect theory can help clarify some of those factors by focusing attention on the situation that confronted Carter and his chief advisors at the time that these decisions were made.

Background

This case begins with the decision not to let the Shah into the country after he left Iran in January of 1979. The events leading up to the departure of the Shah from Iran are beyond the scope of this investigation.[2] Suffice it to say that as the internal political situation in Iran continued to deteriorate rapidly, the Shah proved incapable of reversing the tide of events; in desperation, he decided to leave the country on January 16, 1979.

The official U.S. position concerning the Shah's asylum in the United States was ambivalent from the outset and remained so throughout the crisis. The most succinct characterization of official policy is contained in the Congressional Research Service's report on the situation prepared for then–White House counsel Lloyd Cutler. This report notes the many potential complications that were considered in arriving at a decision on whether or not to admit the Shah into the United States. It is thus worth quoting at length:

The issue of where the Shah would go into exile was one of concern for the United States as soon as he left Iran on Jan. 16, 1979, and was undoubtedly intensified after the fall of the Bakhtiar government and the decision to effect a reconciliation with the Bazargan government. There was evident conflict between U.S. obligations to the Shah in light of longstanding support for his regime and the efforts at reconciliation . . .

. . . On May 22, 1979, Henry Kissinger said that the U.S. owed a "debt of honor" to the Shah and should grant him political asylum . . . the Administration's public position . . . was that the Shah was welcome "in principle" but that there were also questions of timing, security, and U.S. national interests . . .

The decision to admit the Shah raised serious policy questions. At least four factors in this decision can be identified: (1) the U.S. tradition of serving as a political haven; (2) the question of loyalty to a former ally and friend; (3) the new factor of the Shah's apparently deteriorating health; and (4) the possible reactions in Iran and its effect on the reconciliation policy.[3]

At the time that the Shah originally left Iran, he ostensibly had an open invitation to come to the United States. Indeed, plans had already been set for the Shah to occupy the Walter Annenberg estate, Sunnylands, in Rancho Mirage, California.[4] However, the Shah preferred not to come to America at that point; most scholars argue that this was because the Shah hoped to stay close to Iran in the hopes of returning if the revolution there failed and he was reinstated.[5] He spent his first six days in Egypt, followed by three weeks in Morocco, and then he flew on to the Bahamas.

The Shah formally requested admittance to the United States on February 22, through the U.S. ambassador to Morocco, Richard Parker. At this time, leaders in the administration met and decided to encourage him to go elsewhere, although without formally rescinding the U.S. invitation. It was at this point that the administration contacted close personal friends of the Shah, including David Rockefeller and Henry Kissinger, through the Undersecretary of State for Political Affairs, David Newsom, in order to encourage them to convince the Shah not to enter the country. Both men refused to help the administration convince the Shah to go elsewhere. However, Rockefeller continued to help the Shah on a personal basis and eventually succeeded in finding refuge for him in the Bahamas.[6] The Shah left for the Bahamas on March 30.

Without question, there were a number of problems with the timing and communication between the Shah and the administration in the decisions concerning his entrance into the country. Part of the reason for this was that the administration was itself divided. Increasingly, the administration also came under pressure from powerful private citizens, such as Rockefeller and Kissinger, to accept the Shah into the country. Carter resented the pressure that these individuals placed on his administration, but remained uneasy about their ability to intervene against him in the stalled SALT negotiations in Congress as well as in his bid for reelection.[7]

While the administration may have been torn within itself about what to do about the Shah, with Vance opposing entrance and Brzezinski supporting it, it is clear that the Shah's behavior did not help matters. The position of the administration toward the Shah clearly changed as a result of his decision to go to Egypt before coming to the United States. From every perspective, the Shah's decision not to come to the United States directly made his later admission no longer automatic and thus much more difficult to justify. As Gary Sick, National Security Council Staff Advisor on Iran during the crisis, writes:

> Had the Shah come to the United States in January 1979 as expected, his presence would have been regarded as entirely normal. Even Khomeini had expressed no objections . . . the Shah's indecision and procrastination had gradually transformed what would have been a routine event into a political issue . . .
> The Shah had given no indication of a desire to move to the United States, and no further arrangements were made.[8]

The U.S. ambassador to Iran, William Sullivan, shared this perspective on the situation as well:

> Ayatollah Khomeini and his entourage in Paris began to participate in the Shah's departure. Their tactics, at this time, were to encourage his safe and orderly withdrawal from Iran to a place of refuge abroad. In order to make this more palatable to all concerned, the ayatollah issued a statement from Paris to the effect that the leaders of the revolution would welcome the actions taken by any state to provide the Shah with a safe haven and would not take any measures against the interests of any state that provided it. Consequently, at this particular juncture, there seemed to be no risk to U.S. interests in offering the Shah asylum in the United States. On the contrary, it appeared we might even gain some credit with the ayatollah for making the Shah's orderly departure feasible.[9]

However, as Sullivan goes on to explain, the Shah's delay significantly affected the meaning for Iranians of the Shah's admission to the United States:

> So long as the Shah continued to give evidence that he wished to return to the country (Iran), it made our (US) position less tenable. It

would make it particularly difficult for us, in those circumstances, to take the Shah into the United States, because the general presumption in Iran would be that we were hoping to assist him in his ambitions to return to the throne. If he had come to our country at the outset, with the obvious intention of abdicating, that would have been one set of circumstances. But for him to come with the apparent intention of rallying his forces for a return was a quite different situation.[10]

Thus, the Shah's original delay resulted in the explicit decision by the Carter administration not to admit the Shah into the United States when Pahlavi made the formal request from Morocco.

The decision to exclude the Shah was a cautious decision, designed to prevent any hostile action against Americans living abroad, both in Iran as well as in other Islamic countries. In addition, the Carter administration did not want to inflame the whole Islamic region into a fury of anti-American sentiment by admitting the Shah into the United States. This concern proved prescient, indicating that the administration was quite realistic in its assessment of the negative consequences that could follow from admitting the Shah.

The decision to exclude the Shah was also cautious in its attempt not to antagonize the new Iranian government and to do whatever was possible to build a working relationship with them, rather than to participate in its overthrow by attempting to reinstate the Shah, as the U.S. government had done under Eisenhower in 1953.

After refusing entry to the Shah, the United States did try to help him find another place of exile, although this was quite difficult because no other country wanted him. With the help of David Rockefeller, Henry Kissinger, and others, the Shah eventually ended up in Mexico on June 10, 1979. The Shah remained there until the administration changed its position and allowed the Shah's admittance to the United States on October 22, albeit for explicitly medical reasons.

Domain

In the initial decision to refuse admission to the Shah, Carter was operating in a relative domain of gains. This argument may not appear intuitively obvious, because his administration never had the overwhelming popular approval of a president like Reagan; however, within the context of his tenure, late 1978 and early 1979 were the strongest periods of support that Carter experienced as president, aside from the very short initial honeymoon period immediately after his election. Subjective assessment of domain is what is critical in prospect theory. Thus, the argument made here is that Carter felt himself to be in a domain of gains, within his own experience as president. This is true both internationally and domestically, and it is supported by the archival evidence from his administration.

The late 1970s were a time of relative goodwill for the United States internationally. Although there had been a great deal of domestic opposition to their passage, the Panama Canal treaties were widely respected in the international community, and Carter himself was quite proud of this achievement. Despite heavy political cost to the Carter administration, the Senate ratified the second Canal treaty on April 18, 1978, and the signing ceremonies took place on June 16, 1978. The Camp David process was in full swing and brought forth an Arab–Israeli peace treaty that was signed in March of 1979.[11] The SALT process was ongoing, and although the administration encountered trouble with ratification later, there were high hopes at this point that the treaty would survive. Finally, late 1978 was a time of intense negotiations between the United States and China on normalization of relations. Thus, on the international front, the Carter administration felt that it was making progress in a number of important areas.

Carter himself felt relatively good about the world situation just prior to the Shah's request for entry. The timing of the Shah's initial request came on the heels of the conclusion of the Middle East peace treaty between Israel and Egypt. These two events remained linked, even if only by virtue of chronology, in Carter's memory. Carter comments on this explicitly in his memoirs:

> On March 15, the night I returned from the Middle East after concluding the peace treaty negotiations between Egypt and Israel, King Hassan (of Morocco) requested that we accept the Shah. I was not worried about providing him with adequate security, although there were militant anti-Shah groups in the United States. However, primarily because of the intense hatred now built up in Iran among the mobs who controlled the country and the resulting vulnerability of many Americans still there, I decided that it would be better for the Shah to live somewhere else.[12]

Prospect theory would predict cautious behavior in a domain of gains. In practical terms in this case, the prediction would be that Carter would refuse Hassan's request to accept the Shah immediately after the signing of the Camp David accords. Even after sufficient time had passed to allow Carter to analyze events from a distance, he continued to place these two events together in his writing. In other words, it was in the context of an event that Carter considered to be a major foreign policy victory that he decided to exclude the Shah from entry into America. Prospect theory would suggest that Carter would be risk averse in the wake of so great an accomplishment in the Middle East and thus would be predisposed to take a cautious route with regard to the Shah.

During the time that Carter decided to exclude the Shah from America, he was even relatively confident about the situation in Iran:

> In some ways, the situation in Iran had improved during the spring and summer of 1979. On May 5, Iranian Foreign Minister Ibrahim Yazdi had made a major speech, outlining the basis for his country's foreign policy: complete commitment to the Palestinian cause, improvement of relations with the United States, and a noncommittal attitude toward the Soviet Union . . . the government was seeking in many ways to restore normal relations with us.[13]

It is important that Carter thought that his relations with the Iranian government were improving at this time. He did not want to jeopardize this positive movement by taking the risk of admitting the Shah, antagonizing the new Iranian leadership, and possibly endangering Americans living in the Middle East.

The domestic front was relatively stable as well. The election was almost two years off, and Senator Edward Kennedy was not yet a serious Democratic challenger to the nomination. Carter's victories on votes in the Senate ran well over 80 percent in both 1978 and 1979, before plummeting quite significantly in 1980. In 1979, his support among Democratic congressmen was the highest percentage (70 percent) that he enjoyed during any of the four years of his administration.[14]

Thus, relatively speaking, Carter was operating in a perceived domain of gains at the time of his decision to refuse the Shah admittance to the United States in March of 1979. However, by the time Carter allowed the Shah to enter the country in October, the international and domestic situation had changed radically. Carter was under increasing domestic political pressure from conservative leaders to admit the Shah because of his earlier caution. Moreover, he faced mounting opposition within his own party, most notably from Kennedy, for the presidential nomination. By this time, Carter had entered the domain of loss.

The Framing of Options

The original decision in this case was a relatively straightforward one: the Shah could be admitted or he could be excluded. Nonetheless, the decision came to be constantly reevaluated between January of 1979 and July of 1980. As it turned out, a middle ground was found later by offering the Shah entrance for a short duration on the basis of humanitarian concern for his health needs. However, the Shah's medical condition was not known to the administration in March, and so this last option was not considered at the time of the original decision to exclude him.[15]

Two events occurred between the time the Shah left Iran on January 16 and the time of his request to come to America on February 22 that shifted the U.S. perception of the consequences of admitting him. First of all, Khomeini had returned to Iran from his exile in Paris on February 1 to a groundswell of indigenous support. The second event revolved around some rather delicate negotiations that Ambassador Sullivan was undertaking to protect a group of Americans trapped in a remote area of Iran at the time that the formal request for admittance from the Shah was received by the administration.[16] Thus, the likelihood of negative consequences flowing from admitting the Shah to the United States had been greatly increased by these events.

The situation was becoming more complicated for the Shah as well. The Bahamian government, apparently under pressure from the British, refused to extend the Shah's visa after June 10. At that point, Kissinger interceded and found him a place of exile in Mexico.[17]

The Shah's refuge in Mexico after June 10 did not mean that the issue of his entry into the United States was in abeyance. The Carter administration reexamined its decision concerning the Shah almost continually between January and October. Powerful people lobbied for his admittance to the country throughout this period, including David Rockefeller, John McCloy, and Henry Kissinger.

In spite of these influences, President Carter continued to believe that the Shah should not to be admitted into the United States until after the situation in Iran had become more stable. The administration was concerned that if the Shah were admitted to the United States, his entry might jeopardize the safety of Americans living in Iran and compromise any hopes for normal U.S. relations with the new government in Iran.[18]

As with most issues that proved controversial during their combined tenure, Secretary of State Vance and National Security Advisor Brzezinski disagreed strongly on the most appropriate course of action. In turn, each presented a different case concerning the Shah to the president for his consideration. It should be noted that the U.S. Ambassador to Iran, William Sullivan, and Henry Precht, head of the Iran desk at the State Department, generally supported Secretary Vance's position.

In the State Department, the preference to exclude the Shah from the country rested on the hope of avoiding negative consequences for Americans living abroad. While the probability of negative consequences seemed low at the time, it was nonetheless real and difficult to ascertain. The cost of such negative consequences was judged to be potentially extreme. Time proved this assessment to be correct. Vance also believed that admitting the Shah into the country would undermine any hopes the United States might have for forming a normal relationship with the new government in Iran. Vance's position may have been reinforced by his previous perspective on the situation in Iran: he had been much concerned over the Shah's oppressive measures and human rights violations. There was also considerable resentment in the State Department over the Shah's lack of willingness to share any power with the Regency Council prior to his departure; many at State felt that the Shah's obstinance was responsible for the collapse of his regime. Senior officials need not have been vindictive to have appreciated the sense of poetic justice in the Shah's potential demise in the wake of his regime's ruthlessness. Many officials who felt that the Shah was responsible for his own demise held that it was not the responsibility of the United States to save him after his self-immolation.

Vance's argument concerning the Shah's admission to the United States was clear:

In March I made one of the most distasteful recommendations I ever had to make to the President. It was that the Shah, who had left Egypt for Morocco, be informed by our ambassador in Morocco that under the prevailing circumstances it would not be appropriate for him to come to the United States. Had he immediately accepted our original invitation after he left Iran on January 16, there might have been no strong adverse reaction in Iran, assuming he kept a low profile and made no statements about returning to Iran. However, our support of Bakhtiar had inflamed Iranian paranoia about American intentions. Further, in an effort to consolidate his power and focus the energies and hatreds of his warring factions on an external enemy, Khomeini began demanding the return of the Shah to face revolutionary justice. Both U.S. interests in establishing a modus vivendi with the new Iranian government and the safety of Americans in Iran dictated that the Shah should not be allowed into the United States at this time . . .

[R]eports from our embassy in Tehran supported our judgment that he should not now be permitted to enter this country. . . .

Several thousand Americans still remained in Iran. Both they and the embassy staff would be in danger if the Shah came to the United States.[19]

Vance agreed with Ambassador Sullivan's and advisor Sick's arguments that had the Shah entered the country immediately upon his departure from Iran, it might not have created the disturbance that was feared later. Whether or not this is post-hoc rationalization for a policy many found morally distasteful is a matter of controversy, but the fact remains that Vance opposed admitting the Shah in March. Vance, like Carter, was acting in a relative domain of gains; he saw the United States as having nothing to lose by excluding the Shah, and much to lose by allowing his entrance. Vance wanted to prevent the serious losses that he presciently believed would inevitably be precipitated by the Shah's admission.

Vance was supported in his view by many lower level officials involved in day-to-day relations with Iran. L. Bruce Laingen, the U.S. chargé d'affaires in Tehran and senior ranking American diplomat in Iran at the time, was one of the officers who opposed the Shah's admission. Vance sent him a telegram on July 25 asking for his assessment of the situation in Iran if the Shah were admitted to the United States. According to Gary Sick:

> Vance asked for Laingen's assessment of the Iranian government's reaction if the Shah's entry was accompanied by formal renunciation of his claim to the throne and his public agreement to forswear political activity while in the United States. Laingen replied that the Shah's entry would be prejudicial to U.S. interests.[20]

Henry Precht, head of the Iran desk for State, was also asked to provide an assessment of how best to admit the Shah without harming U.S. relations with the new government in Iran. Precht's memo, dated August 1, 1979, offers additional insights into the problems that were foreseen to accompany the Shah's admission to the United States:

> We should inform the new government that we wish to clear our decks of old issues on the agenda. One of these old issues will be the status of the Shah. We could inform the government that we have resisted intense pressure to allow him to come to the U.S. because we did not wish to complicate the People's Government of Iran's problems or our efforts to construct a new relationship. Now with the new government firmly established and accepted, it seems appropriate to admit the Shah to the U.S. The new government may not like it, but it is best to get the issue out of the way. The discussion with the new government of Iran should take place after it is in place some 2–3 weeks and some few days before the Shah would come here . . . the danger of hostages being taken in Iran will persist.
>
> We should make no move towards admitting the Shah until we have obtained and tested a new and substantially more effective guard force for the embassy. Secondly, when the decision is made to

admit the Shah, we should quietly assign additional American security guards to the embassy to provide protection for key personnel until the danger period is over.[21]

According to Gary Sick, not even Henry Precht was convinced that this strategy would work.[22] In fact, the State Department believed that admitting the Shah into the country would present a serious danger to both Americans living in Iran as well as to American relations with the Iranian government.

In short, the issue of the Shah's admittance was framed by State Department officials primarily in terms of the risk his entry posed for the safety of individual Americans living in Iran. It is not insignificant that the majority of the individuals at greatest risk were State Department officials living and working at the embassy in Tehran. Thus, the individuals that officials in Washington were worried about were not abstract citizens but, in many cases, friends and colleagues. Only secondly was the issue framed in terms of American interests in establishing functional relations with the new government in Iran.

In the face of this perspective, even powerful individuals outside the administration who lobbied on behalf of the Shah did so to no avail. For example, John McCloy[23] stated his position to Vance in no uncertain terms concerning the utter necessity of accepting the Shah:

> I very much fear that failure on our part to respond to the Shah's request for permission to reside in the United States would take the form of a conspicuous and perhaps historical example of the unwisdom of other leaders affiliating themselves with United States interests. It could seriously impair our ability in the future to obtain the support of those whom we might well stand in need . . . Moreover, I believe any failure to respond affirmatively would constitute an affront to our long standing tradition of asylum and refuge to those who seek them here . . . It relates to the integrity, the standing and in the longer range, perhaps, to the security of the United States itself. It is important for the country to carry a reputation of steadfastness in respect of its friends, particularly to those who seek refuge here in time of emergency.[24]

Secretary Vance's response was polite and formal, and it reiterated his priorities concerning the fate of Americans living in Iran: "We must be deeply concerned regarding the safety of official and unofficial Americans in the currently unsettled conditions in Iran. Now the risks to both these Americans are great."[25] McCloy's subsequent plea to Vance went unanswered, at which point he forwarded all the relevant correspondence to Brzezinski, who responded warmly and informally, encouraging McCloy to contact him further concerning the issue at any time.[26]

National Security Advisor Brzezinski's sympathetic response betrays his alternate position concerning the Shah. Throughout the decision-making process, the only point upon which Vance and Brzezinski seemed to agree was that it would have been significantly less of a problem to admit the Shah had he arrived immediately upon his departure from Iran. Except for minor disagreements with the Shah's advisors over the most appropriate timing for events to take place, Brzezinski was unflinching in his support for admittance of the Shah from the outset. Brzezinski was not about to bow to what he saw as Iranian attempts at blackmail. He recognized the risks but attached supreme importance to U.S. prestige and credibility in the international community. He was bolstered in his position by Henry Kissinger, David Rockefeller, John McCloy, and other senior statesmen. Brzezinski believed that the United States should honor its commitment to, and show respect for, a leader who had been a staunch ally of the United States for some 37 years and whom the United States had vested interests in continuing to support. He argued that other leaders would be less likely to trust American promises of support in the future if they saw the United States reneging on a pledge to the Shah as soon as it was no longer in its immediate interests to uphold it.

Brzezinski's perspective demonstrates the differences he had with Vance in framing the domain of the central issues involved:

> While earlier it had been axiomatic that the Shah could enter America, before too long his arrival came to be regarded, particularly by the State Department, as a needless complication in our efforts toward improved relations with Iran and a pointless provocation to the radicals. The Shah's own procrastination thus generated an issue where none should have existed . . .
>
> My position never wavered. I felt throughout that we should simply not permit the issue to arise. This was a matter of both principle and tactics. I felt strongly that at stake were our traditional commitment to asylum and our loyalty to a friend. To compromise those principles would be to pay an extraordinarily high price not only in terms of self-esteem but in our standing among our allies, and for very uncertain benefits. I was aware that Sadat, Hassan, the Saudi rulers, and others were watching our actions carefully. Moreover, I felt that, tactically, we could not be blackmailed if we made it clear that what we were doing was central to our system of values, that the matter was

not one of weighing pros and cons or costs and benefits, but was integral to our political traditions.[27]

The major actors in the decision about admitting the Shah saw the situation from quite different perspectives. In terms of prospect theory, they framed the options in different ways. They thus, not surprisingly, reached different conclusions about what should be done. Some of the differences between Vance's and Brzezinski's positions can be discerned from their divergent estimates of the substance of the costs associated with admitting the Shah. There is some reciprocal determinism in this dynamic. Vance and Brzezinski found evidence to support contrary beliefs that they had arrived at previously; they then used this information to reach different conclusions about probable outcomes.[28] The difference lies in framing effects. Vance framed the problems in terms of lives and diplomacy; Brzezinski framed it in terms of reputation and alliances. These different mental accounts led these advisors to seek quite different evidence in support of their preexisting beliefs and to reach quite different conclusions. They also led to quite different presentations of policy positions to President Carter.

Specifically, Vance foresaw serious consequences for American lives and U.S. policy with no tangible benefit if the Shah were admitted. Vance saw a situation with everything to gain and nothing to lose by excluding the Shah and thus adopted the cautious choice of excluding him. This is what prospect theory would predict for someone who saw himself in a relative domain of gains. Vance saw himself as being in the domain of gains as long as no one was killed; he saw any progress in the stabilization of the new regime in Iran as positive movement in a direction that would eventually lead to the release of the American hostages.

Brzezinski, on the other hand, saw a great risk of blackmail and little benefit to American foreign policy from excluding the Shah. He feared an "extraordinarily" high price would have to be paid in terms of national honor and prestige by denying the Shah asylum. Brzezinski saw a situation where the United States had everything to lose and nothing to gain by excluding the Shah, and thus he supported the more risky path of admitting the Shah. Prospect theory would predict this choice for someone acting in the perceived domain of loss. Brzezinski saw himself in the domain of losses because he believed that the United States had already lost credibility in the international community by refusing to admit the Shah immediately.

One way to understand the discrepancies in views between Vance and Brzezinski is in terms of how issues were weighted. Vance put a very high value on the lives of the hostages and relatively less value on any abstract notions of American prestige. Brzezinski, on the other hand, placed great value on American credibility in the international environment and relatively less value on the individual lives of the hostages. In this way, different framing derived from divergent central value structures.

Riskiness of Chosen Option

Admitting the Shah was a riskier choice than excluding him because the variance in possible outcomes was wider. If the Shah were excluded, some officials believed that the reputation of the United States in the international environment would be harmed. Admitting the Shah would demonstrate American credibility in fulfilling promises to allies. If there were no negative reaction to the Shah's entrance to the United States in Iran, there would be little cost associated with demonstrating such faithfulness.

However, it was not clear that approval for admitting the Shah would be universal. While some Western leaders might show disapproval if America proved unwilling to shelter its former ally, many Middle Eastern and Third World countries might view that same behavior as a sign of American commitment to the values of human rights that Carter espoused so diligently. Excluding the Shah may have been morally repugnant to some, but the worst possible outcome was predictable: the Shah would die, and many officials did not consider that outcome to be such a bad thing, given the uncertainty of American relations with the new revolutionary regime in Iran.

On the other hand, admitting the Shah did present a wider variation in both positive and negative directions in terms of possible outcomes. If the Shah were admitted without incident, America could demonstrate her credibility to allies and enemies alike, help an old friend and ally, not harm Americans living in Iran, and show humanitarian concern so that the Shah could get the medical treatment he needed. On the negative side, admitting the Shah could precipitate a severe reaction against Americans living in Iran and sever any hopes for good relations between the new regime and the United States.

Admitting the Shah constituted a riskier choice because of its wider variance in outcome values. To reiterate, American officials were well aware that admitting the Shah posed a significant risk of danger to Americans living in Iran. All the assessments on the situation in Iran that the president received from American officials there confirmed these risks, which were considered to be much less likely to occur if the Shah continued to be excluded from entry into the United States.

In addition to the memos provided by Laingen and Precht that were quoted earlier discussing the risk of the Shah's entry to American interests, other officials noted the risks to Americans of admitting the Shah as well. On March 6, David Aaron, Brzezinski's deputy at the National Security Council, reported to the president that a "guerrilla group could retaliate against the remaining Americans, possibly taking one or more Americans hostage and refusing to release them until the Shah was extradited."[29] Moreover, according to Gary Sick, at a meeting on March 14, Vice President Mondale, David Aaron, David Newsom, Deputy Undersecretary of State, and Frank Carlucci, deputy director of the CIA, "agreed unanimously that the danger to Americans in Tehran would be extreme if the Shah were to come to the United States."[30]

These suspicions were confirmed in early May when Tehran issued its first official warning to the United States on the matter. The Iranian government had been informed of U.S. plans to allow the Shah's children to come to America for their education. At that point, the Iranian government said that "serious problems" would result if either the Shah or his wife were allowed into the United States.[31]

At least partly as a result of these warnings, Carter took the more cautious option and refused to admit the Shah into the United States for fear of the negative consequences of this action to American interests in and with Iran. According to prospect theory, this *cautious* decision is explicable as a result of Carter operating in a perceived domain of gains during that time.

The decision to exclude the Shah was also one that, when reversed in October, brought about exactly the consequences that had been most feared by Vance. Carter made the decision to admit the Shah, only for medical treatment, under pressure from his advisors and the conservative right-wing Republicans. However, humanitarian instincts helped to override caution and Carter admitted the Shah for required medical treatment despite there being no change since March in the objective risk to American national interests. Carter chose to gamble at precisely the time when his re-election campaign began to face an uphill battle, and his environment began to shift from one of gains into one of losses. In this context, prospect theory would predict the observed accompanying shift from caution to risk in decision-making strategy.

The Decision

From the time the Shah left Iran in January, Carter faced the task of integrating and evaluating divergent policy prescriptions and making the choice that he deemed optimal for the values he most wanted to promote. Hamilton Jordan, White House Chief of Staff and one of Carter's closest aides, described the political pressures that faced the president quite succinctly:

> Brzezinski, however, argued forcefully for allowing the Shah to come to the states. "It is unlikely we can build a relationship with Iran," he said, "until things there have sorted themselves out. But it would be a sign of weakness not to allow the Shah to come to the States to live. If we turned our backs on the fallen Shah, it would be a signal to the world that the U.S. is a fair-weather friend."[32]

However, Carter's position was more closely in line with Vance's than Brzezinski's:

> The President and Secretary Vance saw it differently, "As long as there is a country where the Shah can live safely and comfortably," said the President, "it makes no sense to bring him here and destroy whatever slim chance we have of rebuilding a relationship with Iran. It boils down to a choice between the Shah's preferences as to where he lives and the interests of our country."[33]

Carter resented the pressure put on him to admit the Shah by both David Rockefeller and Henry Kissinger, in concert with Brzezinski. He was particularly resentful of Kissinger's prompting because he felt it was being linked to Kissinger's crucial support for the administration's attempt to get the SALT package passed in the Senate.[34] Carter describes the coalition in support of the Shah as follows:

> [Rockefeller, Kissinger, and other supporters of the Shah] had an ally in Zbig, but could not convince me or Cy. Each time, we explained the potential danger to those Americans still in Iran, emphasizing that the Shah had been living comfortably in Morocco, the Bahamas, and now Mexico. Each time, they went away partially mollified, only to return again. Some were merely representing the Shah's interests, while others, like Zbig, thought we must show our strength and loyalty to an old friend even if it meant personal danger to a group of very vulnerable Americans. The arguments raged on, and the question was brought to me at least weekly from some source, but I adamantly resisted all entreaties. Circumstances had changed since I had offered the Shah a haven. Now many Americans would be threatened, and there was no urgent need for the Shah to come here.[35]

Carter's framing of the issue was unique: he neither bought into Brzezinski's construction that America's prestige was the central concern, nor did he fully espouse Vance's position that the safety of Americans in Iran was the main issue. Rather, he devised his own rationale to support the decision to exclude the Shah. Specifically, Carter framed the issue of admitting the Shah in terms of the Shah's preferences as opposed to the interests of the United States. Indeed, as early as January 20, 1979, Carter wrote in his diary that, "I believe the taint of the Shah being in our country is not good for either him or us."[36] This position emerged early and remained consistent in Carter's statements until he agreed to be "overruled" and admit the Shah in October.

The most pointed statement of the depth of Carter's aversion to admitting the Shah comes from a diary entry dated July 27, 1979. Carter notes:

> We finally decided to let Cy contact the embassy in Iran to get their estimate on the possible consequences of letting the Shah come in. I don't have any feelings that the Shah or we would be better off with him playing tennis several hours a day in California instead of in Acapulco.[37]

Thus, Carter was convinced early that it was not in the best interests of the United States to admit the Shah into the country. Carter estimated the probability of harm to Americans that might result from admitting the Shah to be quite high. He also believed that it might take one of several forms: Americans living in Iran might be harmed; or relations with the new, unstable Iranian government might be compromised.

Simultaneously, Carter believed the probability of harm to the United States from excluding the Shah to be "negligible." He did not seem particularly disturbed by potential costs to American prestige or credibility with allies; indeed, these ideas are only ever mentioned by Carter in terms of arguments made to him by Brzezinski. He never appeared to consider them seriously on an independent basis or on their own merit. Furthermore, the only benefit Carter understood to derive from admitting the Shah accrued to the Shah, not to America.

Carter did, however, admit some political responsibility for the Shah. For example, his administration was quite involved in helping the Shah find alternate places for exile and was particularly influential in securing Panama as an asylum after the Shah's stay in New York.[38]

Carter remained firm in this decision for the next eight months despite the persistent lobbying of Brzezinski and others to allow the Shah admittance until new information concerning the Shah's medical condition came to light in October. Up until that time, Carter continued to reject pleas to accept the Shah. Carter sought instead to maximize chances for positive relations with the new Iranian government and to protect Americans living in Iran as best as possible. In prospect theory terms, Carter was not willing to risk what he already had for the prospect of uncertain gains. However, once pressure began to mount against him in the face of an increasingly challenging re-election campaign, Carter proved more willing to take risks to recoup his position in the polls. Once it looked like the Shah was really in bad medical shape, and that his condition would only get worse without treatment, Carter became more amenable to allowing the Shah into the country. More than anything, Carter did not want to be held responsible for the Shah's death because of his refusal to let him into the United States for medical care. In this way, Carter was attempting to keep a bad situation from getting worse by taking a risk in a domain of loss.

Preface to Second Decision

The decision not to admit the Shah was reversed on October 19, 1979. The events leading up to this shift revolved around changes in the Shah's health; Pahlavi was admitted specifically to New York Hospital for medical treatments that the administration was told were unavailable in Mexico. The specifics of the Shah's medical condition were quite complicated. His illness had been a closely guarded Iranian state secret, and the U.S. government was unaware of the severity of his condition until David Rockefeller informed the administration of the serious nature of the Shah's illness in September of 1979.[39] Senior administration officials only became aware that he had cancer on October 18.[40] By this time, the Shah's advisors had retained Dr. Benjamin Kean from New York, a specialist in tropical diseases,[41] to go to Mexico to examine him. Upon arrival, Dr. Kean concluded that in order to determine the source of the Shah's illness, he needed more sophisticated diagnostic equipment, which Kean believed was only available in the United States.

At this point, David Rockefeller's senior aide, Joseph Reed, whose personal physician happened to be Dr. Kean, called David Newsom to inform him of the Shah's condition and formally request the Shah's admittance to the United States for medical diagnosis and treatment.

Second Domain

By October, Carter was in a new domain, one much closer to losses than gains. Public opinion polls showed him at the lowest point ever recorded for a sitting president. Senator Edward Kennedy was challenging him for the Democratic Party's nomination for the presidency, and odds were showing Kennedy to be a two to one favorite over Carter.

Carter was forced to reevaluate his international image as well, which was under renewed criticism from the right for "losing" Iran. With Ronald Reagan appearing to be the next Republican candidate for the White House, Carter was compelled to preempt criticism from conservatives that he would allow the Shah, a formerly loyal ally, to die essentially untreated in Mexico because he cold-bloodedly refused him admission to America for diagnosis and treatment. Carter later acknowledged that this factor probably played a role in his decision to admit the Shah for medical treatment in October.[42]

This change in environment may not have made Carter enthusiastic about admitting the Shah, but it did force him to be more amenable to persuasion by his advisors and ultimately led him to endorse admittance. Carter became more willing to take a gamble to recoup his recent losses in domestic political support, given that Iran was considered "lost" by the right in America.

Carter was trying to avoid additional domestic losses as well. While it may not have *improved* his popularity to admit the Shah, Carter felt that refusing him entrance would make things politically worse, especially with the critical right wing. By admitting the Shah, Carter sought to prevent an even greater decline in his popularity at home by putting the conservatives at bay.

Framing of the Second Decision

Simultaneous with the decision to admit the Shah, American political problems in Iran were increasing. Carter recalled that:

> On the first day of October 1979, [the day he was told of the Shah's illness] . . . Cy [said], "Our Chargé D'affaires [Bruce Laingen] in Tehran says local hostility toward the Shah continues, and that the augmented influence of the clerics might mean an even worse reaction than would have been the case a few months ago, if we were to admit the Shah—even for humanitarian purposes."[43]

Although still opposed to admitting the Shah on political grounds, Vance changed his overall position on the basis of humanitarian concerns and by late October began to argue that the United States must admit the Shah. As Jordan reports:

For the first time, Vance changed his position, stating that "as a matter of principle" it was now his view that the Shah should be permitted to enter the United States for "humanitarian reasons."

The President argued alone against allowing the Shah in. He questioned the medical judgment and once again made the argument about the interests of the United States.

I mentioned the political consequences: "Mr. President, if the Shah dies in Mexico, can you imagine the field day Henry Kissinger will have with that? He'll say that first you caused the Shah's downfall and now you've killed him."

The President glared at me. "To hell with Henry Kissinger," he said, "I am President of this country!"

The controversy continued as Zbig and Vance—together this time—stuck to the arguments of "humanitarian principle." It was obvious that the President was becoming frustrated having to argue alone against all his advisors and against "principle."[44]

Carter remained reticent about admitting the Shah:

Cy made it obvious that he was prepared to admit the Shah for medical reasons. I was now the lone holdout. I asked my advisors what course they would recommend to me if the Americans in Iran were seized or killed . . .[45]

Vance recommended that Carter inform the government of Iran about U.S. plans to admit the Shah. As Vance wrote to Carter:

On Oct[ober] 20, we were faced squarely with a decision in which common decency and humanity had to be weighed against possible harm to our embassy personnel in Tehran. . . .

Following my guidance, on October 20, Warren [Christopher] sent a memorandum to the President that proposed that we:

Notify Prime Minister Bazargan in Tehran of the Shah's condition and the humanitarian need for his hospitalization in the United States.

Unless the Iranian Government's response is strongly negative—in which case I will consult with you again before proceeding—to inform the Shah that we are willing to have him come to New York . . .

Allow the Shah to come here for treatment as arranged by David Rockefeller.

Prepare to respond to press and public inquiries with a statement that the Shah is being admitted for diagnosis and evaluation on humanitarian grounds and that no commitment had been made as to how long he can remain.[46]

Laingen reported the next day that Iranian officials were not pleased by the United States admitting the Shah, but Carter continued to receive reasonable assurances that the embassy in Tehran would be protected by Iranian government officials.

Second Decision

For the decision to admit the Shah into the country, the assessment of negative consequences remained the same, but some of the other factors changed. Specifically, almost everyone in the Carter administration believed that the Shah was on the verge of death and that the treatment he needed was only available in the United States.[47] On the basis of these assessments, Carter agreed to allow the Shah to enter the country for medical treatment.[48] The United States refused an Iranian request that one of its own doctors be allowed to examine the Shah.

In a later interview, Carter commented that:

I was told that the Shah was desperately ill, at the point of death. I was told that New York was the only medical facility that was capable of possibly saving his life and reminded that the Iranian officials had promised to protect our people in Iran. When all the circumstances were described to me, I agreed.[49]

Gary Sick described the choice that confronted the president:

President Carter had months earlier displayed a willingness to look favorably on a request for medical treatment in the United States (with regard to the Shah's wife)—even in the face of a direct warning by the authorities in Tehran. He had said bluntly that he was not prepared to place Americans in jeopardy so that the Shah could play tennis or his wife go shopping in the United States. However, in this case, the President was convinced that the Shah was dying and that he needed urgent medical attention. That was, beyond doubt, the primary reason for the decision, just as it was the sole reason for Secretary Vance to reverse his earlier position on the issue . . .

On the other hand, it would be naive to argue that President Carter and his advisors were oblivious to the political consequences of this decision . . .

President Carter could scarcely have hoped that this decision would suddenly improve his political fortunes. However, he could be certain that if he refused to allow the Shah access to medical treatment in the United States—possibly contributing to his death—he would be severely criticized not only by David Rockefeller and Henry Kissinger but by virtually all Americans, who would have seen his refusal as an abject rejection of humanitarian traditions. President Carter felt exactly the same way. Once the seriousness of the Shah's condition became known, there was simply no question of refusing him medical attention.[50]

Objectively, Carter had more to lose by refusing the Shah admittance once his medical condition was known. As Hamilton Jordan remembered, "We knew it was a risk, but we thought it was a reasonable risk. Obviously, in hindsight, we were wrong."[51]

It is ironic to note that Carter's emphasis on the importance of human rights in foreign policy worked in opposite directions over time in this case as well. In the beginning, an administration that placed such emphasis on human rights could easily justify excluding the Shah on the basis of his widely recognized abuses of human rights during his reign. Later, the Shah's medical condition forced the administration to admit him for treatment to remain consistent with their stated humanitarian goals.

Outcome and Later Decisions

In the end, driven by humanitarian concerns, Carter granted entrance to the Shah for medical treatment. The Shah was admitted to New York Hospital on October 23.[52]

The initial reaction to the Shah's admission was deceptively mild. However, twelve days later, the American Embassy in Tehran was seized by Islamic fundamentalist students. Their claim was that the attack was in response to the Shah's admission to the United States. This began 444 days of captivity for 53 Americans and a sharp decline in the Carter administration's domestic popularity and international effectiveness. While it may be that the students merely used the Shah's entrance into America as an excuse for their deliberate action, the Shah's admittance quickly became the official justification for the protest seizure of the Embassy.

The Shah's plans to return to Mexico on December 2, following his hospitalization, were derailed when the Mexican government refused on November 29 to allow him to return. The only invitation for asylum that the Shah received came from Egypt. Carter didn't think that this asylum was good for Sadat or for American interests in the Middle East:

> The situation is that I want him to go to Egypt, but don't want him to hurt Sadat. Sadat wants him to stay in the United States but doesn't want to hurt me. It is a decision for me to make. Harold [Brown, Secretary of Defense] called back to say that either Fort Sam Houston or Lackland Air Force Base—both near San Antonio— would be the best place for the Shah to go if we have to keep him here.[53]

American public opinion mirrored official ambivalence toward the Shah. According to a Roper poll, 61 percent of Americans felt the United States should admit the Shah. Of those, 45 percent said America should do so because it was the humane thing to do; 16 percent said America should do so because of the U.S. tradition of asylum. Thirty-three percent of Americans believed that the Shah should not be admitted; of those, 15 percent thought the Shah did not need American medical care; 15 percent feared that such an act risked Iranian retaliation. However, 57 percent of Americans also believed that the United States should not return the Shah to Iran for trial.[54]

Direct communication with the White House showed steadily declining support for the Shah's continued presence in America as well. During the week of November 23 through 29, 85 percent of the calls were positive, 15 percent were negative; just a few days later, on December 1, calls were running 83 percent positive and 17 percent negative. While overall mail was running at 87 percent positive for the president on Iran, only 55 percent of mail supported the Shah's asylum in America; 22 percent opposed it. An additional 23 percent wanted some other outcome, such as sending the Shah to Egypt or debating the Shah before the United Nations.[55]

In addition, Carter was under attack from his Democratic opposition for having admitted the Shah. In a UPI interview in San Francisco, Senator Edward Kennedy was quoted as saying, "The Shah was the head of one of the most violent regimes in the history of mankind. How can the United States be justified in taking in a man who wanted to come here and remain here with countless billions of dollars stolen from Iran?"[56] The former U.S. representative to the United Nations, Andrew Young, was equally direct in his opposition. He was quoted as saying, "the United States is harboring a murderer and robber. It is therefore logical that the Iranian people are demanding the extradition of the Shah from the United States to put him on trial for the crimes he has committed."[57]

Thus, the president faced a no-win situation. As a result of the Iranian seizure of the American Embassy, there is no doubt that Carter immediately plummeted into a domain of losses. All of Carter's advisors suggested that the release of the hostages in Iran was dependent upon the Shah's leaving the United States. Carter wanted to handle the Shah's situation appropriately for at least three important reasons: he wanted to facilitate the release of the hostages in Iran; he wanted to eliminate the criticisms from his own party aimed at him for allowing the Shah into America in the first place; and he wanted to demonstrate that American was not willing to succumb to blackmail by the Iranian government. Given the Shah's ill health, Carter refused to return the Shah to Iran for trial for ethical as well as political reasons.

In the first week of December, the Shah was moved to Lackland Air Force base in Texas. At that time, Carter administration officials prepared a document that stated that Carter had "informed the Shah that we would like him to remain in the United States until after all our hostages have been safely returned. I have also informed him that he is welcome to stay thereafter."[58]

Meanwhile, Carter initiated a series of intricate and secret negotiations between White House Chief of Staff Hamilton Jordan and General Omar Torrijos of Panama to secure exile for the Shah in that country. At least partly due to Jordan's efforts, Panama had agreed to accept the Shah in early December.[59] The decision to send the Shah to Panama is related in a document detailing the "original understandings" behind the Shah's admission to America. This document, prepared by White House Counsel Lloyd Cutler, states:

1. *Original Understanding*
   a) Admitted for urgent lifesaving medical treatment not available elsewhere
   b) To depart when treatment, rest and recuperation completed
   c) Treatment completed Dec. 1. When rest and recuperation desirable, could have left then
   d) Because of Mexican switch, moved to Wilfred Hall [Lackland Air Force Base, Texas]. Rest and recuperation now complete.
   e) Therefore obliged to leave if another place available.
2. *U.S. Does not wish to alter this understanding*
   All signals indicate that while not free from risk, departure would help to speed freeing of the hostages.[60]

After the Shah left Lackland for Panama, the official position of the Carter administration refusing the return of the Shah after his departure from the United States was clear and unbending. At the press conference to notify the public that the Shah had left the country, White House Press Secretary Jody Powell was asked, "Do you have any feeling that the United States is taking a chance of an adverse reaction in Iran by the Shah's departure for any other country? Is there any gamble involved here?" Powell replied that, "I know of no reason for any adverse reaction to this development."[61]

The internal State Department memos at the time described the understanding between the U.S. government and the Shah as including the provision that:

> 5. The Shah's departure from the United States does not preclude his returning here, but there is no guarantee he may return. If he asks to return because of a medical emergency, we will favorably consider this request. If he asks to return for non-medical reasons, we will consider his request but can make no commitment whatsoever at this time.[62]

In Panama, the Shah's physical condition continued to deteriorate. There was a great deal of political infighting between the Shah's Panamanian doctors and his American physicians over who held primary authority. The continual bickering over his condition made the Shah suspicious that he would be assassinated on the operating table if he were to have his now-necessary splenectomy in Panama.[63] When word reached the U.S. government that the Shah was thinking of finding a new home because of his fear of being murdered by Panamanian doctors, Jordan and other administration officials flew down to Panama to try to change his mind. Meanwhile, Iran continued to request the Shah's extradition from Panama.[64]

Simultaneously, there continued to be increasing internal political pressure on the administration concerning the Shah. On the one hand, Vance received a new onslaught of letters from John McCloy arguing that the Shah should be returned to the United States, claiming that "no country I can think of is more beholden to him for the consistency of his cooperation unless it might be Great Britain."[65] On the other hand, Carter received a letter from the Family Liaison Action Group, representing the families of the American hostages in Iran, stating:

> If there is any indication that the United States is going to bring the Shah into this country or to put him in a United States military hospital facility, we will, as a group, object strongly and publicly, because

we know such action will ruin what chances may be left for getting our people out of Iran.[66]

In spite of their refusal to readmit the Shah into the United States, the Carter administration remained quite concerned about the political ramifications of the Shah's deteriorating condition. No one wanted to readmit the Shah, and yet no one wanted him to die in a way that made America look bad. The Shah desperately needed medical care that he refused to have undertaken in Panama as a result of his fear of the doctors there. In a secret memo that Hamilton Jordan wrote to Carter and Vance, he outlined the available options. Jordan argued that the Shah going to Egypt "would be highly detrimental to Sadat's domestic and regional position and our own policy in the area."[67] Concerning the Shah's return to the United States, Jordan argued that:

The disadvantages of having the Shah return to the United States for the operation are evident. Our overriding concern would have to be what actions might be taken against the hostages as a result of his entry. At a minimum, we have to accept the possibility of the hostages being held indefinitely, and we would have to contemplate the terrible thought of immediate violence being directed against them as a result of the Shah's return to the states.[68]

Because the other options were so problematic, Jordan tried, without success, to convince the Shah to remain in Panama:

The Shah was undoubtedly going to leave Panama, but he preferred going to Egypt, where he felt he was welcome, over returning to the States without a real invitation. But if President Carter tried to keep him from going to Egypt by encouraging him to come to America, the Shah would accept that invitation in a second.[69]

After speaking with Sadat, Carter agreed to let the Shah go to Egypt despite the president's reservations about inflaming the Middle East by so doing.

Thus, on March 23, the Shah flew to Egypt, a day before the legal deadline for Iran to file extradition papers in Panama. He died there on July 27.

Conclusion

The decisions concerning the Shah were complex and continued to be reevaluated for over a year. In the early stages, the Carter administration adamantly refused to allow the Shah admittance. That decision remained unchanged until October 1979, despite the intense lobbying of National Security Advisor Brzezinski and other powerful constituents to grant the Shah asylum. Both the decision not to admit the Shah and the timing of the reversal provide illuminating examples of prospect theory in action.

The decision to exclude the Shah was reversed in October, when the administration became aware of the serious nature of his medical illness. The Shah was then admitted for medical treatment on the grounds of humanitarian concern. At that time, President Carter's domestic political position was weakening with the Republicans, he was faltering in his bid for renomination in his own party, and he was beginning to shift from a domain of relative gains to one of losses. Prior to the Shah's admission, the administration knew that some kind of attack against Americans in Iran might result from the Shah's entry into the United States. That is the reason why the administration continued to kept the Shah out of the country. Indeed, admitting the Shah provided the excuse for the seizure of the American embassy in Iran. From the perspective of prospect theory, it is not accidental that Carter's shift from a cautious position on admitting the Shah to a more risky one coincided with a shift in his domain from one of gains to one of losses.

After the Shah received medical treatment, he was encouraged to leave the country because the administration believed that the hostage crisis could not be solved while he remained on American soil. After the Shah became dissatisfied with his situation in Panama, the United States again intervened and tried to convince him to remain there. Failing that, they allowed him to go to Egypt, well aware that this action might endanger Sadat's position and thus the delicate balance that had been so carefully orchestrated in the Middle East during the course of the Camp David accords. Nonetheless, Egypt was preferable to the United States because the Shah's return to America was judged to present a potential risk to the lives of the hostages in Iran.

Prospect theory predicts that a decision maker in the domain of gains is likely to make cautious choices. This was certainly the case in Carter's early decision to exclude the Shah. The first decision to exclude the Shah was taken in a time of relative gains for Carter: the election was far off; the Panama Canal treaties had succeeded; the Camp David accords were going well; SALT was still alive; and negotiations over the normalization of U.S. relations with China were progressing. Carter worried about the safety of Americans in Iran, the credibility of his human rights campaign, and the future of U.S.–Iranian relations if the Shah were to enter the country, and thus he made a cautious choice and refused to admit the Shah. In short, Carter felt he had nothing to gain, and something to lose, by admitting the Shah. Thus, he was risk averse in the domain of gains, as prospect theory predicts, and made a cautious choice by excluding the Shah. The variance in outcome was slight with exclusion: at best, Americans abroad would be protected, and Americans at home would be tolerant. At worst, some, though not all, foreign leaders might rebuke the United States for abandoning its former ally, and the domestic right might gain some political strength.

Almost a year later, the situation had altered drastically. By October, Kennedy was mounting a full-scale assault on the Democratic nomination for president; Carter was at his lowest point in the polls. He was also under attack from the right for excluding the Shah. Now, Carter was in a domain of losses. At this point, he took a risk concerning the Shah for justifiable humanitarian reasons. With new information about the severity of the Shah's medical condition, Carter rescinded and granted the Shah entry for medical treatment. At this point, Carter was well aware of the international ramifications of his decision. Indeed, until Carter was persuaded by Vance, he stood alone at the time of the October decision in opposing the Shah's admission. The variance presented by admission was much greater: at best, Carter could save the life of the Shah, ensure protection for Americans abroad, and regain the moral high ground from the domestic right; however, at worst, the Shah could die despite American action, incite domestic Democrats who would oppose his admission on human rights grounds, and endanger Americans abroad in the process. Because this variance in outcome is wider for entrance than for exclusion, admission constituted the more risk-seeking choice. In the end, Carter conformed to the now consensual wishes of his advisors and admitted the Shah, although he first sought assurances from Iranian officials that they would protect the American Embassy in Tehran. Thus, again as prospect theory suggests, decisions made in the domain of losses tend to result in a relatively risk-seeking choice. However, any risk carries the possibility of failure; further failure can lead to more risks. The consequences of Carter's choice, and its failure to produce a positive outcome, plummeted him even further into the depths of political crisis.

After the hostages were seized, Carter again did his utmost to recapture the former status quo by expelling the Shah from the country. By this time, the hostages had become pawns in the Ayatollah Khomeini's internal political plans for the Iranian revolution. It would take over a year, the Shah's death, and the consolidation of Khomeini's control of Iran before the hostages would be released.

Hindsight allows analysts to judge that Carter's first choice, to exclude the Shah, was the right one from the perspective of U.S. long-term political interests. The second decision, to admit the Shah, may have been morally correct, but proved to be politically deadly.

Prospect theory explains not only the choices that were taken, but also explains the change in position that took place over time, in response to shifts in domain. Prospect theory predicts and explains these dynamic shifts: Carter made a risk-averse, cautious choice in excluding the Shah during a relative domain of gains; later, in a domain of increasing losses, Carter tried to recoup his political losses and took a risk-seeking choice to admit the Shah. This gamble led to even more serious losses for the nation and the Carter administration.

CHAPTER 5

The U-2 Crisis

The decisions concerning the Soviet downing of the U-2 were dramatic because they represented the first time that the U.S. government publicly admitted to conducting state-sponsored espionage. More importantly, the U-2 crisis was the first time that an American president was openly caught engaging in deception concerning such policies. As atavistic as it may seem in the wake of Vietnam, Watergate, and their resulting pandemic of cynicism, public exposure of such a governmental cover-up genuinely shocked the American public in 1960.

The Eisenhower administration decisions concerning the Soviet downing of Francis Gary Powers's flight over Sverdlovsk (now Ekaterinberg) on May 1, 1960, were made in a domain of losses. The administration's response included the instigation of the cover-up of American deep-penetration surveillance operations over the Soviet Union in the wake of the public accusation of spying by then Soviet leader Nikita Khrushchev, on May 5, 1960.

In the U-2 case, Eisenhower engaged in risk-seeking behavior by lying to the American public in his official pronouncements following the Soviet downing of the U-2.

The U-2 affair appears as a curious case in Eisenhower's foreign policy decision making. Why did Eisenhower take an apparently unnecessary risk in this situation? The administration did not need to speak out as early as it did; it could have kept quiet until more information was released by the Soviet Union on the status of the plane and the pilot. Moreover, once the administration decided to engage in a cover-up of its spying activities, it need not have issued such a specific, and thus easily refutable, lie; certainly more time and thought could have been devoted to creating a more credible and consistent cover story. The incongruities demonstrated by the administration's erratic handling of the cover-up make the decisions surrounding the U-2 incident a good case for investigation from the perspective of prospect theory.

Prospect Theory

Eisenhower was an enormously popular president of the United States, which was the undisputed hegemonic world power in 1960. As such, Eisenhower had a lot of authority and much freedom to exercise his influence on world opinion. There appears to be no good reason why Eisenhower should have risked his reputation and his aspirations for world peace by injudicious behavior such as lying, and, even worse, getting caught doing so and having to openly admit his mistake.

Prior to the downing of the U-2 in May, Eisenhower was in an enviable situation. Throughout the duration of the U-2 program that began in 1956, Eisenhower remained quite risk averse. He understood the risks he was taking by engaging in the overflights, but he felt the benefits justified the potential risks of discovery and subsequent embarrassment. Eisenhower could have rejected the idea of U-2 overflights, but only by succumbing to pressure for additional military expenditures in response to widespread perceptions of massive Soviet military buildups in the wake of the successful Soviet Sputnik launch. Only by using the information that could be obtained by U-2 surveillance was Eisenhower able to resist domestic opposition and adhere to a restrained military budget. Eisenhower made the calculation that the risk of overflights was justified because he believed that the Soviet Union would not be capable of shooting down the aircraft at such high altitudes, and that even when they were able to do so, no American pilot would be able to survive such an attack, and so there would be no real evidence to tie America to an intentional program of aerial surveillance. As Eisenhower recalled:

> Of those concerned, I was the only principal who consistently expressed the concern that if ever one of the planes fell in Soviet territory a wave of excitement mounting almost to panic would sweep the world, inspired by the standard Soviet claim of injustice, unfairness, aggression and ruthlessness. The others, except for my own immediate staff and Mr. Bissell, disagreed. Secretary Dulles, for instance, would say laughingly, "If the Soviets ever capture one of our planes, I'm sure they will never admit it. To do so would make it necessary for them to admit also that for years we have been carrying on flights over their territory while they, the Soviets, had been helpless to do anything about the matter." We knew that on a number of occasions Soviet fighters scrambled from nearby air bases to attempt an interception, but they could never come close enough to damage a U-2; probably the pilots never even saw one of these attempts. However, I said that while I wholeheartedly approved continuation of the program, I was convinced that in the event of an accident we must be prepared for a storm of protest, not only from the Soviets but from many people, especially from some

politicians in our own country. There would never be a good time for failure.[1]

For these reasons, Eisenhower kept a close rein on the control of these flights and frequently refused to authorize them. On May 31, 1960, a memo reported on Eisenhower's comments that "he had deliberately held the matter on a tight though informal basis and that he had felt this was important from the point of view of leaks."[2] Thus, prior to May, Eisenhower was aware of the risks involved in aerial reconnaissance and sought to minimize them in any way possible.

Once the plane was shot down by the Soviet Union on May 1, however, Eisenhower was instantly plunged into a domain of losses. The previous status quo of silence concerning surveillance had been ruptured. The domestic and international criticism of his administration and its policies was intense. Worst of all, the Soviet response threatened to endanger the success of the long-planned Summit Meeting scheduled to commence in Paris on May 16. At this point, Eisenhower appeared to throw caution to the wind, cover one lie with another, and proceed to engage in a badly planned and poorly orchestrated cover-up. This cover-up was quickly revealed for the transparent web of lies it was and Eisenhower was forced to admit publicly to both spying and lying, thus creating the very outcome he had taken such risks to prevent.[3]

Before the crisis, Eisenhower was in a domain of gains, at least partly because of the intelligence information that the U-2 overflights provided, allowing him to keep track of the true status of Soviet military systems. This information allowed him to defend successfully against requests for huge budget increases for weapons procurement without being concerning about compromising American security interests. Failure to authorize these flights might have endangered his strategy.

In terms of prospect theory, Eisenhower became risk seeking once the downing of the U-2 placed him in a domain of losses. He took a risk that he would not have taken if he had perceived himself to be in a domain of gains at the time. Although Eisenhower was quite popular at the time of the incident, he felt vulnerable to public disclosure of his espionage policies because of the importance of the upcoming Summit Meeting.[4] At this point, Eisenhower did not want to lose what he had worked so hard to attain: the possibility of positive steps toward international peace.

In the U-2 affair, the president's choices changed as the crisis evolved and as the administration's public statements incited furor and controversy. Indeed, as the crisis developed, the interaction between the administration and the world press pushed Eisenhower further and further into the domain of losses and eventually led to his riskiest choice, that of admitting to his previous lies and accepting responsibility for systematic American aerial surveillance of Soviet territory.

Historical Context

Francis Gary Powers's U-2 plane was shot down over Sverdlovsk on May 1, 1960.[5] However, Soviet leaders did not disclose this event until several days later. Their reasoning in delaying the announcement is provided by American Ambassador to Norway Willis in a telegram to Secretary of State Christian Herter following Soviet Deputy Premier Anastas Mikoyan's visit to Oslo in June:

> When the May 1 overflight occurred USSR waited first to see if US would ask about the plane as everyone normally does when a plane is missing. USSR put particular weight on US silence. On May 5 Khrushchev announced shooting down of plane but purposely omitting any details because he wanted to leave open possibility for Americans to make statement. Then came stupid story about pilot losing consciousness . . . Americans did this because they thought plane was lost and believed Russians had no proofs and therefore US could lie at will. There was in fact exploding mechanism under seat of pilot whereby pilot could or should have destroyed himself and plane by pressing a button. Thus Americans thought USSR had not material for proofs but pilot did not act according to instructions. . . . Khrushchev in his May 5 statement opened possibility for President to wash his hands by stating he did not know whether President was aware of this matter. Khrushchev was seeking formula but instead of using this opportunity to get out of this awkward situation Americans just then put into effect maneuvers over whole country.[6]

So, after waiting until May 5, Khrushchev announced in a speech to the Supreme Soviet that the Soviet military had downed an American espionage plane at a high altitude with a direct hit from a single rocket.[7]

In the course of his original announcement about the flight, Khrushchev had in fact proffered an easy way for Eisenhower to get out of the situation by arguing that he must have been unaware of the overflights. He suggested that these flights had been authorized by various Cold Warriors within the Pentagon, clearly referring to Allen Dulles, head of the CIA. A Department of State telegram informed Washington of Khrushchev's speech:

[P]articularly significant was Khrushchev's reference to fact he was willing believe President did not rpt [repeat] not know of this action but he added if this were true they would have all the more cause for concern since this would indicate militarists were in control.[8]

The official U.S. response to the Soviet Union concerning this May 5 disclosure reads:

> The U.S. Government has noted the statement of the Chairman of the Council of Ministers of the USSR, N.S. Khrushchev, in his speech before the Supreme Soviet in May 5 that a foreign aircraft crossed the border of the Soviet Union on May 1 and that on orders of the Soviet Government, this aircraft was shot down. In this same statement it was said that investigation showed that it was a US plane . . . [I]n light of the above the US Government requests the Soviet Government to provide it with full facts of the Soviet investigation of this incident and to inform it of the fate of the pilot.[9]

Ironically, the event caused scarce notice in the Eisenhower administration that day. The president's personal secretary, Ann Whitman, notes in her diary for Eisenhower on May 5 that:

> [White House Press Secretary] Jim Hagerty received news of the shotting [*sic*] down of a plane over Russia, as announced Mr. Khrushchev . . . One of the little highlights: Jim was furious because an hour later he had not heard from General Goodpaster and found out that General Goodpaster had not even informed the President.[10]

Following a routine meeting of the NSC during an evacuation exercise that day, several high-level officials in the Eisenhower administration discussed how to handle Khrushchev's accusations of American espionage. Presidential Staff Secretary Goodpaster recorded the following transcript of the meeting:

> It was agreed that the State Department would have the responsibility at departmental level for handling public statements regarding the U-2. [O]n return of the President and his party to Washington, Mr. Hagerty recommended that there be a statement by the President to the Press. The President agreed to a brief statement from the White House, stating that an inquiry would be made by the State Department and NASA and the results would be made public. I so notified [Acting Secretary of State] Mr. Dillon and [NASA administrator] Mr. Glennan.[11]

The origin of the pre-prepared cover story dated to 1956, when the U-2 program first began. This cover story was never explicitly reviewed by the president or his staff prior to its release, according to the Senate Foreign Relations Committee report:

> The cover story was not discussed in the NSC that day and only in general terms at a smaller meeting which followed. . . . Gates expressed the view on May 5 that "if Mr. Khrushchev had the complete information and the pilot . . . the President should assert the truth" . . . and the "prestige of the Presidency should not be involved in an international lie particularly when it would not stand up with respect to the facts." (p. 129) . . . There was no decision to tell the truth and "it was assumed that the cover story would be continued."
> . . . [C]oncurrently, members of the State Department and CIA were meeting in Washington to decide what should be said. "As soon as we returned to Washington," Dillon said, the statement "was finalized in agreement with CIA and the White House" was obviously kept informed of the contents.[12]

The cover story that was finalized at the Washington meeting provided the basis for the first substantive statement released by the State Department concerning the incident.

Thus, on May 5, the White House stated that the lost plane was being investigated and a report would be issued by NASA and the State Department. The State Department statement read as follows:

> The Department has been informed by NASA that, as announced May 3, a U-2 weather research plane based at Adana, Turkey, piloted by a civilian, has been missing since May 1. During the flight of this plane, the pilot reported difficulty with his oxygen equipment. Mr. Khrushchev has announced that a U.S. plane has been shot down over the U.S.S.R. on that date. It may be that this was the missing plane.
> It is entirely possible that, having a failure in the oxygen equipment which could result in the pilot losing consciousness, the plane continued on automatic pilot for a considerable distance and accidentally violated Soviet airspace. The United States is taking this matter up with the Soviet Government, with particular reference to the fate of the pilot.[13]

This statement failed to note that the plane had been shot down 1200 miles into Soviet airspace, a distance that was indeed "quite considerable."

In these first days of the crisis, members of the administration felt sure that no evidence could be found proving that the U.S. government was conducting intentional aerial reconnaissance over the Soviet Union. Thus State Department spokesman Lincoln Smith felt free to elaborate on the May 5 State Department statement in the question and answer period: "There was absolutely no, N - O, no deliberate attempt to violate Soviet airspace. There never has been . . . it is ridiculous to say that we are trying to kid the world about this."[14]

Although White House Press Secretary Jim Hagerty stated that the White House had been informed of the event by NASA, NASA was not informed that this had been done. Thus, when the press requested a statement from NASA, Walter Bonney, NASA's information chief, generated one based on the prepared story that Richard Bissell, Dulles's special assistant for the U-2 project at the CIA, had given him several days previously. This statement was *not* cleared by the CIA, the State Department, or the White House prior to its release by NASA. At the time that NASA released their version of the cover story, they were unaware of the State Department's earlier press release.

In generating a response to press inquires, NASA used a loose cover story that had been developed when the U-2 program was first begun in 1956. In so doing, NASA was attempting to respond to press inquiries resulting from Hagerty's statement that an inquiry was being undertaken by NASA as well as the State Department. This miscommunication was the result of disorganization as much as anything else, according to testimony submitted by Foster Dulles's aide William Macomber:

> What actually happened is that NASA had the general cover story that had been agreed on with NASA for some time. When they realized that a large number of the press would be descending upon them, rather than to get into a give and take of a press conference, they reduced to writing this cover story which they coordinated with CIA, and which they put out. The problem was that at the time this was being done, this other decision had been taken which was that from now on the State Department was to take it over. It is not inconsistent to have the first statement out of Turkey and the earlier statement out of NASA were consistent with the cover story which in the early stages of is [*sic*] we were trying to preserve. As it became increasingly clear that it was going to be difficult to preserve this, the meeting that has just been alluded to with Secretary Gates and Mr. Dulles took place, and they made an adjustment in their plans. Prior to this point they were trying to preserve the security of the operation. They were following a pre-arranged plan.[15]

The problem with the NASA statement was that it was quite a bit more specific in content than the State Department release. As a result, there were many more details in this statement that the Soviet government could easily refute on an evidentiary basis. The NASA statement read as follows:

> One of NASA's U-2 research airplanes, in use since 1956 in a continuing program to study gust-meteorological conditions found at high altitude, has been missing since about 9:00 Sunday morning, local time, when the pilot reported he was having oxygen difficulties over the Lake Van, Turkey area . . . About one hour after takeoff, the pilot reported difficulties with his oxygen equipment . . . The pilot . . . is a civilian employed by the Lockheed Aircraft Corporation.[16]

This statement went on in great detail about various features, purposes, and locations of other U-2 aircraft. Acting Secretary of State Douglas Dillon was flabbergasted by the NASA statement. He believed it was disastrous because it contained so much information that could be directly disproved: "This statement was absolutely crazy because we *knew* the Russians would jump us on it."[17]

The president had wanted all statements to be issued by the State Department because the explicit goal of all these releases was to try to keep as much of the operation secret as possible.[18] The administration assumed that the pilot would not survive a crash because the plane was judged to be fragile, but also because it contained a self-destruct mechanism that the pilot was supposed to activate after a disabling attack. Ostensibly, this self-destruct mechanism had a time delay for the pilot to eject. Many pilots questioned whether such a delay existed, believing instead that the craft was designed to kill the pilot along with destroying the plane.[19]

The assumptions that guided the administration's policy concerning the potential of a pilot surviving such an attack were codified into training procedures. In Senate Foreign Relations Testimony, CIA Director Dulles characterized the instructions that U-2 pilots received concerning the procedure should they be shot down in hostile territory as follows:

> The pilots of these aircraft on operational missions, and this was true in the case of Powers, received the following instructions for use if downed in a hostile area.
>
> First, it was their duty to ensure the destruction of the aircraft and its equipment to the greatest extent possible.
>
> Second, on reaching the ground it was the pilot's first duty to attempt escape and evasion so as to avoid capture, or delay it as long as possible . . .

Third, pilots were equipped with a device for self-destruction but were not given positive instructions to make use of it . . .

Fourth, in the contingency of capture pilots were instructed to delay as long as possible the revelation of damaging information . . .

Fifth, pilots were instructed to tell the truth if faced with a situation, as apparently faced Powers, with respect to those matters which were obviously within the knowledge of his captors as a result of what fell into their hands.[20]

On May 7, the Soviet government announced that they had the pilot and that he was alive. This information was sent by telegram from the U.S. Ambassador to the Soviet Union to Secretary of State Herter: "Khrushchev has asserted to Supreme Soviet and thus to world at large that pilot in Moscow and is alive and well."[21]

The administration received its first indication of how this surprising turn of events came about in a telegram sent by the deputy ambassador to Moscow to Secretary Herter on May 10:

Investigation has shown that ejection capsule was last inspected in 1956, was "not in good condition", and therefore would not have worked when Powers pushed button. Explosive charge for plane was, however, in order . . . and would have destroyed both plane and pilot if button pushed. Red Star says faulty ejection seat is evidence of "Christian humaneness" of Allan [*sic*] Dulles' espionage agency, which wanted to be sure Powers did not get off alive in case of mishap. Powers "apparently understood" what might happen if he used ejection catapult, says Red Star, but paper does not explain how he actually escaped from plane except to comment that "only chance aided him remain alive."[22]

Another series of meetings were held to determine how the United States should respond to the newly credible charges of espionage in the face of the pilot's survival. At the NSC, a decision was reached on May 9 that stated:

Noted and discussed a statement by the President on the subject, and the admonition by the President that all Executive Branch officials should refrain from any public or private comment upon this subject, except for authorized statements by the Department of State.[23]

On that day as well, Allen Dulles, Richard Bissell, head of Air Force Intelligence Charles Cabell, General Andrew Jackson Goodpaster,

Ambassador to Moscow Charles Bohlen, Hugh Cumming, and Livingston Merchant from the State Department met at CIA headquarters. At that meeting, Dulles offered to take the heat for the president and resign. He argued that the president could accept Khrushchev's May 5 intimation that one of Eisenhower's subordinates had exceeded his authority and the incident could be resolved quickly and quietly, without implicating the president. Dulles's offer was rejected, although some consideration was given to finding a lower-level fall guy, such as Thomas Shelton, head of Powers's unit in Turkey. However, Bohlen and Cumming wanted to continue with the cover-up story and deny any governmental involvement in espionage. This was the position that was ultimately agreed upon at this meeting.[24]

Merchant, Goodpaster, Cumming, and Bohlen then proceeded to another meeting at the State Department with Secretary Herter, Deputy Secretary Douglas Dillon, Assistant Secretary for European Affairs Foy Kohler, and Richard Davis, Kohler's deputy.[25] Dillon began by advocating that Allen Dulles accept responsibility for the incident and resign. Herter and Kohler had just returned from a trip to Turkey and brought with them a more international perspective on the U-2 incident. They believed that the cover story was no longer credible. Kohler argued against Allen Dulles's resignation, feeling that a more honest statement needed to be issued. This position was supported by the American Ambassador to the Soviet Union, Llewellyn Thompson. Thompson had telegraphed Herter on May 7 with the following analysis:

> It is difficult to assess Khrushchev's motives in playing this so hard. I believe he was really offended and angry, that he attaches great importance to stopping this kind of activity, and that he believes this will put him in an advantageous position at the Summit. There is no doubt that we have suffered a major loss in Soviet public opinion and probably throughout the world . . .
>
> A more menacing interpretation is that Khrushchev realizes . . . that he cannot make progress at the Summit and . . . therefore could be exploiting this incident to prepare public opinion for an eventual crisis . . . I cannot help but think, although evidence is very slight, that Khrushchev is having some internal difficulties and this incident affords him a convenient diversion.
>
> Judging by the display which Khrushchev made of evidence in the Supreme Soviet today, I would doubt that we can continue to deny charges of deliberate overflight. Khrushchev has himself stated the dilemma with which we are faced: should we deny that the President himself had actual knowledge of this action?[26]

Herter was particularly adamant in his opinion that the United States had already gone too far in rejecting Soviet charges of espionage. He now felt that the United States had to admit some responsibility, although he still wanted to prevent the president from having to assume ultimate culpability.[27] Goodpaster agreed with this position. Dillon, who had originally endorsed the cover story with Cumming and Bohlen, was persuaded by the others and joined forces with Herter and Kohler in advocating a more truthful statement.

At this point, Cumming notified Dulles of this new decision; Dulles agreed to support the consensus, although it was not his preferred outcome. He did not want a public admission of espionage that would necessitate greater unwanted congressional oversight of his organization.[28]

In the meantime, Herter called Eisenhower, who was at Gettysburg with Hagerty. Eisenhower opposed the idea of being absolved of personal responsibility for the overflights. He wanted to accept full responsibility. Hagerty agreed with Eisenhower's decision, at least partly because he was exquisitely sensitive to the charges of irresponsibility that had been leveled against the president during the 1956 presidential campaign.

Herter told Eisenhower that the president did not need to assume responsibility because Eisenhower had not been involved with the specific decisions about the timing of each flight, including Powers's. Goodpaster spoke to the president as well and endorsed Herter's recommendations. In the end, Herter succeeded in convincing Eisenhower not to accept responsibility for the flights. However, the president felt that the decision might be "a mistake."[29] Indeed, in retrospect, this decision remained Eisenhower's deepest regret about the entire incident. He wrote in his memoirs:

> The big error we made was, of course, in the issuance of a premature and erroneous cover story. Allowing myself to be persuaded on this score is my principal personal regret—except for the U-2 failure itself—regarding the whole affair.[30]

After the original "oxygen loss" cover story had been issued on May 5, Eisenhower felt that another statement at this juncture might be a mistake. Nonetheless he was persuaded by Goodpaster and Herter that a new statement was necessary to respond to Khrushchev's self-congratulatory announcement about capturing the pilot alive.

Thus, on May 7, the State Department issued the following, second cover-up statement:

> The Department of State has received the text of Mr. Khrushchev's further remarks about the unarmed plane which is reported to have

been shot down in the Soviet Union. As previously announced, it was known that a U-2 plane was missing. As a result of inquiry ordered by the President, it has been established that insofar as the authorities in Washington are concerned, there was no authorization for any such flight as described by Mr. Khrushchev.

Nevertheless, it appears that in endeavoring to obtain information now concealed behind the Iron Curtain, a flight over Soviet Territory was probably taken by an unarmed civilian U-2 plane . . .

It is certainly no secret that, given the state of the world today, intelligence collection activities are practiced by all countries . . . The necessity for such activities . . . is enhanced by the excessive secrecy practiced by the Soviet Union . . .

One of the things creating tension in the world today is apprehension over surprise attack with weapons of mass destruction . . . It is in relation to the danger of surprise attack that planes of the type of unarmed civilian U-2 aircraft have made flights along the frontier of the Free World for the past four years.[31]

The statement released on May 7 admitted that the overflights had been sanctioned by the U.S. government *for the previous four years.* However, this statement still offered no official acknowledgment of the president's specific responsibility for Powers's flight. In the wake of this statement, there was a great deal of public clamoring over the president's lack of control over his policies and officials. By this time in the crisis, Eisenhower was quite depressed and commented to his secretary, Ann Whitman, "I would like to resign."[32]

In his attempt at damage control after the furor caused by the revelation of state-sponsored spying, Eisenhower took a risk by engaging in a cover-up. In so doing, he ensured that actions of surveillance and cover-up were traceable directly back to him. After the pilot was acknowledged to be alive and public furor resulted, Eisenhower was faced with a choice of admitting both the espionage and the lies, or claiming to be unaware of the activities of his subordinates. This is a difficult trade-off for anyone to make. On the one hand, no president wants to tarnish his reputation, not to mention compromise the security of his intelligence organizations, by publicly admitting to espionage and cover-up. On the other hand, it can be equally damaging for a leader to appear irresponsible and unaware of the decisions made by underlings about major policy issues, and to seem incapable of controlling his administration.

For someone with a military background like Eisenhower, it was inconceivable to shirk responsibility for his actions or his subordinates'.

Eisenhower considered it ethically reprehensible to blame another for the negative consequences of his own actions. It was against his entire socialization experience to place the blame on his subordinates or to claim ignorance for the activities of those under his chain of command. Thus, he saw no choice but to accept full responsibility for his government's policies. Concerning Eisenhower's decision to accept responsibility, Deputy Secretary of State Douglas Dillon commented:

> He didn't like to blame other people . . . He felt more strongly than a civilian leader might have. He had this thing about honesty and that was a military tradition.[33]

In the end, Eisenhower decided to admit that the U.S. government had not only conducted systematic espionage but that his administration had publicly lied about the practice as well. His decision to accept responsibility was discussed with a group of bipartisan leaders at a breakfast on May 26:

> Senator Fulbright said that he still didn't think it was wise to take full responsibility. President Eisenhower responded that he thought it was, that if he didn't take responsibility someone else would have to. He said that he agreed that Khrushchev had tried to give him an out on this, but that he looked upon it as his responsibility, and he assumed it.
> "Incidentally," he said with a smile, "if anyone should be punished they should punish me first." He said that anyone sitting in his chair wouldn't want to put the CIA on the spot, and would not want to disown the CIA or its Director. He said that in addition to being President, he was also Commander in Chief, and he didn't see how he could duck his responsibility.[34]

Eisenhower believed that he was right in taking responsibility for his actions. However, he also believed that there were some lessons to be learned from his experience with the U-2 incident. In speaking with United Nations Ambassador Henry Cabot Lodge about Lodge's upcoming speech before the United Nations assembly concerning the Soviet charge of U.S. aggression, Eisenhower stated that "we should be guided by the old adage 'not to make mistakes in a hurry' . . . In referring to the U-2 Incident, the president thinks the only real mistake he sees was the statements were made too soon."[35]

On May 9, Herter met again with Dillon, Kohler, Bohlen, Secretary of Defense Tom Gates, and James Douglas, Acting Secretary of Defense, to discuss Eisenhower's change in position and to craft a new statement placing full responsibility in the president's hands:

> The group discussed the wisdom of the President's taking responsibility for the U-2 flights and in Gates' recollection it was unanimously decided that he should. . . . Gates did not recall discussion of any real alternatives. . . . It seemed to be implicitly understood that for the President to assume personal responsibility would be a departure from precedent.[36]

Vice-president Nixon called Herter and said that the administration must "get away from this little-boy-in-the-cookie-jar posture." He ordered that the statement not appear "apologetic."[37] Instead, Herter and his colleagues placed the blame on the Soviet Union for making such overflights necessary because of the Soviet penchant for excessive secrecy. There was no attempt to indicate that the flights would be discontinued, although in practice none had occurred since Powers had been shot down.[38]

Eisenhower summed up the situation at the NSC meeting that day:

> Well, we're just going to have to take a lot of beating on this—and I'm the one, rightly, who's going to have to take it . . . Of course, one had to expect that the thing would fail at one time or another. But that it had to be such a boo-boo and that we would be caught with our pants down was rather painful . . . We will just have to endure the storm.[39]

Later that day, the revised statement acknowledging presidential responsibility was issued as a State Department release under Herter's signature and included the following justification:

> In accordance with the National Security Act of 1947, the President has put into effect . . . directives to gather by every possible means the information required to protect . . . against surprise attack . . . Programs have been developed and put into operation which have included extensive aerial surveillance by unarmed civilian aircraft, normally of a peripheral character but on occasion by penetration. Specific missions . . . have not been subject to Presidential authorization.
>
> The fact that such surveillance was taking place has apparently not been a secret to the Soviet leadership, and the question indeed arises as to why at this particular juncture they should seek to exploit the present incident as a propaganda battle in the Cold War.[40]

While this statement did not admit the full extent of presidential authorization for the operation in general or for Powers's flight in particular, it did nonetheless acknowledge that such flights had been taking place for purposes of obtaining information on the Soviet Union with the president's awareness.

In a further statement released by the president himself on May 11, Eisenhower justified his activities by arguing that "no one wants another Pearl Harbor." Arguing that the Soviet "fetish" for secrecy had required the intelligence gathering operations manifested in the U-2 overflights, Eisenhower declared that he had "issued directives to gather, in every feasible way, the information required to protect the United States and the Free World against surprise attack and to enable them to make effective preparations for defense."[41]

The administration policy of cover-up continued, however, throughout the Congressional investigations into the matter. The concealment approach was explained in an NSC meeting which took place on May 24, 1960:

> Congress could be told that overflights have been going on with the approval of the Secretary of State and our scientific advisors, who have indicated that this method of gathering intelligence is necessary. It should be made clear that basic decisions respecting reconnaissance over-flights of denied territory have been made by the President. However, the impression should not be given that President had approved specific flights, precise missions, or the timing of specific flights . . .
>
> Turning to the timing of the last U-2 flight, the President said there was no good time for failure. The question was had the risk been measurably greater at the time of the flight than it would have been at any other time? . . . The President believed that as long as a powerful government suspected the intentions of another powerful government, intelligence activities would be carried on.[42]

The U-2 incident became the ostensible reason for the collapse of the long anticipated Summit Meeting between Eisenhower, Khrushchev, British Prime Minister Harold Macmillan, and French President de Gaulle which was scheduled to begin on May 16, 1960. This Summit Meeting fell apart in the wake of Khrushchev's demands that the United States apologize for its action with regard to the U-2 overflights, fire those responsible, and pledge never to engage in similar action again. While Eisenhower agreed to the last consideration, he adamantly refused to accede to the first two, and the conference abruptly ended in Paris before it even got under way.[43]

The Soviet Union in general, and Khrushchev in particular, derived enormous international propaganda benefit from the incident; Powers was tried in public and sentenced to ten years confinement.[44]

Domain

The decisions concerning the cover-up of American aerial surveillance following the Soviet downing of Powers's plane took place in the domain of losses. Although things were going well for Eisenhower, and he was benefiting enormously from the intelligence information provided by the U-2 overflights, the downing of the plane itself immediately plummeted the administration into a different position altogether. The American public and the world were outraged by Khrushchev's substantiated revelation of American spying practices.

Prior to the U-2 being shot down by the Soviet Union, Eisenhower was criticized by many influential members in the Democratic party, the media, and the right wing of his own party for being an absentee president. He was often portrayed in the press as not being fully attentive to the affairs of his administration and letting the government be run by inferior advisors. He was depicted as too busy playing golf and relaxing at his farm in Gettysburg to attend to the business of state.[45] White House Press Secretary Jim Hagerty was particularly vexed by these charges and went to great lengths to counter them.

Attacks came from many directions, but were most eloquently and pointedly represented by two-time Pulitzer Prize–winning journalist and commentator James Reston's pieces in the *New York Times*. On May 8, James Reston wrote a stinging editorial that included the following indictment:

> [T]he judgment of the United States government is bound to be questioned . . . [N]ot only the good judgment but the good faith of the government gets involved in controversy. The political fall-out from this controversy is bound to be great . . . [T]he President is not trying to ruin or manage the Summit Meeting. He is not even managing his own departments preliminary to the summit, and this, of course, is precisely the trouble.[46]

Reston continued his attack on the administration in the lead story for the *New York Times* the following day:

> This is a sad and perplexed capital tonight, caught in a swirl of charges of clumsy administration, bad judgment and bad faith.
> It was depressed and humiliated by the United States having been

caught spying over the Soviet Union and trying to cover up it activities in a series of misleading official announcements.[47]

Later in the week, Reston wrote:

> The heart of the problem here is that the Presidency has been parcelled out, first to Sherman Adams, then to John Foster Dulles, and in this case to somebody else—probably to Allen Dulles, but we still don't know . . .
> Institutionalized Presidency . . . disperses authority, removes the President from many key decisions, and leaves the nation, the world, and sometimes even the President himself in a state of uncertainty about who is doing what.[48]

These charges supported the Democratic Party's campaign strategy, designed to portray Eisenhower as a lazy, inattentive president. Prospect theory would predict that it would be precisely under such conditions of loss that a decision maker would be likely to make more risk-seeking choices in hopes of reversing the tide of events. In this situation, loss led Eisenhower to engage in a governmental cover-up concerning the U-2 overflights in hopes of returning to the previous status quo.

The Framing of Options

By the time Powers's flight was shot down by the Soviet military, the U-2 had been in operation as a surveillance aircraft since 1956.[49] Why had the original decision to undertake aerial reconnaissance, which required deep penetration into Soviet airspace, been made? Eisenhower discussed his original reasoning behind authorizing the U-2 flights in a Cabinet meeting on May 26, 1960:

> The President explained that the U-2 was not the only mechanism for obtaining intelligence even though it was one of the good ones . . . He said that he had been told that the U-2 would be overtaken within a matter of months by newer methods. The President added that the U-2 had been especially valuable for building up basic information about things that don't change rapidly. Mr. Gates added that the U-2 was not an alarm clock against surprise attack, rather it provided essential knowledge as to general posture. Allen Dulles recalled that when this U-2 operation had been approved in 1954, it was thought that the Russians would catch up to it in two to three years; actually, it had been of value for much longer than ever expected.[50]

Eisenhower's original decision to engage in overflights was reasonable; he could obtain valuable intelligence that could improve America's security interests at very low cost, by keeping the military industrial complex at bay, as long as the U-2 program could be kept secret.

As CIA Director Allen Dulles, who was in charge of the U-2 program, noted in testimony before the Senate Foreign Relations Committee on May 31, 1960, these flights brought back critical information on Soviet military power:

> Our main emphasis in the U-2 Program had been directed against five critical problems affecting our national security: namely, the Soviet bomber force, the Soviet missile program, the Soviet atomic energy program; the Soviet submarine program, i.e., the major elements constituting the Soviet Union's capability to launch a surprise attack. In addition a major target had been the Soviet Air Defense System with which our retaliatory forces would have to contend.[51]

This type of information was particularly important at this time because of the national hysteria that followed in the wake of the Soviet launching of Sputnik on October 4, 1957. The president could have rejected the idea of U-2 overflights from the outset, but only by succumbing to pressure for additional military expenditures in response to widespread perceptions of massive Soviet military buildups and strategic threat. The information provided by the U-2 served Eisenhower's larger goal of promoting peace by allowing him to keep a cap on weapons spending.

After the Soviet launching of Sputnik, a lot of pressure was placed on the administration from internal planners, as well as external opponents, to address the perceived imbalance in nuclear bombing and missile capability. As Allen Dulles, head of the CIA, noted:

> In the first decade after the war we had only scant knowledge of Soviet missile progress . . . As the techniques of science were put to work, and the U-2 photographs became available after 1956, "hard" intelligence began to flow into the hands of the impatient estimators. Their impatience was understandable, for great pressure had been put on them by those in the Department of Defense concerned with our own missile programs and missile defenses. Planning in such a field takes years.[52]

Because of the perceived risks of discovery, Eisenhower insisted on strict control over the authorization of flights. As Eisenhower recalled:

[E]ach time a new series of flights was proposed, we held a closed meeting to determine whether or not new information on developing technology might indicate the unwisdom of proceeding as before.[53]

Nonetheless, each time a new series of flights was authorized, Eisenhower alone weighed the relative *political* benefits of the information that might result against the potential risk resulting from a mishap. Eisenhower wanted this control not only because of the secrecy of the operation, but because most of his advisors on the matter, such as Allen Dulles, had a vested interest in continuing the flights and were not in a position to evaluate negative consequences in an unbiased manner. As Eisenhower commented at the time:

Such a decision is one of the most soul-searching questions to come before a President. We've got to think about what our reaction would be if *they* were to do this to *us.*[54]

One of Eisenhower's concerns here was that the Soviet government might misinterpret one of these flights as an attack, even a nuclear one. Goodpaster's response to Eisenhower's concern was clear: "It would be approaching a provocation, a probable cause of war because it was a violation of their territory."[55]

Eisenhower recognized the stakes involved in approving the U-2 overflights. As Goodpaster noted:

The President said that he has one tremendous asset in a Summit Meeting, as regards effect in the free world. That is his reputation for honesty. If one of these aircraft were lost when we are engaged in apparently sincere deliberations, it could be put on display in Moscow and ruin the President's effectiveness.[56]

Nonetheless, Eisenhower felt justified in authorizing the flights. As he commented to some Congressional leaders at the time: "Espionage was distasteful but vital . . . The decision was mine. One had to weigh the risks, keep the knowledge in as few hands as possible, and accept the consequences if something went wrong."[57]

The Japanese surprise attack on Pearl Harbor at the outset of World War II was a very powerful analogy for Eisenhower throughout his presidency. One if his primary strategic goals was to ensure that a similar surprise attack from the Soviets never caught America unaware during his watch. Invoking this analogy to Pearl Harbor, Eisenhower explained his original decisions concerning the U-2 to the public in a television address following the failed Summit:

> I take full responsibility for approving all the various programs undertaken by our government to secure and evaluate military intelligence. It was in the prosecution of one of these intelligence programs that the widely publicized U-2 incident occurred . . .
>
> As to the timing (so near the summit), the question was really whether to halt the program and thus forego the gathering of important information that was essential and that was likely to be unavailable at a later date. The decision was that the program should not be halted.
>
> The plain truth is this: when a nation needs intelligence activity, there is no time when vigilance can be relaxed. Incidentally, from Pearl Harbor we learned that even negotiation itself can be used to conceal preparations for a surprise attack.[58]

Even in retrospect, Eisenhower did not believe that the U-2 program itself was a mistake:

> Regarding the U-2 program itself, I know of no decision that I would make differently, given the same set of facts as they confronted us at the time.[59]

Framing of the Cover-Up

Given that the U-2 flights had been authorized for years and held under close scrutiny by Eisenhower, the evolution of the plans for concealment offer an excellent opportunity to examine how framing effects can influence decision making. The espionage program was bureaucratically entrenched, if not widely known. Still, no one seemed to have systematically examined the contingencies associated with failure. Success did breed complacency in this case.

The substance of the advice that President Eisenhower received from his various advisors is critical in understanding the evolution of the cover-up.

Some people remained consistent over the entire period of the crisis. One of these people was the president's brother, Milton, who functioned as one of Eisenhower's most trusted confidential advisors. Milton believed throughout the crisis that Eisenhower should *not* claim responsibility for the overflights. He felt that the president was pressured into approving these flights by the CIA and had been placed in an awkward situation as a result. As Milton wrote in his memoirs:

> About six months before the Powers plane came down in the Soviet Union, *the President at a meeting of the National Security Council suggested tentatively that the United States had obtained all the useful information it could and that the flights should be discontinued.* The heads of the State and Defense Departments and of CIA felt strongly the other way, so a decision for change was postponed. When the Powers plane came down a "cover" story was issued automatically. *The President did not see it or know about it in advance.* When the facts became known the President took full responsibility, something I thought he should not do. His response to me was that if he blamed the situation on a subordinate he would have no choice but to discipline, probably discharge him, and he would not be guilty of such hypocrisy.[60]

John Eisenhower, the president's son, confidante, and assistant staff secretary, took a position opposed to the one espoused by his uncle. John felt that the president had no choice but to accept full responsibility for the entire episode:

> Dad has since been blamed in some quarters for assuming the responsibility. I cannot see how he could have done otherwise. For one thing, it was true; he had approved the flights for periods of a week at a time. (The plane went down on the last day of an approved week.) For another, there was no point in sticking with a discredited "cover story" with the pilot, Francis Gary Powers, in Soviet hands. Finally, the Boss [Eisenhower] instinctively would rather take the responsibility for making an error in judgment than be accused of not knowing what was going on in his administration.
>
> The timing was bad admittedly. However, I cannot think of any good timing for such an occurrence. Our luck had simply run out.[61]

Other officials in the administration were not nearly as consistent in their advice to the president as his family members. The preferred positions on Eisenhower's assumption of personal responsibility for the U-2 flights of senior administration officials ranged from complete disavowal of knowledge to total acceptance of responsibility.

It was in the best interest of many of the president's advisors to continue the flights. Not surprisingly, those advisors with a vested interest in the continuation of the U-2 program were not as convinced as the president that the damage from the Soviet downing of such a flight would be irreparable if discovered.

CIA officials Allen Dulles and Richard Bissell strongly believed in a set of assumptions that argued that: the Soviet military could not shoot a U-2 down; that even if they did they would never make such an event public; that even if they did, a pilot would never survive, and so the United States could plausibly deny responsibility.[62] These assumptions are not logically tied, but they were shared by all who believed that the pilot could not have survived and that an immediate cover story was the best way to handle the initial Soviet accusations of espionage, given that there was presumably no way the surveillance would be uncovered. In short, the probability of each contingency was misjudged, and as a result the consequences of the outcome were severely underestimated.[63]

In the event of charges leveled by the Soviet government, the plan was clear. As Bissell revealed:

> We were quite prepared to say, if the Russians showed photographs of it, either that it wasn't the U-2 or that they had taken the plane and moved it. Now we felt that it would be very difficult for them to disprove that. So the whole point of the story was to explain what had happened—that a pilot had inadvertently crossed the border and been shot down and landed inside, and that they had moved the wreckage.[64]

Goodpaster remembered similar assumptions:

> Allen's [Dulles] approach was that we were unlikely to lose one. If we did lose one, the pilot would not survive . . . We were told—and it was part of our understanding of the situation—that it was almost certain that the plane would disintegrate and that we could take it as a certainty that no pilot would survive . . . and that although they would know where the plane came from, it would be difficult to prove it in any convincing way.[65]

Both these plans assumed a dead pilot. As John Eisenhower noted, a dead pilot was "a *complete* given, a *complete* assumption as far as we were concerned" (emphasis in original).[66] In a conversation with Dulles's successor, John McCone, in 1964, Eisenhower recalled:

> As I understood it, I mean, as was told to me all those years by both (Richard) Bissell and Allen (Dulles), this thing that the plane could

never be recovered . . . they assured me there was really no fear of ever getting back a live pilot if it was knocked down by hostile action in Russia. Even if damaged, they figured that at that height, if he had tried to parachute at 70,000 feet, he'd never survive . . . And the whole cover story was built on the basis that the man would never survive.

McCone: I realize that and I realized it at the time, and it was absolutely wrong. Now, there have been three pilots whose planes have performed just as his did in test flights and so forth where they lost control at 70,000 feet. The wings came off and spiraled down and the pilots ejected and lived. Now, in interrogating Powers as to exactly what happened to him, the same interrogators interrogated the other pilots—and these events happened in Louisiana and Nevada and so forth, and the planes performed and the pilots performed in just identical manners . . .

Eisenhower: . . . I don't want to accuse people of having fooled me. But I do know that they told me that the possibility of anyone surviving—matter of fact, that's the reason I argued against putting out a cover story, and they said, "You just don't have to worry, General. It is perfectly all right because there's nobody there."[67]

In his decisions, Eisenhower was clearly affected by the misinformation in the framing of the options presented to him by Dulles and others.

Riskiness of Chosen Option

As with the other cases, the riskiness of the chosen option is best evaluated according to the variance in outcome it offered. Remaining silent offered a fairly small variance in outcome: at worst, the press might be angered and clamor for more information; at best, nothing would be stated that could later be disproved. Overall, there was little variance at all in outcome as a result of staying quiet; the best outcome can barely be distinguished from worst. Thus, this low variance offered by this option presents a cautious alternative.

Telling the truth offered a wider variation in potential outcome: while it is true that the press would have a field day with the revelation of state-sponsored espionage, the truth would require no cover-up. Moreover, admitting the truth would make sure that everyone knew that Eisenhower was indeed fully in charge of his administration. Given Eisenhower's military culture and training, this was a very important consideration; Eisenhower proved so unwilling to blame subordinates for the U-2 overflights that he preferred to take the brunt of the criticism himself, once the espi-

onage and cover-up were revealed. In the early stages of the crisis, however, the administration feared that admitting the truth would also mean
acknowledging a long history of state-sponsored spying, which might trig-
ger a public outcry. Thus, telling the truth, with a wider variance in outcome, was riskier than remaining silent.

The riskiest choice of all, in terms of variance in outcome, was offered
by lying about the spying. A positive outcome from this option offers the
best possible outcome: no one's reputation would be tarnished, the spying
would remain secret, the public would be placated, and the Summit Meeting could proceed as planned. However, if the cover-up failed, the worst
possible outcome would occur, as espionage was confirmed and cover-up
exposed.

Under this eventuality, the public outcry would extend not only to the
act of spying itself, but to the act of cover-up as well. While this option presented the best possible outcome if it worked, it also offered the worst possible outcome if it failed. Thus, from the perspective of variance in outcome, the Eisenhower administration made the riskiest decision possible.
When the administration did engage in a cover-up and the plan failed, the
worst possible outcome did ensue.

Following the downing of Powers's plane, the administration was
faced with several options. The least risky was to not say anything, or to
claim that an "investigation" was under way. The administration did this
initially, but only for a matter of hours. On the one hand, most officials did
not want to give the Soviet accusation credence through silence. On the
other, many of those same officials in the administration felt that they
could not withstand pressure from the press to issue a more substantive
statement. This disorganization between divisions in the administration
only complicated matters. Thus, two divergent statements were produced
quickly, from NASA and the State Department, before adequate information from the Soviet government became available.

One path available to Eisenhower was to follow Khrushchev's lead.
Given the Soviet leader's opening in his May 5 speech, it would have been
quite easy for Eisenhower to accept publicly Khrushchev's version of
events, castigate and fire a subordinate, such as Allen Dulles, and pledge
that similar events would not occur in the future. This course would have
allowed Eisenhower to retain his popularity for probity and maximized
the likelihood of a successful summit meeting. He could then quietly reinstate the underling in a more discreet position at a later time. Eisenhower
proved unwilling to follow this path; this outcome is at least partly attrib-
utable to Eisenhower's extensive military training and socialization, which
made the prospect of blaming subordinates for his own decisions anath-
ema to him.

Alternatively, Eisenhower could have told the truth about the U-2 flights from the outset. He might have argued that since the Soviet Union had rejected his Open Skies proposal in 1955, he had been forced to undertake aerial surveillance unilaterally in order to prevent the possibility of surprise nuclear attack. He could have seized the diplomatic initiative and invited the Russians to overfly the United States whenever they chose. This kind of initiative would have resulted in disproportionate advantage accruing to America not only because of the tremendous discrepancies between the two societies in terms of their relative openness, but also in terms of their relative technological advances.

Eisenhower was unwilling to pursue either of these paths. Eisenhower believed that the cover-up presented a reasonable possibility of success because of assurances he had received from Dulles and others that the Soviet government would never be able to prove their allegations without a pilot, and that a pilot could never survive. As noted, before the May 7 Soviet announcement, it never occurred to anyone in the administration that Powers might have survived. Eisenhower never requested a probability estimate on the likelihood that a pilot could survive; that possibility was assumed to be zero.[68] As with all probabilities judged to be either certain or impossible, this estimate was given more weight than it normatively deserved.[69] Pseudo-certainty effects in prospect theory demonstrate that highly likely events are often treated as though they were certain, even if that is not objectively the case.[70] Yet every aspect of the initial three cover stories (NASA and State, May 5; State, May 7) was predicated on the faulty and unchallenged assumption that the pilot must be dead, and that therefore U.S. responsibility for the flight could be credibly disavowed.

Faulty and unchallenged assumptions concerning the probability of the pilot's survival encouraged the Eisenhower administration to issue a plethora of cover-up stories. Rather than keep quiet or tell the truth, the administration pursued the path of telling an increasingly intricate series of lies, which were ultimately disproven by the evidence marshaled by the Soviet Union. In short, the risk was more in the lying, and less in the spying.

The Decisions

Prospect theory predicts that people in the domain of losses are more likely to take greater risks than those acting in a domain of gains. Eisenhower might not have so easily agreed to a cover-up statement about the overflights if he had not been in a domain of losses. As mentioned, Eisenhower was relatively cautious concerning the flights themselves. However, once a plane was shot down, Eisenhower faced a much more dangerous situation. He recognized that he would sustain even more serious losses unless he did something to limit the damage. It is in this context that Eisenhower decided to lie. He took a risk that failed. However, had the risk succeeded, Eisenhower stood to recoup all the losses he had sustained after the U-2 was shot down by the Soviet government. Had the risk succeeded, Eisenhower would have ended up with the best outcome possible: continued secrecy surrounding U.S. intelligence programs; and the possibility for a successful summit meeting. In a domain of losses, Eisenhower took a risk to recoup one loss and prevent another. Unfortunately, Eisenhower merely plunged himself further into a morass of deceit and exposure.

More importantly, however, he was influenced by the situation he confronted: an environment in which he was under attack. He thought that by taking a risk, he might be able to recoup the political losses he had sustained to his public credibility.

In the U-2 incident, Eisenhower made some risky choices concerning the cover-up of American aerial surveillance of the Soviet Union. More specifically, Eisenhower was in a domain of losses due to the attacks he had undergone for various charges of incompetence, laziness, and irresponsibility from the Democrats and the press alike. He became more susceptible to taking the kind of risk that eventually forced him to admit responsibility for authorizing state-sponsored espionage and for lying about it. As a result of this susceptibility, the president's best political instincts failed him during the U-2 crisis. All the advice he accepted from his advisors steered him in the wrong direction.

The Outcome

The international ramifications of the U-2 incident were myriad.[71] The Soviet downing of Powers's U-2, and the U.S. admission for the first time not only of systematic state-sponsored espionage, but of lying about this activity, had severe consequences for the president and the country in a number of areas.

Most immediately, it was the putative reason behind the collapse of the summit in Paris that was scheduled to begin on May 16. The meeting never made it past the opening session. It is important to note that the administration itself did not believe that the U-2 incident was the sole reason for the Soviets canceling the summit. In the debriefing following the collapse of the summit, the discussion concerning the Soviet reasoning behind the cancellation of the Summit proceeded as follows:

Mr. Bohlen, as a preface to his remarks, emphasized how everything had to be guesswork as far as the Russian thinking was concerned . . . it was clear during March and April that Khrushchev realized he would not get at the Summit what he wanted regarding Berlin . . . and that the U-2 incident was probably a catalytic agent in view of the traditional great sensitivity of the Russians to any violation of their air space . . . Mr. Bohlen said that these things could not quite be sorted out, but it could be concluded that the Russians had seized upon the U-2 as a reason for sabotaging the conference.[72]

In addition, Khrushchev rescinded his preexisting invitation for Eisenhower to visit the Soviet Union later in the year; this visit had been planned for quite some time in order to reciprocate Khrushchev's visit to the United States the previous September. Moreover, the Soviet Union proceeded to walk out of the Geneva test ban talks on June 27.

Another international consequence of this episode was the cancellation of the president's trip to Japan. The president had been scheduled to tour Japan following his trip to the Soviet Union, but a surge of anti-American violence in Tokyo in the wake of the U-2 incident led Prime Minister Kishi to cancel his invitation to Eisenhower and resign his post.

In the end, Eisenhower's participation in the cover-up precipitated the very domestic criticisms that he had taken such pains to prevent. As James Reston commented in the *New York Times* on May 11, Eisenhower's handling of the U-2 crisis had wrought

. . . almost all the things he feared most. He wanted to reduce international tension and he has increased it . . . He glorified teamwork and morality and got lies and administrative chaos. Everything he was noted for—caution, patience, leadership, military skill and even good luck—suddenly eluded him at precisely the moment he needed them most.[73]

This commentary was followed by another scathing attack on the administration's handling of this crisis on May 13:

The best politics for the G.O.P. this summer lay in creating an atmosphere of peace, an air of progress toward an accommodation with the Russians on Berlin, Germany, nuclear testing, and disarmament . . .

By demanding the right to intrude into the Soviet Union, the President has defied Khrushchev to stop him, put Khrushchev on the spot with the Stalinists who have always been against a detente, embarrassed the allies by making their bases a target of Khrushchev's anger, and repudiated one of Washington's own favorite principles—namely, that each nation has the right to choose its own form of government.

In domestic political terms—to say nothing of international politics—this situation, created largely by accident, bad luck, and bungling, will do the Republicans no good . . .

The fate of one political party in one country in one election is not, of course, the main consideration. The fate of much more is at stake in the present trend of events. But it is a factor. The G.O.P. has, unwittingly, by bad administration, bad judgment, and bad luck, stumbled into a course which is also bad politics.[74]

An opportunity for progress on Berlin, disarmament, and a test ban was transformed into a hardening and deepening of the Cold War at least partly because of the U-2 crisis.

The decision to lie about the spying was a risky decision for Eisenhower to make. He made that choice in the hope of recouping his losses and achieving his goals for increasing peace. He failed in his attempt to recover his loss and received severe political criticism as a result of his acknowledgments of espionage and concealment.

It is important from the perspective of prospect theory that these decisions took place at a time when Eisenhower felt himself to be in a bad situation in the aftermath of the U-2 being shot down. It is precisely under those circumstances that prospect theory would predict that a decision maker would be most susceptible to engaging in risk-taking behavior.

CHAPTER 6

The 1956 Suez Crisis

On July 26, 1956, Egyptian President Gamal Abdel Nasser nationalized the Suez Canal. The ostensible reason for the nationalization was to use the tolls to finance the building of the Aswan Dam. Nasser's action was an act of revenge against the British and the French, who had previously held control of the company that controlled the Canal. This conflict precipitated an international crisis over ownership and operation of the Suez Canal.

The French and British were immediately thrust into the domain of losses by the nationalization of the Canal. The British had recently withdrawn 90,000 troops from the area on June 13, in response to strong American pressure.[1] The French were having trouble with their colonials in Algeria. Both countries saw the seizure of the Canal as prelude to the complete loss of their colonial positions in the African and Asian worlds. Eisenhower's perspective during the Suez crisis stands in stark contrast to the Europeans', at least partly because America had different goals and stakes in the Canal than did the British and French. Eisenhower was in a relative domain of gains, unlike the British and French, who were both operating in domains of loss. According to the predictions offered by prospect theory, this should encourage Eisenhower to make relatively risk-averse decisions as opposed to British and French decisions, which were more likely to be risk seeking in nature.

At the time of the Suez crisis, the United States had the military power to force its will on Egypt, and yet Eisenhower chose not to do so. Indeed, the United States made no military attempt to force Egyptian President Gamal Abdel Nasser into any concessions concerning the Canal. The British, French, and Israelis, on the other hand, did intervene militarily into Egyptian territory. Why did Eisenhower chose not to use American military power to support his allies?

In terms of prospect theory, the Suez crisis offers an exemplary case of Eisenhower taking a small, sure gain over a risk that, while offering the possibility of a somewhat larger gain, also presented the possibility of a much larger loss. On the one hand, small, sure gains were made in American stature and prestige in the Third World through American

135

military restraint. This sure gain was in contrast to the gamble that Eisenhower might have taken, and that the British and French did pursue. On the other hand, such a gamble, offered by the option of participating in the allied military intervention, presented the possibility of consolidating the Western alliance and potentially intimidating future aggressors, if successful. However, if the option failed, it also offered the prospect of inflaming the region and potentially instigating war with the Soviet Union. In the end, Eisenhower was cautious and avoided involving the United States in a military action that might precipitate a larger war.

Eisenhower's behavior contrasted markedly with the British and French decision makers who, in clear domains of loss, took great risks and subsequently sustained great losses. The British in particular endured the fall of their cabinet, a severe oil shortage, and an almost complete collapse of their banking system as a direct result of their military involvement in Suez.

In the United States, the Suez crisis provides a good example of risk-avoidant decision making. Enormous pressure was put on Eisenhower by his allies to engage in some kind of risky military action to support them, up to and including going to war with Egypt. Yet Eisenhower refused to accede to his allies' request.

Background

The history of the Suez Canal, and the Suez Canal Company, which was charged with operating it, is somewhat complex.[2] The Canal physically exits within Egyptian territory, but the Company that handled the operations of the Canal was owned by an international group that functioned under the Constantinople Convention of 1888. The control that this Company held over the rights of the Canal was legally similar to the control held by someone who has easement rights within a property owned by another. Thus, when Nasser nationalized the Canal, there was no international legal recourse for the British or French to oppose his action as long as he continued to operate the Canal efficiently. Nasser did continue to operate the Canal efficiently, and he promised to pay remuneration to the owners of the Canal Company as well.

The British and French, however, felt that they held historically justified rights to controlling interest in the Canal *Company*.[3] In spite of these treaties and claims, there really was no legally sanctioned *organization* authorized to run the Canal Company. The discussion that took place in the National Security Council meeting on August 9 makes clear that the

Eisenhower administration was well aware of this technicality, as stated by Secretary of State John Foster Dulles:

> There had never been an international authority in charge of the Canal; the 1888 arrangements had placed operations in the hands of a private Company with an international composition, but had not set up a public international organization.[4]

The Suez Canal was an extremely important international passageway at the time of the crisis. About 1.5 million barrels of oil a day transitted the Canal, about 1.2 million of which were destined for Western Europe. This figure amounted to about two-thirds of Western Europe's total oil supplies.[5] About a third of the ships that passed through the Canal at the time were British, and about three-fourths belonged to NATO countries. Relatively few vessels that passed through the Canal, however, were technically of American registry. American vessels only accounted for 2.7 percent of the total net tonnage that transitted the Canal in 1955.[6] Under existing arrangements, Egypt received about $17 million a year in proceeds from the Canal, while the Company made a total of about $31 million a year in profit.[7]

The Suez Canal region had been politically tense for some time prior to the outbreak of the crisis. Egypt had closed the Gulf of Aqaba, as well as the Canal, to Israeli shipping several years prior. Moreover, the Suez Canal crisis was further complicated by preexisting legal arrangements between the relevant powers. For instance, the Tri-Partite Agreement of 1950 had been signed by the United States, Britain, and France. The original intention of the treaty when it was signed was to prevent the major powers from selling large amounts of weapons to states in the region. The agreement also committed these countries to act together, with or without the sanction of the United Nations, to oppose any aggression in the Middle East that might alter the borders established by Israel and its Arab neighbors in their armistice.

The ostensible immediate precipitant of the crisis was the U.S. refusal to fund the Egyptian project to build the Aswan Dam. An offer had been made by the U.S. government to Egypt through the World Bank on December 16, 1955, to help fund this project. Eisenhower's diary describes the offer and its subsequent withdrawal as follows:

> When we made our first offer . . . to help build the Aswan Dam, it was conceived of as a joint venture of ourselves and the British. . . .
> Egypt at once did two things:

(1) They sent back to us a whole list of conditions that would have to be met before they would go along with this plan and some of these conditions were unacceptable;

(2) They began to build up their military forces by taking over equipment provided by the Soviets, and they went to such an extent that we did not believe they would have a sufficient balance of resources left to do their part in building the Dam.

We lost interest and said nothing more about the matter.

Suddenly . . . Nasser sent us a message to the effect that he had withdrawn all of the conditions that he had laid down, and was ready to proceed under our original offer. Since conditions had changed markedly and we had thought the whole project dead, we merely replied that we were no longer interested.[8]

A press release withdrawing the offer to build the Dam was issued by the U.S. government on July 19, 1956:

At the request of the government of Egypt, the United States joined in December 1955 with the United Kingdom and the World Bank in an offer to assist Egypt in the construction of a high dam on the Nile at Aswan . . . It would require an estimated 12 to 16 years to complete at a total costs of $1,300,000,000, of which over $900,000,000 represents local currency requirements . . .

Developments within the succeeding 7 months have not been favorable to the success of the project, and the U.S. government has concluded that it is not feasible in present circumstances to participate in the project. Agreement by the riparian states has not been achieved, and ability of Egypt to devote adequate resources to assure the project's success has become more uncertain than at the time that the offer was made.[9]

Following American withdrawal of their offer, Nasser nationalized the Canal, claiming that its revenues were now necessary to support the building project.[10] Nasser indicated he expected to make $100 million a year in profit from the Canal.[11] Existing overall profit only amounted to about $52 million a year. As Eisenhower notes in his memoirs, if Nasser did not raise fees, it would have taken him 367 years to pay for the Dam project with tolls alone.[12] Thus, American officials were prone to believe that the Aswan Dam project provided a convenient excuse for an inevitable action.

The British and French immediately condemned Nasser's action and focused on reasserting international control of the Canal. Prime Minister

Eden's first telegram on the matter to President Eisenhower revealed that military options were being investigated from the outset:

> As we see it we are unlikely to attain our objective by economic pressures alone . . . We ought in the first instance to bring the maximum political pressure to bear on Egypt . . . My colleagues and I are convinced that we must be ready, in the last resort, to use force to bring Nasser to his senses.[13]

At the time of the nationalization, Britain had about a six-week supply of oil on hand, which was slightly more than the French had available.[14]

Eisenhower's initial reaction to Nasser's decision was to attempt to defuse the situation in order to lessen the likelihood of a military clash. He dispatched Secretary Dulles to London with a plan for an International Board to operate the Canal. Twenty-four countries met in London on August 16 to discuss this plan. Those countries included the original signatories of the Constantinople Convention along with the main maritime powers and the major users of the Canal. Eighteen nations approved the proposal. Prime Minister Menzies of Australia led a delegation of five representative nations to Egypt on September 3 to present the plan to Nasser. Six days later, Nasser rejected the plan.[15] The second attempt to defuse the crisis was a proposal to create a Suez Canal User's Association to operate the Canal. The Western powers met again in London on September 19 through 21 to discuss this proposal.[16] Simultaneous with this Second Conference, the British and French referred the Suez problem to the Security Council of the United Nations. The United States had opposed involving the United Nations in the dispute. The Eisenhower administration feared that if the United Nations failed to resolve the crisis, such demonstrable impotence would irreparably damage the reputation and efficacy of the still-young international organization.

Once the British and French had turned to the United Nations for help, the United Nation's Secretary General Dag Hammarskjöld helped develop Six Principles for the future of the Canal. These were based on the conclusions of the First London Conference and the Menzies mission ideas and suggestions. These principles stated:

> Any settlement of the Suez question should meet the following requirements:
>
> 1. There should be free and open transit through the Canal without discrimination, overt or covert—this covers both political and technical aspects;

2. The sovereignty of Egypt should be respected;
3. The operations of the Canal should be insulated from the politics of any country;
4. The manner of fixing tolls and charges should be decided by agreement between Egypt and the users;
5. A fair proportion of the dues should be allotted to development;
6. In case of disputes, unresolved affairs between the Suez Canal Company and the Egyptian Government should be settled by arbitration with suitable terms of reference and suitable provisions for the payments of sums found to be due.[17]

Egypt rejected the British claim that the London Conference and the Menzies proposals met these six requirements, and a stalemate emerged.

By this point, sensing American opposition, the British and French had ceased communication with the United States concerning their military plans. British and French troops were massing on Cyprus, and Israeli troops were concentrated near the Jordanian border, which Eisenhower knew about because of information provided by U-2 overflights. The United States was aware that the volume of electronic communication between Israel, France, and Britain had increased as well, but was not apprised of the content of these communications. The Eisenhower administration assumed, wrongly, that Israel was planning to attack Jordan, with whom the Israelis had independent conflicts.[18] In actuality, the allies were planning an attack on Nasser.

Britain and France had orchestrated a plan beforehand with the participation of the Israelis. Secretary Dulles described the sequences of events to the National Security Council "as a series of concerted moves among the British, French, and Israelis, the French actually conducting the concerted planning and the British acquiescing."[19]

Eisenhower was surprised and infuriated by the subsequent development of events, and most especially by what he saw as British deception. As Anthony Nutting, British Minister of State for Foreign Affairs, described British preparations:

> Nobody was kept more completely in the dark than the President of the United States. After Eden's initial confession that he wanted war had provoked Eisenhower to indignant protests, the President was treated as an unreliable ally. The more he warned Eden that American and world opinion would not support him if he appeared to be trying to browbeat a smaller nation into submission, the more determined Eden became to conceal his hand from the Americans.

And after the decision to gang up with Israel had been taken, Eisenhower was told nothing at all.[20]

Eisenhower only learned the truth of allied plans after Israel attacked the Egyptians on October 29. In an overwhelmingly successful campaign, the Israelis succeeded in killing or capturing 30,000 Egyptians by November 3. As prearranged, Britain and France invoked the Tripartite Agreement of 1950 to call on Israel and Egypt to stop all hostilities, withdraw troops ten miles from the Suez Canal, and allow occupation of the Canal zone by Anglo-French forces in order to keep the peace. If these conditions were not met, Egypt would face allied military intervention. Note that Britain and France did not require withdrawal to the original borders required by the armistice clause of the Tripartite Agreement, as defined by the 1950 agreement they invoked, but ten miles away from the Canal. Not surprisingly, the ultimatum was accepted by Israel on the condition that the Egyptians accept it as well. Egypt refused.

The British and French used Egypt's refusal on October 31 to justify their invasion of the Canal area. The president was outraged. He went on television and announced:

> The United States was not consulted in any way about any phase of these actions. Nor were we informed of them in advance. As it is the manifest right of any of these nations to take such decisions and actions, it is likewise our right, if our judgment dictates, to dissent. We believe these actions to have been taken in error. For we do not accept the use of force as a wise and proper instrument for the settlement of international disputes.[21]

Despite various UN attempts to instigate a cease-fire, the international situation continued to deteriorate. The Soviet Union had recently invaded Hungary but Soviet Premier Nikolai Bulganin took time out to send notes to France, Britain, and the United States on November 5 that contained thinly veiled threats to use nuclear weapons against Britain and France if they failed to withdraw from the Suez region.[22] The Soviet letter to Eisenhower proposed that the United States and the Soviet Union join forces against the allied European powers in the region. Eisenhower reacted with fury to the Soviet proposal:

> Those boys are both furious and scared. Just as with Hitler, that makes for the most dangerous possible state of mind. And we better be damn sure that every intelligence point and every outpost of our

armed forces is absolutely right on their toes. We have to be positive and clear in our every word, every step. And if those fellows start something, we may have to hit 'em—and, if necessary, with *everything* in the bucket.[23]

Eisenhower was very concerned about the infiltration of Soviet influence into the region during the crisis and feared the potential for the Soviet Union to catalyze a major conflict. Eisenhower received information from head of the CIA Allen Dulles that "Nasser has apparently received assurances from the Soviet Ambassador in Cairo that Russia is prepared to support Egypt all the way, even risking World War III."[24]

In his planning, Eisenhower clearly considered the risk of war with the Soviet Union to be a real one. Notes from a policy meeting on November 6 describe Eisenhower's response as follows:

The President said our people should be alert. If the Soviets attack the French and British directly, we would be in war, and we would be justified in taking military action even if Congress were not in session . . . The President asked if our forces in the Mediterranean are equipped with atomic anti-submarine weapons.[25]

The United States, despite its opposition to the Anglo-French intervention, forcefully rejected Soviet proposals for joint action in the region to contain European allied military action. While Eisenhower clearly did not support allied military intervention in the Middle East, he adamantly refused to tolerate Soviet interference in the Middle East either. Eisenhower's trepidation about the Soviet Union using this crisis to gain access to the region in ostensible defense of Egypt was one of the main reasons Eisenhower wanted to preempt further conflict in the area.

Through the intermediation of the United Nations, a cease-fire was announced on November 7. However, British forces refused to withdraw from the area until a UN peacekeeping force was in place. The first of these forces arrived in the region on November 15. By this time, the economic situation in Europe had deteriorated significantly. The oil shortage was becoming severe. There was a serious run on the pound sterling in Britain, and Western Europe was running short of oil reserves.[26] Eisenhower put intense pressure on the Europeans to withdraw their forces from the region, refusing to deliver any oil or allow any financial assistance until the British and French had withdrawn their troops from the area.[27] The British, who expected stronger American support, found Eisenhower's behavior surprising, but bowed to American pressure and withdrew the last of their forces on December 22. American pressure on Israel was less effective, and Israeli withdrawal from Gaza was not completed until March 7, 1957.[28]

During hostilities, the Egyptians sunk at least eight ships in the Canal to prevent passage of Western ships. In addition, they sabotaged the oil pipeline into Iraq and destroyed three major pumping stations.[29] Cleanup of these areas took several months. The Canal itself was not reopened to traffic until April 8, 1957.

Domain

Immediately prior to and during the Suez crisis, President Eisenhower was clearly in the domain of gains. He was an overwhelmingly popular president who had been highly successful throughout his first term. His position prevailed in 79.1 percent of the votes in Congress during his first four years in office. He held strong party loyalty in Congress. In 1956, he obtained more than 80 percent agreement from Republicans on a regular basis.[30]

In the State of the Union address that Eisenhower made on January 5, 1956, seven months prior to the nationalization of the Canal, he appeared pleased with the picture of the nation he portrayed:

> Our country is at peace. Our security posture commands respect. A spiritual vigor marks our national life. Our economy, approaching the 400 billion dollar mark, is at an unparalleled level of prosperity. The national income is more widely and fairly distributed than ever before. The number of Americans at work has reached an all-time high. As a people, we are achieving ever higher standards of living— earning more, producing more, consuming more, building more, and investing more than ever before.
>
> Virtually all sectors of our society are sharing in these good times . . .
>
> Our defenses have been reinforced at sharply reduced costs. Programs to expand world trade and to harness the atom for the betterment of mankind have been carried forward. Our economy has been freed from governmental wage and price controls. Inflation has been halted; the cost of living stabilized.
>
> Government spending has been cut by more than ten billion dollars. Three hundred thousand positions have been eliminated from the Federal payroll. Taxes have been substantially reduced. A balanced budget is in prospect. Social security has been extended to ten million more Americans and unemployment insurance to four million more. Unprecedented advances in civil rights have been made. The

long-standing and deep-seated problems of agriculture have been forthrightly attacked.[31]

In the midst of the Suez crisis, Eisenhower won the election on November 7, 1956, by an electoral margin of 457 to 73 votes and a popular vote of over nine million votes. This was a larger margin than he had had in the 1952 election. He won 41 states.[32]

In addition, Eisenhower's international popularity and approval ratings *during* the crisis rose to new heights, higher than his August 1955 post–Summit Meeting ratings: 77 percent among West Germans (26 percent increase); 73 percent among Italians (17 percent increase); 76 percent among the British (6 percent increase); and 35 percent among the French (5 percent increase).[33] This popularity was at least partly a result of the success of Eisenhower's Suez policy. As Secretary Dulles noted at an NSC meeting on November 1, "[T]he position of avoiding resort to a solution by force. This has been a policy which has evoked greater international support for the United States than we have secured at any time in our history."[34]

In a meeting on October 30, just a few days after the Israeli attack on Egypt and the Soviet invasion into Hungary on October 26, Eisenhower

> mentioned that he had thought the world picture was brightening for some time except for the Eastern European tier of countries and for the situation in the Middle East. He even thought he saw possibilities of improvement in the Middle East, although the present developments were adverse. The President indicated that he feels that if the Eastern tier of states can be made independent and neutral, the possibilities for a constructive era of world development would be greatly enhanced.[35]

Eisenhower was concerned about the Soviet invasion of Hungary but initial reports were not indicative of how dire the situation would become. In fact, Eisenhower was eager to use the Soviet invasion for propaganda purposes; he wanted to show what happens to small countries that fall under Soviet influence. The notes from the November 11, 1956, NSC meeting report that: "[T]he President said, it remained wholly inexplicable to him that any state in the world, Syria included, would play with the Russians after witnessing what had happened in Hungary. It was for this reason, continued the President, that we must go on playing up the situation in Hungary to the absolute maximum, so the whole world will see and understand."[36] Such a "demonstration effect" served to make the Soviet Union look bad in the international arena and provided a superordinate enemy and overarching goals to inject desperately needed cohesion into the Western alliance when it was most required.

In spite of his concerns about Soviet behavior in Eastern Europe and about allied behavior in the Middle East, Eisenhower had the power and freedom to assure America's security. The United States at this time was undoubtedly the preeminent military and economic power in the world. America possessed overwhelming strategic and conventional force. The United States was not subject at this time to dependence on foreign oil reserves to the extent that the British and French were. Moreover, unlike its allies, America had almost no financial interest in the Suez Canal Company.

Eisenhower was in a very secure position internationally as well as domestically at the time of the Suez Crisis. Eisenhower was satisfied with the reference point. Clearly in the domain of gains, Eisenhower had the personal and political power to advocate virtually any policy he chose. His caution in the Suez crisis can be seen as noteworthy and deserving of explanation because Eisenhower possessed the power to be belligerent at low cost to possibly large positive effect. Yet according to the predictions of prospect theory, this positive position would make him relatively risk averse. And, in fact, Eisenhower proved unwilling to seriously disturb an international situation that he largely found to be satisfactory and mostly conducive to U.S. interests.

The Framing of Options

Eisenhower faced two major options in handling the Suez crisis. First, he could have joined forces with the French, British, and Israelis and engaged in military action against Nasser. Second, he could have forced the Europeans into accepting Egypt's nationalization of the Canal.

The first option Eisenhower considered was to join the allies in forcing Nasser out of the Canal Zone. Eisenhower felt military action would not be well received domestically, and this was a concern because of the impending election. Moreover, Eisenhower felt that "imperialist" aggression against a leader with as much local charismatic power as Nasser might drive Arab countries into Nasser's arms.[37] If this happened, Eisenhower feared that Nasser could lead the Arab world to fall under Soviet sway; Eisenhower's most pressing concern revolved around this kind of Soviet involvement in the region.[38] He felt that supporting allied forces against a nation that was, after all, taking a legal action was unwise.[39]

Eisenhower did not share the British and French fears that Egypt would close off the Canal to Western ships. From the outset, the allies claimed that the Egyptians would be unable to run the Canal efficiently;

this view was no doubt reinforced by remnants of colonial condescension. Eisenhower disputed this claim from the beginning. He had studied the workings of the Panama Canal and was convinced that the Egyptians could run the Suez Canal as effectively and efficiently as the British or French. Indeed, Eisenhower proved to be correct in his assessment of the situation. As far as Eisenhower was concerned, as long as Egypt gave just compensation for the property it seized, and allowed free and open access to the use of the Canal, no other state had a legitimate basis upon which to mount a military campaign against it.[40]

The other major option Eisenhower contemplated was pressuring American allies to accept the nationalization of the Canal. This option required no military force, and it secured American's position as the dominant world power in the region. Inducing the allies to accept nationalization of the Canal accomplished more than preventing alienation from the Third World: it secured American influence in the Middle East and thus decreased the chance of Soviet infiltration into the area.

This is the option Eisenhower chose. At the beginning, Eisenhower did what he could to defuse the crisis through legal means and a negotiated compromise.[41] Indeed, Eisenhower remained quite averse to placing any overt pressure on the allies until all other methods of peaceful resolution had failed. When negotiated peace-seeking strategies failed and armed conflict erupted, Eisenhower did everything he could to stop the fighting. Indeed, when he first heard about the attack on Egypt, Eisenhower was angry enough to contemplate openly supporting the Egyptians. As Goodpaster recalled:

> The President said we must indicate we are considering ways and means of redeeming our pledge to the Middle Eastern countries. If the British back the Israelis they may find us in opposition. He said he did not fancy helping Egypt in the present circumstances but he felt our word must be made good. Mr. Wilson again asked how clear cut our pledge is to the Middle Eastern countries, and the President recalled that we had told Israel quite recently that they did not need from us the arms they were seeking because of the assurance inherent in our pledge.[42]

Eisenhower coerced his allies into capitulating to Nasser by withholding desperately needed financial assistance and oil supplies until after they had withdrawn their armed forces from the area.[43] In this way, Eisenhower overtly pressured his allies into a negotiated peaceful withdrawal of forces from the Suez Canal region.

External Influences on Framing

An American president's perspective on any given crisis is necessarily informed by his international position. This was particularly true in this case, because the central dispute surrounded an *international* right to access. British Prime Minister Anthony Eden and French Premier Guy Mollet placed the most direct pressure on Eisenhower to change his position during the crisis and join them in military action against Nasser. These leaders framed the issue in terms of Western prestige and credibility in the region. Eden and Mollet were concerned about securing their broader colonial interests and access to their oil supplies, among other things. They saw Nasser as a modern-day Hitler and were thus determined not to appease his demands, in their fear that such capitulation would lead to greater losses in the region. Because allied British and French views were so central to American decision making in the Suez crisis, each perspective will be examined in turn.

Prime Minister Eden, and later Macmillan, were primarily interested in maintaining British prestige and influence in the area. The same can be said of Prime Minister Mollet of France; France's major concern was that by accepting the nationalization of the Canal and the rights of sovereignty upon which the nationalization had been justified, France would send an unacceptable message to their Algerian colonials that sovereignty was a legitimate basis for independent action. France did not want to set a precedent in Egypt that would encourage the Algerians to oppose French rule in Northern Africa. The Israelis, for their part, were anxious to eliminate the preexisting enemy base for fedayeen raids and to reverse the Egyptian decision to exclude their ships from transit through the Canal.[44]

Robert Bowie, Assistant Secretary of State, eloquently described the differences in framing between the Europeans and the Americans:

> I think basically it was the difference in the way in which Washington and London and also Paris defined the problem. Eisenhower said: we must try to separate the issue of keeping the Canal in operation from the question of the risks from Nasser in other respects, especially in the Arab world. This obviously was something that Eden did not accept. He felt the seizure of the Canal was so to speak a first step, and he repeatedly invoked the memory of Hitler and the necessity of dealing with these kinds of things early . . . the French and the British attitude was . . . How can this issue be handled in such a way as to cut down Nasser? Therefore, the efforts of the United States to prolong negotiations seemed like temporizing to the British and French,

whereas the efforts of the British and French to bring the thing to a head seemed to be constantly getting in the way of the Eisenhower–Dulles effort to produce an atmosphere in which negotiations might succeed . . . With Eisenhower and Dulles focusing mainly on the question of safeguarding the use of the Canal, the use of force did not seem a particularly sensible way to achieve this. They were fearful that force just would not succeed in accomplishing this aim . . . they feared that it would be extremely difficult to operate the Canal in the face of Egyptian hostility . . .[45]

The point Bowie raises about Eden is particularly important. It is clear that the Munich analogy influenced Eden's and Mollet's analysis of the Suez Crisis. Eden really did see Nasser as a latter-day reincarnation of Hitler. Eden believed that concessions to Nasser would only lead to greater aggression on Nasser's part throughout the rest of the Middle East.[46]

Eden's perception points to an important difference in the focus of concern regarding Nasser between the United States and its Western allies. In terms of prospect theory, Eden and Mollet were acting in domains of loss precipitated by the nationalization itself. Eden and Mollet were quite preoccupied with returning the Canal to the old status quo, when the Western powers held controlling interest of the Canal Company. These leaders were concerned that submission to a loss in Egypt would only encourage their colonial interests to challenge Western control of the colonials' sovereign rights as well.[47] According to prospect theory, Eden and Mollet would be expected to take extreme risks in order to recoup their losses and return to the old status quo.

As Bowie notes in another context:

The allies were focusing almost entirely on the costs of *not* destroying Nasser as a threat to their position in the Middle East. The U.S. assessed the Canal dispute and the stakes mainly in relation to its efforts to build world stability and order and to contain Soviet expansion.[48]

In short, Britain and France were operating from a different reference point than the United States was. For Eden and Mollet, the only acceptable reference point was the *old* status quo. In prospect theory terms, Eden and Mollet had failed to renormalize to the new status quo. In essence, Britain and France were trying to recoup their losses and thereby return to the status quo ante; they assumed the situation would get worse unless Nasser was removed from power. For America, the new status quo was really no different than the old in terms of direct national interest; payments for tolls would go to Egypt instead of Britain and France, but ships would continue their unimpeded transit through the Canal just as well. The United States had not sustained the loss of property, possession, and shares in the stock of the Canal company that Britain and France had endured. In fact, the United States appeared to reinforce the new status quo; Eisenhower believed that things would get worse if military action was used against Nasser, especially if this action prompted the Soviet Union to intervene militarily as well.[49] Eisenhower felt that the new status quo was a perfectly appropriate reference point, whereas his European allies did not. They believed that the operative reference point was the *old* status quo.

In spite of these factors, Eden was quite astute in trying to manipulate American fear about Soviet influence in order to garner support for Britain's actions against Nasser. Eden assumed, perhaps as a result of wishful thinking, that Dulles's statement to him on August 1 that "Nasser must be made to disgorge what he was attempting to swallow" was sympathetic to his position.[50] Eden derived from this statement that if push came to shove, the United States would support military action against Nasser. The obvious miscommunication is clear from Eden's memoirs:

> I still believed that the United States Government held firmly to their determination that Nasser must be made to "disgorge." This being so, I considered that they must be allowed as free a hand as possible in selecting methods. The User's Club could be the American choice . . . we were frustrated, and the User's club assumed a different form from that which we had been led to expect.
>
> In the meantime I had received a disquieting message from Mr. Eisenhower on September 3. Hitherto he and his officials had always given us to understand that the United States would not take exception to the use of force . . . The fact that we had taken military precautions, had, furthermore, been approved from time to time. Now the President told me that American public opinion flatly rejected force. He admitted that the procedures of negotiation on which we were then engaged would probably not give Nasser the setback he deserved . . .[51]

Eisenhower's communication led Eden to plead for American support of the British position in a letter dated September 6:

> [T]he seizure of the Suez Canal is, we are convinced, the opening gambit in a planned campaign designed by Nasser to expel all Western influence and interest from Arab countries . . .

> You may feel that even if we are right it would be better to wait until Nasser has unmistakably revealed his intentions. But this is the argument which prevailed in 1936 and which we both rejected in 1948 . . .[52]

This letter points to another important difference in the way the British and the Americans assessed the situation in the Middle East.

Eden had not yet adjusted to the idea that Britain's colonial influence had waned. Indeed, his idea of the larger status quo was outdated, and his attempts to force Nasser into submission were based on an attempt to recoup British colonial power and regain lost influence and territory. Eden wanted the new reference point to be similar to the old status quo; he wanted Middle Eastern politics to continue to revolve centrally around British interests.[53] In terms of prospect theory, Eden had a different idea of what constituted the appropriate reference point than did Nasser or, indeed, Eisenhower. As opposed to these others, Eden felt strongly that definitive influence in Middle Eastern politics rightly belonged to Britain.

As a result of these outdated larger beliefs about the appropriate status quo, the British and French governments continued to plan for military action against Egypt. Such planning proceeded despite the fact that military action was *not* supported by the majority of the British population at the time. An August 1956 British poll showed that

> roughly one and one half times as many people advocate economic and political sanctions as advocate the use of force . . . A surprising 23% of the people blamed past British weakness for the current crisis as compared with 3% blaming the US.[54]

Thus, it is unlikely that Eden was driven to military intervention by public demand.

The Eisenhower administration understood that the British leadership was, however, less interested in public opinion than in regaining lost British prestige. As Secretary Dulles noted in one National Security Council meeting, the British were operating off a larger mental account than public opinion:

> [B]oth the British and French looked at this crisis in broader terms than the Suez Canal itself. These two countries were greatly concerned with Nasser's growing stature in the Middle East, and the resultant jeopardy to their whole position in the Middle East and North Africa. Secretary Dulles admitted that the U.S. plan could be

made to appear to be a victory for Nasser, or at least so the British and French argued. They therefore felt that they must come out of the crisis with some action that would cut Nasser down to size.[55]

Dulles appeared to have an intuitive understanding that the size of the perceived context drastically affected the two allies' response to the Suez crisis; the larger the context, the more drastic the required reaction. Just after the Israeli attack, Dulles noted:

Unfortunately the problem was being placed by the British and French in a larger context of their entire Middle East position. Under those circumstances, a solution was more difficult.[56]

British leaders undoubtedly assumed that a great triumph in the Middle East by British forces would restore all the prestige and popularity that Nasser had cost them by nationalizing the Canal.

State Department officials mention this feature a number of times in almost classical prospect theory terms. When asked what an acceptable outcome might look like for the British, Secretary Dulles replied that "it could *only be a return to the situation* in the Canal Zone *that had existed* a few years ago in which terrorist attacks by the Egyptians were unceasing, with nearly 90,000 British troops present there."[57] Later in that same meeting, Goodpaster noted that the president had joined in Dulles's analysis by arguing that "he recognized the intensity of British feeling—specifically their feeling that *they have been going down and down in the Middle East and that they are now reaching a point where they must strike back.*"[58]

Information coming back to the State Department from the embassy in London shared this view as well. In a telegram sent on September 1, an official notes that the British

seem increasingly to have convinced themselves that military operations could be confined to narrow area of Egypt and could be swiftly successful at small cost in men and treasure. *On this assumption they foresee military defeat Nasser as restoring Brit position and prestige Middle East permitting favorable solution Brit problems with Saudi Arabia, Jordan, Syria, Etc.*[59]

In terms of prospect theory, the British, like the French, were faced with an unacceptable *new* status quo after Nasser nationalized the Canal. The British and French were thus immediately plummeted into a domain of loss and, as a result, became quite risk-taking in their choices. The variance for their action was quite wide, and thus quite risk seeking: if they succeeded, they could regain control of the Canal from Nasser, as well as strengthen their colonial status in the region; if they failed, they stood to lose not only control of the Canal, but loss of men, material, status in the region, access to vital oil supplies, financial solvency, and even govern-mental stability. From the perspective of prospect theory, the British and French were governed in their actions by loss aversion: they sought to recoup what they had lost, even at a potentially high future cost if the ven-ture failed. They engaged in a risky military venture that failed, at least partly because Eisenhower refused to support the venture. In this way, the British lost much more than they would have had they merely been willing to accept the nationalization of the Canal at the outset. Because Eden and Mollet placed the Suez crisis in a larger mental account, they perceived a greater loss, took a greater risk, and sustained a greater setback than if they had renormalized more quickly to the new status quo after Nasser nationalized the Canal.

The Suez crisis was especially destructive for Prime Minister Eden, both personally and professionally. It cost him his health and eventually led to his forced resignation from the British government on January 8, 1957. In the midst of the crisis, Eden became quite ill, went on vacation to Jamaica,[60] and was replaced by the former Chancellor of the Exchequer, Harold Macmillan. Macmillan faced serious political and military crises that were characterized on November 19 by an American Embassy official as follows:

> Macmillan said that it was evident that British government may be faced within next few days with the terrible dilemma of either (A) withdrawing from Egypt, having accomplished nothing . . . without having secured the free operation of the Canal or even being in a posi-tion to clear it, or (B) renewing hostilities in Egypt and taking over the entire Canal . . . and to avoid the complete economic collapse of Europe within the next few months. The danger of course in the minds of the British Cabinet of adopting the first alternative is the loss of prestige and humiliation would be so great that the govt must fall, while the second alternative would obviously involve the risk of bringing in the Russians and resulting in a third world war.[61]

The French were somewhat less engaged with the Americans during the course of the crisis than the British, but they held the Americans more responsible for its instigation. In a series of telegrams sent to Secretary Dulles, Ambassador Dillon delineates the French reasoning for holding the United States responsible for the crisis:

Mollet said that French opinion was particularly disturbed because they had the feeling that they were being abandoned by the US after US had started the whole affair by their withdrawal of aid for Aswan Dam. Mollet said the French fully approved of this action by the US but felt that the US should also accept the consequences.[62]

Dillon made clear what the French thought those consequences might be, unless the United States supported France and Britain in military action against Nasser right away:

> He [Mollet] felt that the US was embarking on the same course of error by appeasement that had been followed toward Hitler in the 1930s . . . He said he had never been so disturbed and worried for the future and was certain that if we did not take action to stop Nasser now we would be faced with the same problem 3, 6, or 9 months hence, only the Western position by that time would have greatly deteriorated.[63]

Indeed, Mollet was not above invoking a little Cold War blackmail in order to encourage the U.S. government to support French military action against Egypt. Mollet intimated to Dillon that the French had rebuffed a Soviet offer to "bring about peace in Algeria, in concert with Nasser" if the French would agree to abandon total support for NATO.[64] By rebuffing this offer, Mollet felt entitled to expect American support against Nasser as payment for rejecting such a tempting Soviet offer.[65]

Despite a long history of personal friendship with British leaders forged during World War II when Eisenhower was commander of allied forces against Germany, the president remained relatively immune to pressures from the British and French to join in their military ventures in Egypt. Eisenhower recognized the source of their actions as being rooted in interests and concerns that he did not share. Where the British and French saw an overwhelming threat to legitimate Western rights and interests, with a domino potential for even greater losses unless Nasser was stopped immediately, Eisenhower saw a legitimate nationalist claim to sovereign rights, and a threat of Soviet influence and Arab pan-nationalism if the Western powers used military force to subdue Nasser.

Eisenhower believed that his allies were not assessing the situation objectively and were instead caught up in nineteenth-century politics. Eisenhower's understanding of the British position did not prevent him from changing his personal evaluation of Eden based on the prime minister's behavior in the crisis. As Eisenhower's secretary noted in his diary afterward:

About Eden, he said that he had always liked him—but that he had
not proved himself a good first man. He had had so many years under
Churchill—and learned from him—but was unable to carry the load
himself. He said that Eden's great popularity stemmed from his resignation (from Parliament?) at the time of the appeasement of Germany
. . . that Macmillan and Eden were somewhat alike in the fact that
both could not bear to see the dying of Britain as a colonial power.[66]

In a conversation with Dulles while the Secretary was in the hospital for
the treatment of stomach cancer, Eisenhower commented:

One of the most disappointing things was to start with an exceedingly
high opinion of a person and then have continually to downgrade this
estimate on the basis of succeeding contacts with him. He indicated
that Eden fell into the latter category.[67]

However, Western leaders saw different realities. Differing perceptions are most clearly evident in allied leaders' responses to Nasser himself.
Eisenhower did not believe that the British were malicious or unjustified in
their opposition to Nasser. However, he did feel that the British response
was overreactive and probably misguided:

My conviction was that the Western world had gotten into a lot of
difficulty by selecting the wrong issue about which to be tough. To
choose a situation in which Nasser had legal and sovereign rights and
in which world opinion was largely on his side, was not in my opinion
a good one on which to stand.[68]

Eisenhower argued that Macmillan and Lloyd were not really assessing
the situation clearly: they "were so obsessed with the possibilities of getting
rid of Nasser that they were handicapped in searching objectively for any
realistic method of operating the Canal."[69]

Did the Europeans hold a different perspective than Eisenhower simply because they estimated different payoffs from various actions? The
question of payoffs is incorporated into prospect theory within the concept of the weighting function. The weighting function speaks directly to
variations in payoffs and how the perceived likelihood of each option
affects how heavily that option is subjectively weighted. Events that are
judged to be extreme in probability, either certain or impossible, are
greatly overweighted in importance. Options that offer a high probability
of achieving their desired outcome assume greater importance than they
rationally might merit in actual decision making. Pseudo-certainty effects

make highly likely events be judged as though they were certain, although that may not be the case. If the Western leaders assumed that the probability of Nasser asserting control over larger areas of the Middle East was high, they may have treated this assumption as though it were reality, due to the pseudo-certainty effect. In this way, a likely event was treated as though it were inevitable, when in reality it was only highly probable and indeed proved not to occur.

Eisenhower was more comfortable with the status quo, including Nasser's rule, than were either Eden or Mollet; this is at least partly because the European leaders perceived a different, and worse, reference point. Eisenhower mentioned the international importance of the reference point in a backhand way when he commented that "Any immediate recourse to the United Nations seemed to [Britain and France] to be risky delay, thus allowing a situation to exist long enough to imply world acceptance of its permanence."[70]

In addition, each leader framed the issue in fundamentally different ways. Each leader worked from a different reference point in international relations and this difference in starting points accounts for the radically different goals and means that each side adopted to accomplish its objectives. Britain and France saw a challenge to their credibility and a threat to their power in the region and sought to rectify the balance through force; Eisenhower wanted to present a challenge to Soviet influence in the region through brokering peaceful negotiation and through the use of diplomatic and financial pressures to bring about a resolution to the crisis without engaging in a wider war.

Throughout the crisis, Eisenhower's biggest concern was that the Soviet Union would become involved. In fact, the fear of Soviet involvement influenced Eisenhower's decision-making process during the Suez crisis more than the pressure applied by the Western allies. In early August, Secretary Dulles argued that Eisenhower "felt that the United States should make it clear that we would be in the hostilities if the Soviet came in."[71] Apparently there was no subsequent discussion at the meeting that such an assurance of intervention might instead *encourage* the British and French to provoke the Soviet Union into entering the conflict in order to induce American military support.

There is some evidence to support this contention. On October 31, following the British and French military intervention into the Middle East, David Lawrence told Secretary Dulles that "the answer re why they did not consult us is they were afraid America would intervene forcibly to kill the scheme as in the early days."[72] On the same day, records of a telephone conversation between United Nations Ambassador David Lodge and Dulles reported that Lodge's "belief is they were counting on the Russians getting into it and then we get in to get them out. L. [Lodge] said it would be fine if we make them understand they cannot take us for granted."[73]

It is clear that the Soviet Union dreaded the same outcome that the Americans feared. On November 5, shortly after the Western allies intervened militarily in Egypt, Bulganin sent a letter to Eisenhower in which he stated, "If this war is not stopped, it is fraught with danger and can grow into Third World War."[74] Eisenhower's fear of Soviet action was apparently sustained by his belief that the Soviet Union was more likely to take a risk because it was in a bad position. Two days after he received Bulganin's note, Goodpaster noted Eisenhower's response: "we should give the Soviets a clear warning. The President said his concern is that the Soviet Union, *seeing their position and their policy failing so badly in the satellites, are ready to take any wild adventure.*"[75]

A day later, Eisenhower had given more thought to the matter. Notes taken of an NSC meeting report that "He just couldn't help believing that the Russians would play their game short of anything which would induce the United States to declare war on them."[76]

Riskiness of the Chosen Option

Expected variance proves helpful in analyzing the options that were available to Eisenhower. The option of supporting the allies in their bid against Nasser possessed a wider variation in potential outcome than the one that would accept nationalization of the Canal. Since variance was greater with military intervention, this would have been the more risk-seeking choice, which Eisenhower avoided.

The first option, supporting the Western allies, held some positive possible outcomes. If Nasser could be ejected, the Canal would be returned to Western control. The Western alliance would demonstrate strength and cohesion, and Western prestige and status would be supported. In addition, such action might intimidate future aggressors from taking unwarranted action against American interests.

However, if this option failed, very bad outcomes might occur. If the Soviet Union intervened in support of the Egyptians, however remote this possibility, a third world war might result. Moreover, even if the effort was a success and the Soviet Union did not intervene, it was not inconceivable that Nasser could still emerge as a hero in the face of Western imperialist assault, and American influence in the region would plummet to a new low.

The option of pursuing peaceful resolution to the crisis offered some positive and negative outcomes as well. On the negative side, it presented an uncomfortable schism in the Western alliance and risked allowing

Nasser to gain status and prestige at a cost to Western influence. However, a policy of peaceful resolution also reduced the danger of bloodshed and increased the likelihood that Americans would be viewed in the Middle East as defenders of law and justice.

Officials in the administration were not unaware of the wide range of possibilities that the crisis might produce. Treasury Secretary George Humphrey was centrally involved in salvaging the British financial situation when he described the situation well by commenting at an NSC meeting in late November that "the possibilities, for good and for evil, which could come out of the present situation were such that they could scarcely be exaggerated. The range was complete from great success to genuine disaster."[77]

The most desired outcome for the British and French of reasserting control of the Canal was best offered by the option of military intervention. The probability of achieving total political, if not military, success with this option was low. Moreover, the worst possible outcome, instigating a war with the Soviet Union, was also possible with this option. Because of this wide variation in possible outcome values, military action remained the riskier path. Peaceful resolution, on the other hand, constituted a more risk-averse choice than military intervention.

Eisenhower took this cautious route. He first pursued peaceful compromise through a variety of ultimately failed negotiating plans. When the British, French, and Israelis intervened militarily anyway, Eisenhower continued his policy of refusing to engage in armed conflict. Rather, he withheld vital oil and financial resources from the Western alliance until the British and French were forced to withdraw their forces from the area.[78]

Eisenhower's assessment of the risks associated with military action were supported by an evaluation of the situation by the Joint Chiefs of Staff, prepared for the Secretary of Defense, in which the Chiefs argued that "unsuccessful U.S. military action would be most damaging and must not be permitted to occur."[79] Indeed, in developing a policy position for the London Conference, Dulles stated: "It was finally agreed that re-routing should be the 'next to last' resort. War is being regarded as the last resort."[80]

In a cable Eisenhower dictated to Eden the day after the Israeli invasion, but never sent, he mentioned his discomfort with the risks involved in the use of force:

> I must say that it is hard for me to see any good final result emerging from a scheme that seems to antagonize the entire Moslem world. Indeed I have difficulty seeing any end whatsoever if all the Arabs should begin reacting somewhat as the North Africans have been operating against the French.[81]

Eisenhower recognized that long-term strategic risks associated with the reckless use of force in the Middle East outweighed any possible benefit that could be gained through reestablishing lost control over the Canal.

In one press conference he gave during the course of the crisis, Eisenhower said:

> Any outbreak of major hostilities in that region would be a catastrophe for the world. As you know, all of Western Europe had gone to oil instead of coal for its energy, and that oil comes from the mideast. That region is of great—as a matter of fact, it is of extraordinary importance to all of the free world, so that just for material reason alone we must regard every bit of unrest there as a most serious matter.[82]

There is much evidence that Eisenhower and his Cabinet believed that the risks associated with armed intervention in Egypt were much greater than those concomitant with alienating Western leaders. On Sept 11, Eisenhower's secretary reported that he claimed he "cannot minimize seriousness of the situation. We are 'sitting on a keg of dynamite.'"[83]

Eisenhower's action in the Middle East involved restraint in a situation where the United States could quite easily have exerted decisive military force. Had the United States so desired, it could have rapidly forced Nasser into submission. Eisenhower could have quickly generated support for military action had he wished to do so; he was, after all, an overwhelmingly popular president with a secure base of support. In spite of this, Eisenhower, having been battered and made heroic by his battlefield commands in World War II, knew only too well that the American people did not want another war. He was particularly conscious of this in the middle of his reelection campaign. As White House Chief of Staff Jim Hagerty noted a month before the election:

> [T]he American people and the people of the world expect the President of the United States to do something dramatic—even drastic—to prevent at all possible costs another war.
>
> This question of peace or war—in Egypt or anywhere else—is the number one question in the minds of American people. For a peaceful settlement of the Suez problem, the people of our nation would support the President in any way . . .
>
> Peaceful settlement must be the only answer in these days of nuclear weapons.[84]

Thus, while Eisenhower may have been taking a calculated political risk in opposing allies, this option presented much smaller domestic political risks than engaging in military action in the Middle East. In this case, Eisenhower took a small, sure gain in the Arab world over a gamble that offered the possibility of a larger gain through strengthening the Western alliance and intimidating potential aggressors.

The Decision

In spite of allied pressure to view the Suez crisis as a threat to Western prestige, Eisenhower framed the issue somewhat differently. Eisenhower was less concerned with symbolic issues involving colonial status than were either Eden or Mollet, and Eisenhower gave more legitimacy to Egypt's claim of sovereignty over the Canal than did his Western allies.

Over all else, Eisenhower opposed the use of force. Moreover, he supported the United Nations in the newfound organization's attempts to facilitate resolution of international conflict through peaceful mechanisms. As Eisenhower stated in a press conference early in the crisis:

> I think this: we established the United Nations to abolish aggression, and I am not going to be a party to aggression if it is humanly possible or likely to be—to avoid it or I can detect it before it occurs.[85]

Eisenhower was very concerned with safeguarding the prestige and credibility of the fledgling United Nations to make sure it did not fail in its ability to facilitate peaceful resolution of the crisis.[86] In a surprisingly strong statement of support, Eisenhower wrote after some Israeli raids into Jordan that he wanted to make sure that "Ben Gurion should not make any grave mistakes based upon his belief that winning a domestic election is as important to us as preserving and protecting the interests of the United Nations."[87]

Eisenhower was a pragmatist; most strategically, he wanted to secure access to Middle Eastern oil for the Western powers. As Secretary Dulles commented in a National Security Council Meeting:

> [I]f Middle Eastern oil were lost to the West, rationing of oil in the United States would be an immediate result, with curtailment of automobile production, and a severe blow to the United States economy. Secretary Humphrey said there could be great anger against the UK on the part of the people of the United States if such a result came from unilateral British Action.[88]

Oil supplies to Europe continued to dominate the highest level political discussions throughout the crisis. At all times, Eisenhower was well aware that he held the trump card in all these matters because the Europeans had a greater dependence on Middle Eastern oil than the Americans.

Eisenhower did not dismiss all allied concerns out of hand, however. He disagreed with their interpretation of events and their preferred methods of action but continued to believe that the overarching enemy of the whole Western world was the Soviet Union. Eisenhower describes these differences in detail. Because they are so important in illustrating his thought processes with regard to his decision in the Suez crisis, Eisenhower's memoirs will be quoted at length:

> Obviously we were anxious to sustain our continuing relations with our old and traditional friends, Britain and France. But to us the situation was not quite so simple as those two governments portrayed it. The basic premise of their case was that Egypt, with no authority under international law, had unilaterally flouted a solemn treaty. Next they asserted that the seizure by the Egyptians of the Canal Company would seriously damage the interests of the West . . . because the efficient operation of the Canal requires trained and professional personnel that the Egyptians could not supply . . . A final consideration, which I suspected was the overriding one, was obvious fear of the great increase in Nasser's prestige if he were able to carry out his design successfully. His influence would become so immense, in their view, that he would eventually become, in effect, an Arab dictator controlling the Mediterranean . . .
>
> Our reasons for differing from our allies were roughly as follows :
>
> We doubted the validity of the legal position that Britain and France were using as justification for talk of resorting to force. The weight of world opinion seemed to be that Nasser was within his rights in nationalizing the Canal . . . the waterway, although property of the Canal Company, lay completely within Egyptian territory *and under Egyptian sovereignty.* The inherent right of any sovereign nation to exercise the power of eminent domain within its own territory could scarcely be doubted, provided that just compensation were paid . . . The main issue at stake therefore, was whether or not Nasser would and could keep the waterway open for the traffic of all nations, in accordance with the Constantinople Convention of 1888. This question could not be answered except through test.
>
> Next, we believed that a resort to force, in settling questions such as this one, at such a stage, would be unjustified and would automatically weaken, perhaps even destroy, the United Nations.[89]

Eisenhower did not feel that Nasser posed the kind of Hitler-like threat that Eden and Mollet feared. Eisenhower also thought beyond the immediate conflict and feared that force alone could not support a sustained British or French presence in the region:

> The use of occupying troops in foreign territories to sustain policy was a costly and difficult business. Unless the occupying power was ready to employ the brutalities of dictatorship, local unrest would grow into guerrilla resistance, then open revolt, and possibly, wide-scale conflict. We of the West, who believed in freedom and human dignity could not descend to use of Communist methods.[90]

Eisenhower's assessment of the situation differed significantly from the one provided to him by foreign leaders. Eisenhower felt that he had complete support from his administration officials and from the American people in his preference for peaceful resolution and thus was encouraged in pursuing his values against allied opposition.

Eisenhower felt that the issues at stake in the crisis were subtly different from those perceived by his allies. The president noted this explicitly in a conversation with the French Ambassador to the United States on September 10, when he stated that:

> [T]he United States also had a deep interest in preventing an illegal and forceful seizure of the Canal, but that our interest, while strong, was less direct than that of the French or British. . . . [W]e are not apparently too directly concerned as Britain and France, and it would be hard to convince our own people of the justification for going further than we had already done.[91]

Eisenhower expressed an additional concern in a letter to his friend Swede Hazlett:

> Whether or not we can get a satisfactory solution for this problem and one that tends to restore rather than further damage the prestige of the Western powers, particularly of Britain and France, is something that is not yet resolved. In the kind of world that we are trying to establish, we frequently find ourselves victims of the tyrannies of the weak.
>
> In the effort to promote the rights of all, and observe the equality of sovereignty as between the great and the small, we unavoidably give to the little nations opportunities to embarrass us greatly. Faith-

fulness to the underlying concepts of freedom is frequently costly. Yet there can be no doubt that in the long run faithfulness will produce real rewards.[92]

In a later letter to Hazlett, Eisenhower emphasized that risk should never be driven by fear of the future:

> The real point is that Britain, France and Israel had come to believe—probably correctly—that Nasser was their worst enemy in the Mid East and that until he was removed or deflated, they would have not peace. I do not quarrel with the idea that there is a justification for such fears, but I have insisted long and earnestly that you cannot resort to force in international relationships because of your fear of what might happen in the future. . . . I think that France and Britain have made a terrible mistake.[93]

Eisenhower managed to stay oriented to the present throughout the crisis and took the cautious path. He pursued peaceful negotiations, avoided armed conflict on the part of the American government, forced the Western allies to withdraw their forces from the region, and avoided war with the Soviet Union.

The Outcome

A cease-fire was announced in the Suez by the United Nations on November 7. UN peacekeeping forces began to arrive in the area on November 15.

The U.S. government put enormous pressure on its Western allies to withdraw from the region. It withheld shipments of oil supplies and denied loans through the Import-Export bank and the World Bank until European troops withdrew from the Canal Zone. By this time, the French needed about $260 million from the World Bank in order to pay for oil. The British expected to obtain about $560 million from the World Bank as well as $600 million in credit from the Export-Import bank in order to help stabilize the pound sterling and pay for oil as well. As Goodpaster notes:

> American pressure was conducted in a very direct manner:
> The President said the sequence as he saw it was as follows: First, we are ready to talk about help as soon as the pre-condition (French and British initiation of withdrawal) is established; second; on knowing that the British and French forces will comply with a withdrawal undertaking at once, we would talk to the Arabs to obtain the

removal of any objections they may have regarding the provision of oil to Western Europe; third; we will then talk about the details of money assistance with the British.[94]

The British troops withdrew completely by December 22. Once the British troops were withdrawn, the United States began shipping 200,000 barrels of oil daily to Britain; this amount eventually increased to 300,000 barrels daily until the Canal reopened in April 1957.

The Israeli withdrawal from the Gaza Strip was not completed until the following March. Delay was at least partly because America was not able to exert the same kind of financial and energy pressure on Israel that it had been able to exert on Britain and France. For one thing, Israel was not as desperate for American oil supplies as were the Europeans so the United States had less leverage with which to encourage the Israelis to comply with settlement conditions.

A common interpretation of the crisis argues that Britain and France were humiliated by their failure to enlist U.S. support for their actions.[95] A more subtle but profound impact of the crisis was the shift in power in the Middle East. Prior to the crisis, Britain had been the main outside force in the region. After the crisis, the United States emerged as the dominant outside power. Dulles and Eisenhower were quite sure they wanted everyone to accept this American position as the new status quo. On November 2, Dulles stated that "we should avoid any implication that we are simply going back to the situation that formerly existed in the area."[96] In fact, by challenging Nasser to preserve the previous status quo, Britain and France helped transform the region into a new status quo dominated not by Nasser nor by the British and French, but solidly by the Americans. By January 1, the new American position was solidified:

> The Secretary stated that the prestige of the United States had increased in the Mid-East because of our conduct in the crisis but had decreased among the colonial powers of Western Europe.
>
> Looking to the future, Secretary Dulles stressed *the importance of preventing the Soviet from recouping its position by a victory in the Middle East.*[97]

Conclusion

The last several months of 1956 were particularly dramatic ones for the postwar world. The combination of the invasion of Hungary by the Soviet Union, the invasion of Egypt by the Israelis and later by the British and French, and the presidential elections made it a particularly stressful time for President Eisenhower. This stress is demonstrated by the fact that many of the major decision makers in this crisis were incapacitated at various junctures by severe health problems.[98]

The Suez crisis was dramatic because it triggered many memories and analogies for all of the participants. The British and French possessed powerful interests in preserving their colonial prowess. The British had only recently left the region in July; the French were still contending with colonial uprisings in nearby Algeria. European leaders considered Hitler to be a salient and emotionally powerful comparison for Nasser, and many of them felt that it was essential not to appease the Egyptian leader in his aggressions, as such submission would undoubtedly provoke him to new assaults.

The Suez crisis was also dramatic because of the implicit threat of Soviet intervention. When Bulganin raised the specter of nuclear war, schisms in the Western alliance were viewed as particularly dangerous. A major war was averted because of firm and consistent pressure by Eisenhower against his Western allies.

Eisenhower was in the domain of gains at the time, possessing overwhelming political popularity domestically and leading the predominant economic and military power in the world. He made a cautious decision in supporting Nasser against Eisenhower's old and trusted allies in Europe. Eisenhower believed his choice to be the best legal, military, and ethical one he could make.

Prospect theory would predict that Eisenhower would be inclined to be risk avoidant during so many challenging international situations precisely because he was so firmly entrenched in the domain of gains. The Suez crisis shows how essential it is to establish the domain of action, which determined what each actor saw and how he evaluated the environment he confronted. Operating in a domain of gains, Eisenhower made risk-averse decisions, as predicted by prospect theory; in this way, Eisenhower actively, though cautiously, "waged peace."

Prospect theory can also explain the rash actions taken by Eden and Mollet in the same international context as the more cautious action taken by Eisenhower. The British and French were in the domain of loss; they took serious risks and lost. Eisenhower was in a domain of gains, and behaved more cautiously. Prospect theory explains the actions of all three Western leaders.

CHAPTER 7

Conclusions

Everyone confronts many risks, in various forms, every day. In many instances, risks go unrecognized or are underestimated. For instance, it is notoriously difficult to get people to change their eating, exercise, and smoking patterns in order to lower their risk of stroke or heart attack in the future. In other instances, objectively trivial risks are blown out of proportion. Even disasters that are large in terms of financial impact, such as the 1989 and 1993 California earthquakes, can result in a comparatively small loss of life, relative to, say, the number of motor vehicle deaths in the same state during those years. Finally, in some cases, people do not have enough experience with particular risks to know whether or not they are acceptable.

This section relates some of the findings in the case studies to larger issues of risk assessment in the political world. It also strives to integrate some seemingly peripheral concerns, such as emotion, into the analysis of risk propensity. Discussion begins with a contrast between experts' notions of appropriate risk assessment and laypersons' characterizations of acceptable risk. The role of emotion in decision making is addressed next. Evaluations of the relative merits and limitations of the application of prospect theory to international relations are offered last.

Risk Assessment versus Risk Perception

What distinguishes risks people fear and act upon from those they ignore? Why do the experts' judgments differ in their assessments of risk from the concerned layperson's perception of what constitutes an acceptable level of risk? The source of much of the discrepancy in risk analysis between experts and laypersons involves this very difference between risk assessment and risk perception.[1] Most experts, in assessing risk, use rational models to define "acceptable risk." In practical terms, invoking this procedure means that risk is typically analyzed in terms of the number of impairments or deaths caused per year in a certain geographical area, like the United States, or within a specific population group, like women, for a given product or event. As with most rational models, more advanced models adjust for assessments that involve the probability and severity of the risk. In some circumstances, assessments can include estimates of damage to future generations, such as when radiation exposure is assumed to increase the incidence of birth defects in subsequent generations. However, in many cases, probability and severity are unknown in advance. Even with sincere effort and adequate planning, it is often impossible to determine what measures need to be taken to reduce the death rate from various natural hazards and man-made disasters.

So how do laypersons understand risk?[2] Risk assessment offers a rational basis upon which a decision maker can evaluate options; risk perception provides an identical service from a differing, more nonrational, perspective. Most people think about risk in ways that are much more in line with risk perception than with formal risk assessment models.

In their seminal work on risk perception, Paul Slovic and his colleagues take issue with the rational models of risk perception advocated by analysts such as Chauncey Starr.[3] Starr uses a model quite similar to the decision analyst's notion of "revealed preferences" that often argues that what actually comes into being represents an acceptable level risk almost by virtue of its very existence. In other words, Starr and, later, his followers contend that society has reached an "essentially optimum" balance between risks and benefits. Slovic and his colleagues have demonstrated, through a psychometric approach that they label "expressed preferences," that Starr's characterization is misguided.[4]

Slovic and his colleagues argue that the public's perception of risk is both predictable and quantifiable, however drastically it may depart from rational "expert" assessments.[5] Two aspects of their argument are crucial here. First, there are some risks that people systematically overestimate and others that people systematically underestimate.[6] The curve for these values is similar to the decision weight curve (fig. 2) found in prospect theory.

Second, researchers have found that risk perception can be thought of as involving a two-factor space (see fig. 3).[7] Slovic has come to call these factors the "unknown" factor and the "dread" factor.[8] In essence, the unknown factor means that people tend to be more affected by, and thus overestimate, risks that are seen to be unobservable and novel, and whose effects are relatively unknown to the victim or to science. An example of this kind of threat might be exposure to invisible chemicals in drinking water.

The second factor, dread, refers to perceived lack of control, potential for catastrophic consequences, certainty of fatal effects, and inequitable distribution of risks and benefits. In more concrete terms, people are more willing to accept risks that they see as voluntary, controllable, and natural.

For example, risks associated with sporting injuries are rarely viewed as ominous. On the other hand, risks that are man-made or result from novel technologies are often greatly feared. In this category, biological and chemical weapons are considered highly unacceptable, even though the people who have *died* as a result of their use in the last several decades appear to be mostly restricted to Kurdish settlers in Iraq.[9]

The dread factor appears to be more important in people's assessment of risk than the unknown factor. Slovic posits that one of the reasons for this is that many of these kinds of threats are seen to possess "signal value."[10] In other words, accidents such as Three Mile Island and Chernobyl, the explosion at the chemical plant in Bhopal, India, and the toxic contamination at Love Canal serve as indicators to people of how much worse a particular hazard might become if it is not controlled immediately. In other words, some crises are somehow recognized as harbingers of worse consequences to follow.[11] Such beacon events are acknowledged to presciently indicate the catastrophic nature of particular risks and to disclose new information about the risks inherent in a particular event or technology. Other crises, particularly those resulting from familiar sources, are seen to represent nothing more than themselves. So, for example, a car accident tells others nothing new about the nature of automobile technology and is not assumed to increase the likelihood of other accidents occurring.[12] However, an accident involving genetic mutation could easily be interpreted as a dangerous warning of the potential for this technology to precipitate even more disastrous accidents in the future. Because genetic engineering is not well understood and its consequences not well calibrated, any information about its harmful consequences appears to portend poorly for the ability of scientists to monitor safety concerns adequately in the future.

But what do risk assessment and perception of technological and environmental hazards have to do with political realities? Aside from the obvious response that many political decisions involve these very issues, the more important point is that concern about the "unknown" or "dread" aspects of any risk are not irrelevant to a decision maker, even if they are considered nonrational to a decision analyst. Risks that involve unknown outcomes present a challenge to values, and it is often the case that values are not limited to the number of lives lost per year. Even more significantly to politicians, such values can also help to win or lose an election. Other values, which include fear of the unknown and dread catastrophes, can play important and salient roles in political decisions. These factors are neither irrelevant nor irrational to consider in approaching the value trade-offs inherent in most political decision-making processes.

In some sense, the understanding of risk in terms of dread and

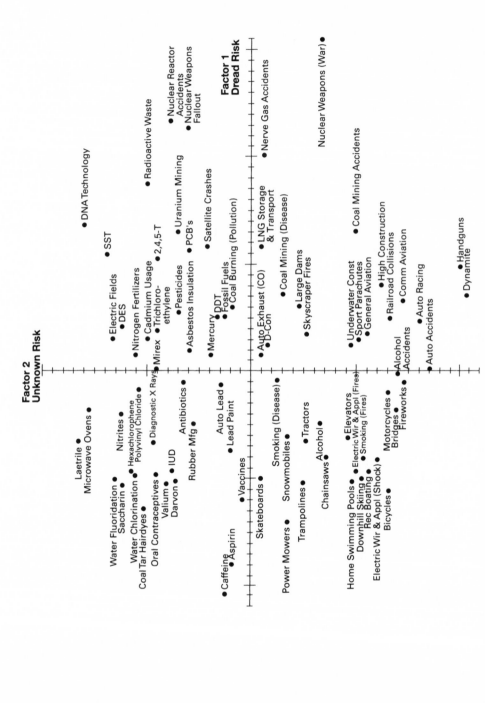

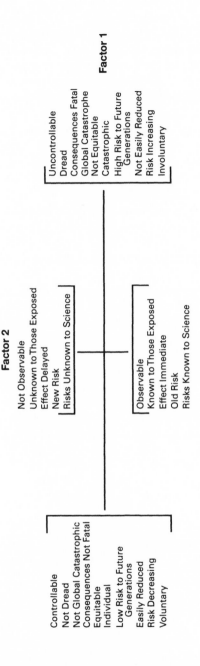

Fig. 3. Risk perception. (Reprinted with permission from Paul Slovic, "*Perception of Risk,*" *Science* 236 (1987): 282. Copyright 1987 American Association for the Advancement of Science.)

unknown factors can be seen as kinds of heuristic biases, ways people automatically come to think about and evaluate the risks they encounter. As with the tendencies demonstrated in prospect theory, policymakers are not immune to these heuristic tendencies by virtue of their role. Indeed, decision makers are more likely to approach risk problems like laypersons than like decision analysts. And it is not clear that embodying this more psychologically holistic approach is inappropriate; many of the empirically important factors, which decision analysts regard as irrational to consider, have important political consequences. It is not clear, after all, that scientists and formal models have a monopoly on determining the appropriate hierarchy of societal values.[13] In fact, decision makers are not irrational to consider factors that are considered irrelevant in risk assessment by classical modelers; such dread or unknown factors can make or break political careers.

This model of expressed preferences in risk perception provides additional empirical grounding for the descriptive accuracy of prospect theory. It is yet another example of how the situation, the very nature and character of the risk itself, is more definitive in the perception of risk than the perceiver's "personality." Scholars and decision makers alike often argue that risk-taking is most closely correlated with the personality of the individual leader. While it may be easy to fall prey to the fundamental attribution error in analyzing risk propensity, prospect theory cautions against such a tendency. Prospect theory demonstrates that the situation is more important to understanding the psychological mechanisms behind risk-taking than the personality of a particular individual. In the language of prospect theory, the situation is characterized as domain and categorized in terms of gains and losses. Dread and unknown factors related to the nature of the risk itself exacerbate these situational forces. In the end, these situational forces are neither "irrational" nor "irrelevant"; they are merely empirical realities that run counter to the normative models.

The Role of Affect

Another influence on judgment and decision making that often runs contrary to normative modeling is emotion.[14] Prospect theory stresses the central role of cognitive effects on judgment and decision making. As a result, the role of emotion or motivation has received relatively less attention in the treatment of risk propensity here. The unfortunate result of this emphasis is that people can emerge sounding rather like machines; the image conjured up is one of a rather flawed computer circumnavigating decisional pitfalls on two legs. Obviously, that is an inaccurate portrayal of the complexity of human consciousness.

From a psychological perspective, cognitive strategies have evolved and are maintained because they are, by and large, very useful and efficient processes for understanding, interpreting, and integrating the vast amount of information people encounter every day.[15] Heuristic cognitive strategies are largely effective in helping individuals to assimilate information quickly, make accurate judgments easily, and generally allow people to make effective sense of the world. Problems arise because these strategies encourage systematic perceptual biases, under certain circumstances, such as when uncertainty or risk are centrally involved in decision making.

In spite of this disclaimer, some people may feel that the processes that have been described in this book do not adequately reflect their subjective experience of decision making. Individuals may agree that situational factors affect the sort of options considered, and that thinking about things plays an important role in decision making, but many people still believe that a lot of important decisions in their lives are greatly affected by how they *feel* about particular things. Few Americans in the twentieth century will admit that they chose their mate, for example, on the basis of ostensibly superficial considerations such as wealth, physical attractiveness, or status, although these forces may have a larger impact than most people would be willing to acknowledge openly. Rather, people prefer to believe that they married because of "love" or they chose their career path because of "interest." These emotive notions invoke a more psychodynamic kind of psychology that focuses, if not primarily on sex and aggression, at least on "hot" motivations like greed, anger, fear, shame, guilt, or lust, rather than on "cold" cognition like probability assessments, utility calculations, attributional biases, and risk propensity.

Indeed, it is as misleading to assume that emotion has no role in cognition as it is to assume that cognition has no role in emotion. Although early motivational theorists were eclipsed in their influence by the rise of social cognition research,[16] the lay understanding of psychology still places greater emphasis on feelings than on thoughts. Recently, a more interactionist approach has begun to hold sway, and researchers are willing to acknowledge the mutual impact of affect and cognition on human behavior.[17] Nonetheless, most lay people still do not respond to the cognitive perspective as enthusiastically as researchers might advocate; Freud's perspective still holds the most sway on the Oprah Winfrey show.

As a result, the role of affect in judgment and decision making does deserve some further direct discussion. People often believe that they are greatly affected by their emotional states and can readily give many examples of being influenced by something as seemingly trivial as a passing mood. Others are willing to validate the definitive impact of affective disturbances. For example, people who are less efficient following the death of a family member are usually given leeway by others who understand the effect of emotions on performance. On the other hand, many people believe that they should not be affected by their emotional state and try to be as "rational" as possible in their approach to decision making. When someone takes this approach, problems arise when part of the outcome should involve a consideration of how a person might *feel* about something. For example, when a person makes a job choice based solely on the characteristics of the job itself, he may be very unhappy when he takes a job in a place where he hates living; in this case, the person's failure to take feelings into account can produce a much worse outcome than if he took his emotions seriously in reaching his decision. In this way, lack of consideration for emotion in decision making typically fails for cognitive as well as emotional reasons.

Moreover, as prospect theory indicated, loss aversion may lead people to evaluate improperly the risks they confront because they do not want to pay the price of loss from an emotional standpoint. For example, a politician does not want to be publicly humiliated or chastised or to lose the next election for personal as well as professional political reasons. Such a politician may thus be motivated to believe that the risks he takes to recoup losses are not as severe as the political consequences of appearing to passively accept the loss. In this situation, such a leader may not realize that if the risk fails, he will be worse off than if he had quietly absorbed the loss from the beginning because he wants to believe that the gamble will succeed. In this way, such a leader may create a self-fulfilling prophecy and bring about the reality he fears the most: public humiliation, chastisement, and defeat.

Throughout this process, unmotivated and motivated biases can *combine* with political forces to make it easier for leaders to perceive inaccurately the magnitude or scope of the risks they confront, or undertake, in an attempt to save political face. Motivated biases involve responses that are based on strong emotions, such as fear, greed, anger, hate, or revenge. Unmotivated biases include the situational effects that have been delineated throughout this study. More specifically, high risks may not be fully appreciated not only because of the cognitive properties of loss aversion, but because of motivated biases, such as revenge, as well.

Political pressures can engender motivated biases on the part of decision makers just as easily as cognitive factors can reinforce political predispositions. It is easy to imagine a leader becoming so angry at a particular enemy for getting the better of him in some public way that subsequent risks will be taken to "win" out of sheer desire for revenge. In this way, influence becomes overdetermined as political, cognitive, and motivational factors each reinforce one other. Political exigencies can raise emotional issues that work to strengthen the direction and impact of underlying cognitive tendencies. People are often impassioned about politics and become committed to the process, seduced by the power, and frightened of the fall. Forceful emotional elements, including greed, hatred, and revenge, combine to produce deep loyalties and even deeper antagonisms that only serve to fuel the flame of political ambition in the direction of greatest self-promotion.

This motivational phenomenon is particularly important in political situations that involve heated debates about emotional issues, abortion providing a paradigmatic domestic example. Politicians need to be responsive to their constituencies in order to stay in office, and yet they are also affected by their own attitudes and feelings on the particular issue. In addition, politicians are often constrained by the thoughts and feelings of colleagues whose support they need on other issues that they may feel strongly about. Indeed, in highly polarized issues, it may be impossible to please everyone by seeking the middle ground, because certain issues are inevitably categorized in zero-sum terms.[18] In these situations, framing can become nine-tenths of the battle—as the linguistic distinction between "anti-abortion" and "pro-life" nicely demonstrates.

Moreover, evidence strongly suggests that people are often unaware of what really influences their behavior.[19] In this regard, the cognitive arguments presented here are particularly important for two reasons. First, it can be shown experimentally that people are affected by various factors that they are not even aware exist. Just because people are not conscious of the operation of these cognitive processes does not mean that such biases do not have an enormous impact on their behavior. The psychophysical analogy is instructive in this regard. People are not aware of the perceptual processes that translate various stimuli into sight and sound, and yet there is irrefutable evidence for the systematic operation of these mechanisms. No one questions the reality or value of what they see or hear on the basis of their failure to understand the nature of the neuropsychophysiological processes involved in translating various stimuli into sight and sound. Yet people remain prone to question the psychological reality of unconscious processes that might affect conscious thought for these very reasons.

The importance of bringing these psychological effects to the fore in decision making is analogous to recognizing the fundamental attribution error. Prospect theory attempts to rectify the underestimation of situational variables in risk propensity. By calling explicit attention to these cognitive biases in judgment and decision making, it becomes possible to understand the way certain forces can affect behavior, even when people remain unaware of the systematic operation of both cognitive and affective biases. And, as with substance abuse, awareness of the process constitutes the first step toward intervention.

Second, these findings are important because they run contrary to normative admonitions. When informed, most people agree that trivial forces, such as framing effects, should not have an impact on the substance of their decisions, or at least not as big an impact as they can be demonstrated to possess. Many people will be prompted to reevaluate their judgments and decisions once they have been made aware of the ways in which their behavior violates normative axioms. Nonetheless, most people will not spontaneously seek out the potential sources of perceptual error prior to decision making unless it is explicitly brought to their attention. Perhaps even more significantly, if people are not continually reminded, they tend to relapse into their natural, powerful, biased cognitive tendencies in judgment and decision making.

Cognitive biases are not the only influences that matter. But people are more likely to be aware of emotional factors than cognitive processing ones. Cognitive biases are not stressed because they matter *more* than emotional ones; they are emphasized because people do not pay them the attention they merit. People often overestimate the role of affect while underestimating the role of these more cognitive and situational factors in their attributions concerning their own judgments and decisions. In many cases, people are not accurate in their intuitions about the overriding importance of affect; as with probability, sometimes the importance of emotion is overstated, and at other times its significance is underestimated.[20] While affect is certainly more than a cognitive illusion, emotions do not always function the way people *feel* like they do.

Affect is *not* irrelevant in judgment or decision making, although it is often the case that people think emotion is not a good *enough* reason on which to base serious decisions. Yet affect matters in two major ways. First, people act solely on the basis of their emotions, however irrationally based, in many instances. Such emotion-based action is the basis for much self-destructive behavior; smoking and drinking, which might feel good but are not good for you, are classic examples. Second, affect becomes important when people *believe* that it makes a difference in their behavior. These beliefs can then have an impact on choice; the person may act *as though* affect makes a difference, and so affect ends up making a difference. However, from a social cognition position, affect is greatly overestimated in explaining and justifying judgment and decision making, if not in other areas of life, just as cognitive processes tend to be greatly underestimated.

Affect clearly plays *some* role in judgment and decision making. Tversky and Johnson, for example, found to their surprise that inducing negative affect increased subject's estimates of the frequency of other undesirable events. This was true regardless of the similarity of the estimated events to the target event.[21] This finding is consistent with work on mood and memory that has demonstrated that mood-congruent memories are more accessible than mood-incongruent ones.[22]

Mood can influence the cognitive estimates that subsequently effect judgment and the choices upon which they are based. Even in the areas where people realize that their emotions affect them, they are not quite aware of the precise way in which their mood actually does influence their judgments and choices. Memory processes may provide the key to understanding the overlap between affect and cognition in judgment and decision making.

Evaluation of Prospect Theory[23]

From the perspective of prospect theory, human decision-making processes are best conceptualized in terms of reason-based choice, as opposed to norm-based choice, which rational theories of decision making advocate.[24] In reason-based choice, there need not be any numerical value associated with a particular choice decision, but there are often qualitative reasons that are invoked both to construct and to justify a choice or resolution. Indeed, these reason-based choices may be more appropriate for examination of uncontrollable events, such as those that take place in the real world, outside of the confines of a controlled laboratory experiment. While reason-based analyses may lack the parsimony of more formal modeling, they have many redeeming qualities. First, reason-based choice is closer to the way people think about their own decision-making processes than are the normative mathematical models advocated by rational choice theorists. Second, reason-based choice permits a full examination of framing effects in the context of each choice set. This is worthwhile because analysis of framing effects allows for the nature of conflict and value trade-offs to be made explicit in the decision-making process. Finally, reason-based choice allows for a consideration of nonnormative factors, such as affect, which can be quite powerful but are often ignored or purposely excluded from more norm-based analyses.

Relative Strengths

The relative strengths of a prospect theory approach can be summarized in four basic categories. These include the dynamic nature of the theory; its empirical basis and descriptive accuracy; its situationalist emphasis; and its explanatory power.

Dynamic Nature

One of the most useful aspects of prospect theory is the dynamic nature of its predictions. Many theories of international relations, including classic realist and neorealist approaches, are static in nature. Prospect theory provides explanations and predictions that allow for change over time in response to changes in the external environment.

In prospect theory, the independent variable has to do with the context in which a decision maker is acting, usually constructed in terms of relative gains or losses. Prospect theory predicts that when a decision maker is choosing in the context of gains, she is most likely to be cautious in her choices; on the other hand, if she is acting in the face of recent losses, she is likely to be more risk seeking in her decisions. Thus, prospect theory provides a ready framework on which to examine substantive changes in decision making that take place over time. Many policy gambles in the political arena, especially in the area of bargaining and negotiation, take place over time. During this evolution, many forces in the environment may precipitate changes in a decision maker's risk propensity. Prospect theory offers one interpretation as to why such changes take place.

Additionally, prospect theory offers provocative insights into phenomena that are dynamic processes by their very nature. For instance, escalation of commitment in the face of sunk costs is not consistent or explicable from a standard normative perspective. Nonetheless, the reality of the incorporation of sunk costs into future decisions holds up robustly to the mirror of introspection. Prospect theory demonstrates that people who are averse to losses, particularly if they feel responsible for having made the decisions that led to them, are more likely to attempt to recoup sunk costs through further escalation than those who are not confronted with a similar previous loss.[25]

Moreover, prospect theory illuminates other aspects of time perspective in decision making as well. It helps explain why particular decisions might be spaced the way they are, or announced in a certain order, in order to buffer bad news with more positive information to soften the blow. Couching negative information in a positive context is a particularly salient consideration in reporting emotionally negative information. Certainly intuition supports that body counts are much more tolerable in the context of a victory celebration than a military rout.

Empirical Support

Most rational theories of decision making start with a set of assumptions that remain essentially unchallenged. These assumptions are necessary in order to derive the normative predications and prescriptions that these rational theories offer. However, when these assumptions are called into question, the descriptive accuracy of the relevant theory is fundamentally challenged.

Prospect theory represents exactly that kind of fundamental challenge to normative theories of decision making. Because prospect theory is based on empirical studies, it does not require these kinds of implicit and unexamined assumptions in order to support its predictions. Empirical and descriptive support for prospect theory has been extensive, robust, and consistent. Prospect theory makes no normative claims. Unlike rational choice theories, it does not claim that people *should* behave according to the tenets of the theory, merely that they *do* behave that way. This is in contrast to rational theories that argue that people *should* behave in line with their prescriptions, but that have been unable to marshall any systematically clear evidence that people actually *do* act in such ways.

In the descriptive realm, prospect theory is fundamentally incompatible with normative theories that conflate descriptive and normative aspects. Yet standard theories of rational choice have been remarkably slow to respond to the challenges inherent in prospect theory concerning descriptive accuracy and empirical support. The strongest responses argue that if the predictions of rational models are accurate, it does not matter whether the assumptions are true. While that may be an adequate response if an analyst's interest is limited to prediction, it is woefully inadequate if the quest is for an understanding or explanation of the process of decision making itself.

As Tversky argues:

> The rational theory of choice seems to provide a better account of people's normative intuition than of their actual behavior . . . the descriptive analysis of choice is concerned with principles that govern actual decisions; the normative analysis of choice is concerned with human intuitions about what constitutes rational behavior.[26]

It is not possible to argue that normative approaches to decision making are descriptively accurate. Normative theories, while often elegant in form and rigorous in prediction, are not able to accurately capture the process of decision making itself with any reliability or richness.

Situationalism

The fundamental attribution error argues that people tend to have a basic bias in their attributional style and inferences concerning the assessment of causality in the world around them.[27] This bias suggests that people tend to overestimate the impact of personality while simultaneously underestimating the impact of the situation upon behavior, including choice.

Most theories of international relations avoid this bias by excluding people from the analysis, as for example Waltz does when he argues that the distribution of power in the international environment determines outcome regardless of the leaders involved.[28] However, literature that has focused on the decision-making level of analysis has not been so fortunate in escaping the pervasive nature of this bias in its analysis. A great deal of political psychology literature has suffered from the tendency to overestimate the impact of a given leader on a particular outcome while simultaneously underattributing cause to situational factors. Many psychohistories, as exemplified by Nathan Leites's infamous work on the Bolsheviks, are rife with explanations for decisions based on the personality or psychopathology of a particular person or culture that is assumed to have a pervasive impact on all members of a particular group.[29] There is, of course, great difficulty in pursuing this line of research well because of the exhaustive amount of information about the personality of a leader and the information available to him at the time of a particular decision that is required in order to conduct an accurate analysis. This problem is often compounded by the pervasive influence of retrospective bias in memoirs and oral histories as well.

Prospect theory avoids this bias not by eliminating the leader from consideration but by reintroducing the impact of the situation, in the form of domain, on the decision maker's choices. An analyst need not know so much about the idiosyncrasies of a particular leader in order to be able to predict and explain behavior on the basis of the situation confronting that leader. But an analyst need not eliminate the leader either, since a decision maker's framing of options, especially when evoking powerfully vivid, salient, concrete historical analogies, can be critical if the analyst is interested in examining framing for explanatory purposes. In this way, the power and impact of the situation is reintroduced into political psychology without losing the individual altogether or falling prey to an overestimation of the effect of his "personality" on outcome.

Explanation versus Prediction

Prospect theory by its nature as a psychological theory of decision making is necessarily approximate and incomplete at times. However, prospect theory's virtue lies in its superior explanatory power. This can be useful in two specific instances.

First, prospect theory may be able to address issues and problems that standard theories of rational choice cannot explain adequately. For example, the following situations are often difficult to explain, much less justify, from a normative perspective: when sunk costs are overweighted in evaluating escalation decisions; when the same alternatives produce different choices when framed in different ways; when choice depends on the other options available. Rational choice theories cannot explain such behavior because they argue that such behavior can not be justified in decision-making contexts. Normative theories rely on implicit assumptions in order to derive their predictions, and yet outcomes are often notoriously inconsistent with the premises upon which rational theories rest. Prospect theory offers a useful tool for analysis and explanation of behavior that can neither be predicted nor explained adequately from a more rational perspective.

Second, it may well be that prospect theory is better suited for certain types of questions and problems while rational choice models provide a better fit for different kinds of issues and concerns. For example, studies that use a large number of cases in order to make quantitative arguments about the probability of certain outcomes may indeed be best suited for an analysis conducted according to formal quantitative models. However, if an analyst wants to trace the process of a particular decision, or is interested in investigating a particular case in depth, prospect theory offers richer and more flexible tools to proceed with such analysis. Some problems are not addressed by classical rational models because they do not easily "fit" into large number studies; these kinds of investigations may be precisely the cases that are particularly amenable to examination through the lens of prospect theory, but remain particularly inexplicable from a more normative perspective. And these difficult or anomalous cases may, in fact, be among those that are most interesting and significant in furthering understanding of a particularly important or uncommon phenomenon such as escalation in the face of sunk costs or launching preemptive war.

Relative Weaknesses

Obviously prospect theory has its disadvantages in application to cases in international relations. Several of these obstacles are particularly troublesome in attempting to examine political phenomena from a psychological perspective in general and through the lens of prospect theory in particular. Only some of these limitations will be addressed here, but these include the difficulty of operationalizing the variables; the fact that political and psychological imperatives often converge in determining causation; the relative lack of parsimony; and the difficulty of undertaking a contextual application of psychological findings to political phenomena.

Operationalization

Operationalization is a particularly difficult aspect of applying prospect theory to cases in international relations. The challenges take place in the construction of both independent and dependent variables; operationalization of domain and risk propensity present unique methodological quandaries.

Even a relatively simple assessment of domain as gains or losses can be more complex than it appears at first pass. Gains or losses may be straightforward but can be substantively altered by the placement of the reference point. Usually the reference point is theoretically placed at the status quo, but it can be theoretically justified at the level of a decision maker's aspirations or expectations about a particular outcome as readily as it can be based on the losses that most recently occurred and have yet to be assimilated. There are indications that individuals adjust, accommodate and renormalize to gains faster than to losses.[30]

Nonetheless, it is possible to make a fairly good argument based on relatively straightforward indicators, especially if the situation is extreme. Documents that can be particularly helpful in this regard include public opinion polls, general economic indicators such as GNP, inflation and unemployment figures, as well as political indicators such the number of congressional overrides. Regardless, this can be a difficult variable to solidify. The evidence will likely be different from case to case, and the choice of indicators must in any event be justified theoretically.

Second, the operationalization of risk propensity is even more taxing to consolidate. Risk propensity, whether acceptant or averse, can be assessed in a number of ways. An analyst can make such a judgment of propensity relative to the other options available at the time of the choice, but these comparisons are notably affected by framing issues that are notoriously difficult to predict in advance, much less control for in retrospect.[31] An analyst may decide to make an assessment of risk based on more economic models. In this way, for example, one might assess the risk propensity of various options based on each one's variance around a particular mean outcome, as was done in this study. In this view, choices that offer wider variances are considered to be more risky. It is critical that these variables do not become tautological in their operationalization or definition. However, it may still be very difficult to analyze domain and risk propensity even once an analyst does decide which methods to employ in measuring them.

The problem of accurate measurement is further compounded by the fact that most leaders do not talk about their decisions in terms of the probabilities and utilities of various outcomes; outcomes may be too uncertain for such terminology to be helpful to a political leader trying to make a decision or justify a policy choice. Indeed, one of the reasons normative models are so psychologically unappealing is because they do not accurately reflect the intuitions that most people have about how they go about making decisions and which factors they take into account in reaching a decision. Thus, in a real-world context, where explanations and justifications and options can not be fully controlled, much less accurately manipulated as in a laboratory setting, it is not at all surprising that leaders do not offer their assessments of domain and risk propensity in quantitative forms.

Overdetermination

As Jervis has pointed out, it is often the case the political and psychological realities can converge to favor the same decision.[32] In such cases, it may be superfluous to consider the impact of psychological factors on political outcomes.

In real-world politics, unlike the laboratory, decisions have real consequences, some negative and others positive. These consequences may be all that is needed to justify or explain a particular action or decision; psychological factors may be simply redundant. If political and psychological factors reinforce each other, one need not resort to psychological factors in order to explain the reasons for political decision making. For example, if a leader knows that a loss in a war is likely to be punished at election time, he may be particularly averse to allowing the possibility of that outcome, either by avoiding war from the outset or by pursuing victory at all costs if it occurs. In such a case, it is not irrational for a leader to demonstrate reluctance to incur political loss through mechanisms that might be methodologically indiscriminate from loss aversion. An analyst need only invoke political realities in order to explain behavior that, while not necessarily rational from a cost–benefit standpoint, is nonetheless totally rational from the perspective of personal political survival.

Thus the cases that will be most helpful in determining the accuracy and viability of using prospect theory over and above reasonable political imperatives are those where political behavior deviates from what would be expected solely from the standpoint of political expediency or rational calculation. Cases where the political and psychological predictions converge are less likely to support the utility of prospect theory for analyzing political decision making independent of political motives. In such cases, it may be sufficient to attribute the outcome of the decision process to political motives and constraints, and an analyst need not invoke prospect theory, seeing it as superfluous explanation.

Lack of Parsimony

Prospect theory, as a psychological theory, is inherently prone to approximate and incomplete predictions. The only honest way to respond to this criticism is to admit it. However, this does not makes prospect theory irrelevant. Prospect theory can be used to explain cases where outcomes diverge from what would be expected from a rational choice perspective. Prospect theory can also be used to illuminate process variables in depth, as well as questions and problems that are more concerned with explanation than prediction. As previously noted, prospect theory may be better suited for case studies in this respect, while formal rational models may be more useful for large number quantitative studies of probabilistic variables and outcomes.

Difficulty of Contextual Application

There is no question that the most difficult problem with any application of psychological theory to political phenomena is the question of translation from the laboratory to the real world. The challenges of contextual application are myriad. And here the reference is *not* to the fact that the original experimental studies were paper and pencil tests conducted on college sophomores. Paper and pencil is not an inaccurate model for how many people go about making decisions. And college sophomores are no less intelligent or educated, on average, than the majority of the population. However, extrapolating a phenomenon from a controlled environment with carefully designed and manipulated variables to a real-world event or decision with infinite complexities and uncontrollable factors can appear a seemingly insurmountable task at times.

The central question is whether an analyst can apply any kind of psychological theory to a complex environment where significant variables cannot be carefully controlled or measured as they would be in a laboratory setting. In the context of international relations, the answer at first pass must be no. The environment is too complex, the variance too uncontrolled, and too many alternative hypotheses must be manipulated as possible explanations before an analyst can assume that her theories account for even a part of the variance observed. However, generalization of laboratory phenomena to the real world is not the entire basis upon which to evaluate the utility and viability of a psychological theory to an analysis of political decision-making processes.

Leaders are people. That implies that they share the basic structure of human cognitive functioning, including the biases delineated earlier in terms of judgmental heuristics and prospect theory. With regard to international relations, then, the central question concerning utility must be whether *any* of the components of the theory or its implications are helpful in shedding light on the phenomena of decision making in general or on risk propensity in particular. This is especially important if the theory can do so in areas where other theories have proved fruitless in their explanatory or predictive attempts. Here the answer is not nearly so clear-cut or discouraging. In fact, studies like this are designed precisely to test the extent to which prospect theory *can* shed light on complicated phenomena in the real world.

The true contribution of psychological theories, such as prospect theory, to international relations is that they offer new explanatory concepts and theoretical tools that can be enormously useful in thinking through existing political phenomena in a novel, creative, or insightful way. Once this perspective on judging viability is offered as one way to appropriately evaluate the worth of prospect theory for an understanding of international relations, the theoretical picture becomes much brighter.

What are the elements of psychological theory in general and prospect theory in particular that help generate more intelligent discussion of the relevant phenomena? There are several that emerge as the most promising candidates. First, framing effects of all sorts appear to be a key consideration in both the manipulation and explanation of certain seemingly nonnormative or suboptimal choices. Second, loss aversion appears to be a hugely robust and widely generalizable phenomenon in a variety of areas, of which politics is only one. And finally, in cases where the data neither fit nor refute any particularly theoretical perspective from the standpoint of prediction, psychological variables may offer key insights into a richer explanation of how such outcomes came to occur.

Conclusion

Psychological theories do not exist for the sake of political analysis alone any more than economic ones do. Yet both economic and psychological theories can be put to good use in political analysis when they offer unique perspectives and insights that are not available from existing viewpoints.

In many ways, prospect theory does not so much simplify political analysis as complicate it. The theory raises a broad array of psychological considerations that may be particularly relevant to certain kinds of analysis or explanations of the political decision-making process.

The relative advantages of introducing these factors into an analysis of political decision-making processes are several. Prospect theory offers a dynamic, empirically sound, situationalist explanation for decision making under conditions of risk. It offers insights into important phenomena, such as framing effects and loss aversion, which would not be obviously approachable from the standpoint of rational choice or other theories of decision making. Moreover, these insights appear to account for many of the very phenomena that remain inexplicable from other theoretical perspectives.

The relative disadvantages of prospect theory are notable, however. It is a difficult theory to operationalize in historical and political context. It often offers predictions that are superfluous to more elegant or parsimonious rational or political imperatives. And the contextual application of laboratory findings is challenging at best.

However, there are two important concerns that are brought to light by this examination of the relative strengths and weaknesses of applying prospect theory to international relations. One is the importance of reasons in decision making, as opposed to the imperatives offered by normative considerations. The second is the contextual importance of decision making that emphasizes that people are not necessarily value maximizers with preexisting preferences, but rather problem solvers whose preferences are constructed as part of creative solutions to the challenges and problems that individuals face.

When most normal people think about how they make important decisions, they often invoke a variant on Benjamin Franklin's suggestion of writing down a list of pros and cons, weighing each consideration by its importance, and choosing the side with the greater total.[33] While formal models may mimic that procedure in design, they certainly do not resemble it in process. Reasons matter to people; when individuals make decisions, they want to have a sense that they know why they make a particular choice and often need to feel justified in their choices, especially if they think they will have to explain it to others in the future, as politicians often must. Rational models of choice do not offer such succor to decision makers; instead, formal models offer utilities and values and calculations that only vaguely resemble the subjective sense of decision making that the individual feels like he confronts. In this regard, reason-based choice offers a superior model for analyzing decisions in context, taking full account of the various historical and political forces that tend to offer reasons and justifications for decisions, not merely calculations and predictions. Formal models may be more appropriate for economic and even experimental psychological analyses, but they are probably poorly suited for nonexperimental data such as that which most commonly occurs in real-world political contexts.

Second, hard decisions are hard precisely because they involve some element of conflict over goals, values, and options. Easy decisions do not force such challenges. But hard decisions require careful consideration precisely because of the trade-offs involved in giving up some of one thing in order to have more of another or some similar dynamic. If preferences and values are constructed more than elicited, as strongly indicated by the empirical evidence, then people make choices in the relative absence of clear preexisting preferences, values, or goals. In such a context, where perhaps many decisions involving trade-offs must be made simultaneously, it is inevitable that decision making becomes quite complex and confusing very quickly. Under such conditions, Krantz may be correct when he argues that:

> the normative assumption that individuals *should* maximize *some* quantity may be wrong. Perhaps . . . there exists nothing to be maximized . . . [B]ecause the calculations are impossible in principle: People do and should act as *problem solvers, not maximizers,* because they have many different and incommensurable . . . goals to achieve.[34]

As problem solvers, and not value maximizers, individuals can claim more freedom to be as complex and unpredictable in theory as they unquestionably are in reality. And if theory seeks to understand and explain human behavior as opposed to simply predicting it, in political decision making or elsewhere, then psychological considerations are as intricate a part of that phenomenon as anything can be.

In the end, it is not even clear that people normatively *should* make decisions on the basis of rationality. As with risk assessment and perception, where societal values encourage appropriate appreciation of dread and unknown factors in a way admonished by rational calculations, rationality itself may not provide the most valuable measure of optimal choice behavior; after all, deifying rationality as the criterion upon which to evaluate the utility of behavior represents nothing more than a choice among values. In some alternative universe, it is possible to imagine that the place now held by rationality might easily be replaced by "emotional-ity," for example. However "irrational," the cognitive strategies that have evolved over time have done so for a reason; namely, they are largely effective and efficient strategies for understanding and responding to the world. It is decidedly unclear whether, normatively, anyone would be bet-ter off if capable of surrendering these strategies in service of achieving more "rationality."

Notes

Chapter 1

1. This distillation is based on reviews in A. Pollatsek and Amos Tversky, "A Theory of Risk," *Journal of Mathematical Psychology* 7 (1970): 541; and Jon Elster, *Rational Choice* (New York: New York University Press, 1986).

2. For an example of this kind of argument applied to Soviet foreign policy, see Jan Triska and David Finley, *Soviet Foreign Policy* (New York: Macmillan, 1968). For a similar argument about risk propensity as a "national" attribute, also applied to the Soviet case, see Hannes Adomeit, *Soviet Risk-Taking and Crisis Behavior* (London: George, Allen and Unwin, 1982).

3. The literature on these topics offers an array too vast to begin to list in any comprehensive fashion. For representative examples on: why nations go to war, see Bruce Bueno de Mesquita, *War and Reason* (New Haven, CT: Yale University Press, 1992); on arms control and weapons procurement, see Coit D. Blacker and Gloria Duffy, *International Arms Control: Issues and Agreements* (Stanford, CA: Stanford University Press, 1984); and on crisis management, see Sean Lynn-Jones, Steven Miller, and Stephen Van Evera, eds., *Nuclear Diplomacy and Crisis Management* (Cambridge: MIT Press, 1990).

4. Two of the most prolific and insightful writers in this areas are Herbert Simon and James March. Representative examples of their work include: Herbert Simon, "Information Processing Theory of Human Problem Solving," in W. K. Estes, ed., *Handbook of Learning and Cognitive Processes*, vol. 5 (Hillsdale, NJ: Erlbaum, 1978); and Herbert Simon and James March, "Bounded Rationality, Ambiguity, and the Engineering of Choice," *The Bell Journal of Economics* 9 (1978): 587–608. For an application of some of these principles to presidential decision making, see Alexander George, *Presidential Decisionmaking in Foreign Policy: The Effective Use of Information and Advice* (Boulder, CO: Westview Press, 1980).

5. This study concentrates on a unitary actor embodied by the president. Significant advisors are analyzed from this perspective as well. Prospect theory is less easily applied to the dynamics of *group* decision making, except to the extent that all members are assumed to share similar biases in risk propensity, although each may possess a different understanding of such crucial features as appropriate frame for discussion, applicable reference point, domain of action, and so on. For discussion of prospect theory applied to group decision making, see Tatsuya Kameda and James Davis, "The Function of the Reference Point in Individual and Group Risk Decision Making," *Organizational Behavior and Human Decision*

Processes 46 (1990): 55–76; and T. Kiesler, S. Kiesler, and J. Siegel, "Group and Computer-Mediated Discussion Effects in Risk Decision Making," *Journal of Personality and Social Psychology* 52 (1987): 917–30. For an excellent analysis of the dynamic of group decision making from a non–prospect theory perspective, see Irving Janis, *Groupthink: Psychological Studies of Policy Decisions and Fiascoes,* 2d ed. (Boston: Houghton-Mifflin, 1982). An analyst could investigate Janis's cases from a prospect theory perspective but such an analysis would tend to place more emphasis on the individual leader's risk propensity and less on the dynamics of group process.

6. Lee Ross, "The Intuitive Psychologist and His Shortcomings: Distortions in the Attribution Process," in *Advances in Experimental Social Psychology,* vol. 10, ed. Leonard Berkowitz (New York: Academic Press, 1977), 174–77.

7. Daniel Kahneman and Amos Tversky, "Prospect Theory: An Analysis of Decision Under Risk," *Econometrica* 47 (1979): 263–91.

8. Daniel Kahneman, Paul Slovic, and Amos Tversky, *Judgment Under Uncertainty: Heuristics and Biases* (New York: Cambridge University Press, 1982).

9. This is not to say these assessments are useless or insignificant. Probability assessments are particularly crucial in the area of epidemiological research and treatment planning. Even with sophisticated modeling techniques, predictions can be woefully misguided. Remember that CDC officials feared that the Ebola Fever epidemic of 1977 might kill thousands, but only 153 died in Zaire before the disease disappeared in that round. Meanwhile, in the early years of the AIDS epidemic, it was not judged to pose a widespread problem, but it has claimed hundreds of thousands of lives. For more on how these early judgments of probability affected health policy in a way that failed to foster greater preventive efforts, see Randy Shilts, *And the Band Played On* (New York: Penguin Books, 1988).

10. The following discussion is distilled from Kahneman, Slovic, and Tversky, *Judgment Under Uncertainty.*

11. Sarah Litchenstein, Paul Slovic, and Baruch Fischhoff, "Judged Frequency of Lethal Events," *Journal of Experimental Social Psychology* 13 (1977).

12. I am grateful to Lee Ross for this example, which I first saw dramatically demonstrated in his social psychology class.

13. Some of the ways this manipulation might be done include adding and deleting options that are more or less similar or dissimilar to the preferred options. See Amos Tversky, "Elimination by Aspects," *Psychological Review* 79 (1972): 294–96.

14. For the most concise description of the original experiments on which prospect theory is based, see Daniel Kahneman and Amos Tversky, "Choices, Values, and Frames," *American Psychologist* 39 (April 1984): 341–50. For criticisms concerning the external validity of classroom experiments, see Ebbe Ebbeson and Vladimir Konecni, "On the External Validity of Decision-Making Research: What Do We Know About Decisions in the Real World," in *Cognitive Processes in Choice and Decision Behavior,* ed. T. Wallsten (Hillsdale, NJ: Erlbaum, 1980), 21–45.

15. The following discussion derives from Kahneman and Tversky, "Choices, Values, and Frames," 341.

16. Theda Skocpol and Margaret Somers, "The Use of Comparative History in Macro-Social Inquiry," *Comparative Studies in Society and History* 22 (April 1980): 174–97. For one of the best demonstrations of this method in comparative politics, see Jeffrey M. Paige, *Agrarian Revolution: Social Movements and Export Agriculture in the Underdeveloped World* (New York: Free Press, 1975).

17. I am grateful to Paul Fischbeck for this useful analogy.

18. The distinction between decision values and experience values is discussed at greater length in Kahneman and Tversky, "Choices, Values and Frames."

19. Amos Tversky and Daniel Kahneman, "Rational Choice and the Framing of Decisions," *Journal of Business* 59 (1986): S252.

Chapter 2

1. The following discussion derives from a compilation of Daniel Bernoulli, "Exposition of a New Theory on the Measurement of Risk," *Econometrica* 22 (1954): 23–36 (original work published 1738); Kahneman and Tversky, "Choices, Values, and Frames"; and notes from a class on judgment and decision making given by Amos Tversky in the fall of 1987 at Stanford University.

2. Psychophysics has had a long and important tradition in the history of psychology. First comprehensively explicated in print by Gustav Fechner in his 1860 publication *Elements of Psychophysics,* the study of psychophysics originally sought to systematically, and mathematically, explore the relationship between the physical and psychological worlds. Fechner's experiments, which drew on earlier work by Ernst Weber, investigated the relationship between stimulus and sensation, following the observation that the two phenomena did not increase in direct proportion to one another. He demonstrated that the relationship between the intensity of physical stimulus and sensate perception was a concave function. This is significant, given Bernoulli's similar finding in his application of this approach to money and probability. Ironically, Fechner's contribution to psychophysics was more seminal to the birth of the experimental method in psychology than to later explanations of the nature of sensation and perception.

3. The following discussion derives from a combination of J. von Neumann and O. Morgenstern, *Theory of Games and Economic Behavior,* 2d ed. (Princeton: Princeton University Press, 1947); and notes from Amos Tversky's fall 1987 class on decision making at Stanford University.

4. This shift also allowed the analysis to be applied to the single play of a game. In earlier models, the analyst was restricted to a calculation that required multiple plays of a game, like the throwing of a die, in order to determine preferences.

5. Definitions for transitivity, dominance, and invariance come from Kahneman and Tversky, "Choices, Values and Frames."

6. For succinct summaries of this extensive body of work, see Kahneman and Tversky, "Choices, Values, and Frames," and Amos Tversky and Daniel Kahneman, "The Framing of Decisions and the Psychology of Choice," *Science* 211 (1981): 453–58.

7. Daniel Kahneman and Amos Tversky, "The Psychology of Preferences," *Scientific American* 248 (1982): 160–72. Also ibid.

8. The following discussion of prospect theory draws most heavily on Kahneman and Tversky, "Prospect Theory: An Analysis of Decision Under Risk," and Kahneman and Tversky, "Choices, Values and Frames," as well as extensive personal communication and class discussion on prospect theory with Amos Tversky.

9. For a more extensive discussion of the history of psychophysics in psychology, a good succinct account can be found in E. Heidbreder, *Seven Psychologies* (New York: Century Co., 1933).

10. Tversky and Kahneman, "Rational Choice and the Framing of Decisions."

11. I am grateful to an anonymous reviewer for helpful comments concerning utility and prospect theory.

12. Tversky and Kahneman, "The Framing of Decisions and the Psychology of Choice."

13. B. McNeil, S. Parker, H. Sox Jr., and A. Tversky, "On the Elicitation of Preferences for Alternative Therapies," *New England Journal of Medicine* 306 (1982): 1259–62.

14. Tversky and Kahneman, "Rational Choice and the Framing of Decisions."

15. The following discussion essentially paraphrases the discussion in Kahneman and Tversky, "Prospect Theory: An Analysis of Decision Under Risk."

16. Amos Tversky and Daniel Kahneman, "Advances in Prospect Theory: Cumulative Representation of Uncertainty," *Journal of Risk and Uncertainty* 5 (1992): 297–323.

17. This is true unless you believe that all value is not in whether you win or lose, but how the game is played. If this is true, your preferences require a different utility function than that of those betting money on the outcome of the game.

18. Kahneman and Tversky, "Choices, Values and Frames," 346.

19. George Quattrone and Amos Tversky, "Contrasting Rational and Psychological Analyses of Political Choice," *American Political Science Review* 82 (September 1988): 729–30.

20. Tversky, "Elimination by Aspects: A Theory of Choice."

21. Kahneman and Tversky, "The Psychology of Preferences," 166–68.

22. Tversky and Kahneman, "The Framing of Decisions and the Psychology of Choice," 457–58.

23. As Kahneman and Tversky mention in this quote, shifting the frame of a problem can also change the very experience of its outcomes. This is what Tversky and Kahneman refer to in their discussion of the use of framing as a potential mechanism of self-control: is drinking, eating, or smoking considered a "treat" for a job well done, or an "unwarranted indulgence," demonstrating a lack of willpower? Clearly, a treat is enjoyed in a different way than an indulgence that produces shame, guilt, and regret. This framing phenomenon is well captured by the old adage of seeing a glass as half empty or as half full. Cognitive therapy for depression, for example, is fundamentally based on mentally reframing experience in a more positive light. For more on this approach, see Aaron Beck, A. John Rush, Brian F. Shaw, and Gary Emery, *Cognitive Therapy of Depression* (New York: Guilford Press, 1979).

24. This is not to discount the possibility that framing can be used in a motivated way, in order to structure and influence the choice of others. However, it need not be invoked in a motivated fashion in order to produce systematic and nonnormative results. I am grateful to Jon Mercer for helpful comments on the motivated possibilities for framing effects.

25. Paul Slovic, Baruch Fischhoff, and Sarah Litchenstein, "Facts vs. Fears: Understanding Perceived Risk," in *Societal Risk Management: How Safe Is Safe Enough?*, eds. R. Schwing and W. A. Albers Jr. (New York: Plenum, 1980).

26. McNeil, Parker, Sox Jr., and Tversky, "On the Elicitation of Preferences for Alternative Therapies."

27. Baruch Fischhoff, "Predicting Frames," *Journal of Experimental Psychology: Learning, Memory, and Cognition* 9 (1983): 104.

28. The seminal demonstration of this effect can be found in R. E. Nisbett and T. W. Wilson, "Telling More than We Can Know: Verbal Reports on Mental Process," *Psychological Review* 84 (1977): 231–59.

29. For more on how behavior itself (giving an explanation) can help to create a change in attitude ("I wrote it, therefore I must believe it to be true"), see Daryl Bem, "Self Perception Theory," in *Advances in Experimental Social Psychology,* vol. 6, ed. Leonard Berkowitz (New York: Academic Press, 1972), 1–62.

30. I am grateful to Robert Jervis for this insight.

31. This explanation derives from Kahneman and Tversky, "Prospect Theory," 277.

32. Tversky and Kahneman, "The Framing of Decision and the Psychology of Choice," 456.

33. M. Argyle and J. Crossland, "The Dimensions of Positive Emotions," *British Journal of Social Psychology* 26 (1987): 127–87.

34. For more on the endowment effect and its implications for willingness to trade, see Daniel Kahneman, Jack Knetsch, and Richard Thaler, "Experimental Tests of the Endowment Effect and the Coase Theorem," *Journal of Political Economy* 98 (1990): 1325–48.

35. The previous discussion is drawn from Kahneman and Tversky, "Prospect Theory," 280.

36. Study by Richard Zeckhauser, as cited by Scott Plous, *The Psychology of Judgment and Decisionmaking* (New York: McGraw-Hill, 1993), 99.

37. Kahneman and Tversky, "Prospect Theory," 282–83.

38. For a theoretical analysis of why this occurs, see Amos Tversky and Daniel Kahneman, "Extensional versus Intuitive Reasoning: The Conjunction Fallacy in Probability Judgment," *Psychological Review* 90 (October 1983): 293–315.

39. Slovic, Fischhoff, and Litchenstein, "Facts vs. Fears: Understanding Perceived Risk." While the rates of homicide have clearly risen in the last decade, so have the rates of suicide. Thus, even if the specific numbers in this article are a bit dated, the underlying principle remains accurate.

40. Kahneman and Tversky, "Choices, Values and Frames," 345.

41. Ibid., 345.

42. This discussion is distilled from Kahneman and Tversky, "Prospect Theory," 288–89.

43. J. J. Christensen-Szalanski, D. Beck, C. M. Christensen-Szalanski, and T. Koepsell, "Effects of Expertise and Experience on Risk Judgments," *Journal of Applied Psychology* 68 (1983): 278–84.

44. W. H. Loke and K. F. Tan, "Effects of Framing and Missing Information in Expert and Novice Judgment," *Bulletin of the Psychonomic Society* 30 (1992): 187–90.

45. L. Dube-Rioux and J. Russo, "An Availability Bias in Professional Judgment," *Journal of Behavioral Decision Making* 1 (1988): 223–37.

46. S. Fiske, D. Kinder, and W. M. Larter, "The Novice and the Expert: Knowledge-Based Strategies in Political Cognition," *Journal of Experimental Social Psychology* 19 (1983): 381–400.

47. C. Koopman, J. Snyder, and R. Jervis, "Theory Driven versus Data Driven Assessment in Crisis: A Survey of *International Security* Readers," *Journal of Conflict Resolution* 34 (1990): 694–722; C. Koopman, R. McDermott, R. Jervis, J. Snyder, and J. Dioso, "Stability and Change in American Elite Beliefs about International Relations," *Peace and Conflict: Journal of Peace Psychology* 1 (1995): 365–82. These findings are readily explicable within the well-established finding of belief perseverance; see C. Lord, L. Ross, and M. Lepper, "Biased Assimilation and Attitude Polarization: The Effects of Prior Theories on Subsequently Considered Evidence," *Journal of Personality and Social Psychology* 37 (1979): 2098–2109.

48. I am grateful to an anonymous reviewer for helpful comments on individual differences.

49. For more on how other kinds of argument and evidence cannot definitely establish *causal* determinism and often fall prey to various forms of counterfactual bias, please see Philip Tetlock and Aaron Belkin, *Counterfactual Thought Experiments in World Politics: Logical, Methodological, and Psychological Perspectives* (Princeton, NJ: Princeton University Press, 1996).

50. I am grateful to Paul Fischbeck for explanation and clarification of the issues involved in the operationalization of the risk variable.

51. Tversky and Kahneman, "The Framing of Decisions and the Psychology of Choice," 456.

52. Kahneman and Tversky, "Prospect Theory," 286–87.

53. I am grateful to Amos Tversky for clarification of this point.

54. Daniel Kahneman, Jack Knetsch, and Richard Thaler, "Experimental Tests of the Endowment Effect and the Coase Theorem."

55. These ideas derive from Amos Tversky and Dale Griffin, "Endowment and Contrast in Judgments of Well-Being," in *Strategy and Choice,* ed. Richard Zeckhauser (Cambridge: MIT Press, 1991).

56. It should be noted, however, that the theory argues that reverse behavior is possible, indeed expected, when the probabilities are extreme (either certain or impossible). It can be very difficult, however, to get an accurate assessment of relative probabilities at this fine a level from available information. Moreover, taken to an extreme, this caveat can render the entire theory as unfalsifiable as global systems such as psychoanalysis or Catholicism. If a case fails in its prediction, one need only argue that it is because the probabilities were extreme. Although this

may really be the cause in certain instances, it is important to guard against this danger of unfalsifiable theory. Therefore, the mitigating circumstances offered by extreme probabilities must be treated carefully in any application of prospect theory to international relations.

Chapter 3

1. Selected Hearings, President to Congress, "Hostages in Iran, Selected Congress, 11/79 [CF, O/A 749] [2]," Box 61, WHCF, Jimmy Carter Library.

2. This quote, as well as the information on the earlier seizure, from Memo, Gary Sick to Jerry Schecter, "American Hostage in Iran, 11/7/79–11/30/79" Box 75, WHCF, Jimmy Carter Library.

3. Memo, David Aaron to Carter, October 31, 1979, "Staff Office," Box 154, WHCF, Jimmy Carter Library.

4. A good account of the entire Iranian hostage crisis can be found in Gary Sick, *All Fall Down* (New York: Penguin Books, 1986). Specific references to the seizure of the hostages by the students are made in chapter 10, especially on page 230.

5. Thirteen of the hostages, all either black or female, were subsequently released on November 18 and 19. One additional hostage, Richard Queen, was released on July 11, 1980, for medical reasons that were later diagnosed as multiple sclerosis. AP Chronology, "American Hostages in Iran-Chron (Partial)," Box 75, WHCF, Jimmy Carter Library.

6. A complicated legal document, mediated by the Algerians to bring about the release of the hostages in exchange for the unfreezing of Iranian assets in United States banks, was called the Declaration of Algiers. This statement was released by White House Press Secretary Jody Powell on January 21, 1981, after three weeks of intensive negotiations that required Secretary of State Warren Christopher to fly to Algiers. Declaration of Algiers, 1/21/81, "CO-71, 4/26/80–1/20/81," Box CO-32, WHCF, Jimmy Carter Library. Gary Sick has since claimed that the Reagan campaign was independently negotiating with the Iranian Revolutionary Council over the timing of the hostages' release in order to negatively affect Carter's bid for reelection. He argued that the Carter administration was unaware of these illicit negotiations involving the exchange of hostages for arms through Israeli intermediaries. See Gary Sick, "The Election Story of the Decade," *New York Times,* April 15, 1991. ABC News *Nightline,* in collaboration with the *Financial Times* of London, has conducted a series of investigations into these allegations. Much of the evidence offered in support of Sick's arguments is circumstantial and thus the accuracy of his claims remains inconclusive.

7. Executive Summary, Special Operations Review Group to Joint Chiefs of Staff, "Iran Rescue Mission, 4–8/80," Box 92, Counsel, Jimmy Carter Library.

8. *New York Times,* June 25, 1979, 1.

9. All statistics above from record, "American Hostages in Iran, 11/7/79–11/30/70," Box 75, WHCF, Jimmy Carter Library.

10. Memo, Bob Beckel to Hamilton Jordan, November 8, 1979, "11/8/79 [1]," Box 155, WHCF, Jimmy Carter Library.

11. Foreign Policy Issues, 12/3/79, Box 157, WHCF, Jimmy Carter Library.

12. Roper Reports, December 1, 1979, "Iran 11/79," Box 34, WHCF, Jimmy Carter Library.

13. ABC News-Harris Survey, filed January 31, 1980, "Hostages in US Embassy in Iran, 1979–80," Box 63, WHCF, Jimmy Carter Library.

14. "And Reagan Catches Carter," *Time,* April 14, 1980, 28.

15. In the president's defense, Carter's statement of progress on hostage negotiations made on April 1 had been prompted by what was viewed at the time as a genuine breakthrough by the administration and was not simply designed to manipulate the outcome of the primaries in Wisconsin and Kansas that day. Hamilton Jordan, *Crisis* (New York: Putnum, 1982); Jody Powell, *The Other Side of the Story* (New York: William Morrow and Company, Inc., 1984). This contention is also supported by a wide variety of archival evidence on the Iranian hostage situation in the Jimmy Carter Library.

16. All statistics in this paragraph are from *Time,* April 14, 1980, 28.

17. Norman Ornstein et al., *Vital Statistics on Congress, 1984–5* (Washington, American Enterprise Institute for Public Policy Research 84): 178, 181.

18. Pierre Salinger, *American Held Hostage* (Garden City, NY: Doubleday and Company, 1981): 235.

19. Sick, *All Fall Down,* 347.

20. Cyrus Vance, *Hard Choices* (New York: Simon and Schuster, 1983): 381–408.

21. State Department Telegram, "Vance to Amembassy Rome/Ottawa, March 26, 1980, Iran 4/80," Box 35, WHCF, Jimmy Carter Library.

22. AP week-by-week Chronology, August 24, 1980, "American Hostages in Iran-Chron (Partial)," Box 75, WHCF, Jimmy Carter Library.

23. According to the AP statement, "Ten of 15 Security Council members vote in favor of economic sanctions against Iran but the Soviet Union, as a permanent member, vetoes the resolution" AP week-by-week Chronology, "American Hostages in Iran-Chron (Partial)," Box 75, WHCF, Jimmy Carter Library. For a succinct discussion of United Nations involvement in the crisis, see Vance, *Hard Choices,* 400–406.

24. For judgment of the International Court of Justice and official U.S. response, see Background memo, United States State Department, "Iran-ICJ, 2/79–3/80," Box 88, Counsel Files, Jimmy Carer Library and Draft Statement, "Iran-ICJ, 5/80," Box 89, Counsel Files, Jimmy Carter Library.

25. Zbigniew Brzezinski, *Power and Principle* (New York: Farrar, Straus, and Giroux, 1985): 493.

26. It will be remembered from the discussion in the theory chapter that frames are difficult to predict, as well as complex to explain. See Fischhoff, "Predicting Frames."

27. Vance, *Hard Choices,* 408–9.

28. Brzezinski, *Power and Principle,* 495. The fact of the matter is that rescue raids have a high historical failure rate; the Iran rescue mission may offer an almost classic example of the availability heuristic in foreign policy, where base rates were underestimated in light of a salient successful case. In this instance that notable

case was Entebbe, a rescue raid that was successful, although it took place in quite different terrain.

In the case of American rescue attempts, the historical track record is dismal at best. The Son Tay raid on a Vietnamese war camp, which included soldiers who later participated in the Iran mission, failed because the prisoners had been moved to another location prior to the arrival of the rescue team. The raid on the Palestinians who took nine Israeli athletes hostages during the 1972 Munich Olympics resulted in the death of all the hostages and five of the right-wing terrorists. The 39 hostages in the Mayaguez incident were indeed freed, but it appears that their release was under way *prior* to the rescue mission itself. Even so, that mission cost the lives of 41 American soldiers, and another 50 were wounded. Another relatively similar case, that of the Hammelburg raid to release prisoners of war in Germany during World War II, was only partly successful as well, because fighting with German forces subsequent to the raid was heavy.

In fact, Entebbe and Mogadishu stand as relative anomalies in the history of these kinds of missions both for their success and their lack of casualties: three hostages and one Israeli officer were killed at Entebbe; and three terrorists were killed by the West Germans in Somalia. The key to both these successful raids was total surprise combined with a relatively isolated area of attack. In spite of the critical geographical differences, Entebbe was the operative analogy for most of the principals involved in the Iranian rescue mission. For a quick rundown of these other cases, see Warren Christopher et al., *American Hostages in Iran* (New Haven: Yale University Press, 1986), 386. *Time* magazine also offers a brief description of some of these cases in the May 5, 1980, issue, 19, 25. For a more extensive analysis of the Mayaguez incident, see Paul Ryan, *Iranian Rescue Mission* (Annapolis, MD: Naval Institute Press, 1985), 142–44.

29. For Carter's shared view, see Gary Sick, "Military Options and Constraint," in *American Hostages in Iran,* 161. For Carter's speech request, see Jordan, *Crisis,* 252.

30. This information and the following analysis of the understood hierarchy of risks derives extensively from a telephone interview by the author with Gary Sick in July 1990 in New York City.

31. As National Security Advisor Zbigniew Brzezinski comments, it is crucial to keep in mind the distinction between military and political risks throughout this analysis (interview by author with Zbigniew Brzezinski, July 1990, in Washington, DC). In this case in particular, these political and military risks increased and decreased inversely. Moreover, it was clear that there was a trade-off between domestic and international imperatives as well; while the allies were cautious, the American public was impatient.

32. Sick's arguments are also supported by author interview with Harold Saunders in Washington, DC, in July 1990.

33. At this point, I want to reiterate that the following characterization of the five options that were considered, and who supported which position and why, derives from a telephone interview conducted by the author with Gary Sick in New York City in July 1990. The following discussion draws heavily upon that conversation. It must be noted, however, that there is no information in any of the printed

or archival material, or any of the other interviews I conducted, that contradicted Sick's analysis in any way. Thus, in the following discussion of the options that were considered, interested readers are directed to the relevant memoirs, noted elsewhere, in order to either confirm or expand upon specific analysis presented here.

34. Interview by author with Harold Saunders in Washington, DC, in July 1990.

35. Prospect theory does not directly discuss the role of emotion in decision making. Nonetheless, it is an important topic. For more on the role of affect in decision making, see that section in the concluding chapter. For a work that discusses those issues in greater depth, see Irving Janis and Leon Mann, *Decision Making* (New York: Free Press, 1977).

36. For some of these actions, see Statement by the President, April 7, 1980, "Iran-Leg 4/1–16/80," Box 89, Counsel Files, Jimmy Carter Library; Press Conference No. 56 by the President of the United States, April 17, 1980, "Press 4–11/80," Box 92, Counsel Files, Jimmy Carter Library; Memos, "Isolation Package" and "Non-Military Options," "Hostages in U.S. Embassy in Iran, 1980 No. 1 [CFR, O/A 749] [1]," Box 62, WHCF, Jimmy Carter Library. Also Memo, "Additional Options for Economic Measures against Government of Iran," "Iran-Freeze 10–12/79," Box 87, Counsel Files, Jimmy Carter Library. For a comprehensive narrative of these actions, also see Sick, *All Fall Down,* especially 339.

37. Proclamation, November 12, 1979, "CO-71, 7/1/79–11/30/79," Box Co-31, WHCF, Jimmy Carter Library. Amount of oil from Talking Points, "Iran-Freeze 10–12/79," Box 87, Counsel Files, Jimmy Carter Library.

38. Declaration, Jimmy Carter to Congress, November 14, 1979, "CO-71, 7/1/79–11/30/79," Box CO-31, WHCF, Jimmy Carter Library.

39. Noted in Declaration, Jimmy Carter to Congress, December 4, 1980, "Co-71, 4/26/80–1/20/81," Box CO-31, WHCF, Jimmy Carter Library.

40. Statement by the President, April 7, 1980, "Iran-Leg 4/1–16/80," Box 89, Counsel Files, Jimmy Carter Library.

41. Press Conference No. 56 by the President of the United States, April 17, 1980, "Press 4–11/80," Box 92, Counsel Files, Jimmy Carter Library.

42. Memos, "Isolation Package" and "Non-Military Options," "Hostages in U.S. Embassy in Iran, 1980 No. 1 [CFR, O/A 749] [1]," Box 62, WHCF, Jimmy Carter Library. Also Memo, "Additional Options for Economic Measures against Government of Iran," "Iran-Freeze 10–12/79," Box 87, Counsel Files, Jimmy Carter Library. See also Statement by the President, April 7, 1980, "Iran-Leg 4/1–16/80," Box 89, Counsel Files, Jimmy Carter Library. Press Conference No. 56 by the President of the United States, April 17, 1980, "Press 4–11/80," Box 92, Counsel Files, Jimmy Carter Library. Memos, "Isolation Package" and "Non-Military Options," "Hostages in U.S. Embassy in Iran, 1980 No. 1 [CFR, O/A 749] [1]," Box 62, WHCF, Jimmy Carter Library. Also Memo, "Additional Options for Economic Measures against Government of Iran," "Iran-Freeze 10–12/79," Box 87, Counsel Files, Jimmy Carter Library. For a comprehensive narrative of these actions, also see Sick, *All Fall Down,* especially 339.

43. This is noted above in the State Department telegram to Rome/Ottawa.

Allied response was also noted above in the joint action that placed May 17 as the deadline for the release of the hostages. See note 24.

44. Letter, Honecker to Carter, December 31, 1979, "CO-71 1/1/80–4/25/80," Box CO-32, WHCF, Jimmy Carter Library.

45. Both argue this in their respective books: Sick, *All Fall Down;* Brzezinski, *Power and Principle*. Both spontaneously emphasized this point to the author during interviews as well.

46. This reasoning is reminiscent of Jervis's arguments concerning irrational consistency in service of the avoidance of value trade-offs in decision making. See Robert Jervis, *Perception and Misperception in International Politics* (Princeton, NJ: Princeton University Press, 1976). Also note that it may be easier to calculate the risks associated with military action than with political failure. This bias may predispose decision makers to take advantage of concrete options that offer an estimable chance over options that present inestimable probabilities of unknown outcomes.

47. This is consistent with the human rights campaign, which directed Carter's foreign policy emphasis throughout his administration.

48. The rescuers did not have the information about the location of the hostages within the rather large compound until less than twenty-four hours before the mission. Even then the information was obtained by accident. The Iranian students had released a Pakistani cook from the compound who happened to sit next to a covert CIA operative on a flight out of Tehran; on the long journey, the cook unintentionally provided the crucial location information to the operative. (So much for the optimal nature of rational planning; this was pure chaos theory in action.) For the dramatic story, see Zvi Lanir, Baruch Fischhoff, and Stephen Johnson, "Military Risk-Taking: C3I and the Cognitive Functions of Boldness in War," *Journal of Strategic Studies* 11 (1988): 96–114.

49. It is interesting to note that insurance companies considered the risk of American military action in the region to be so serious that rates for maritime shipping were increased enormously and rapidly. Lloyd's of London, for example, declared the Arabian Sea to be a War Zone and increased rates for ships going into the area by 400 percent. Needless to say, this action had the premeditated effect of reducing trade to the region. See Selected Hearing, Carter before Congress, "Hostages in US Embassy in Iran Selected Congress [CF, O/A 749] [2]," Box 61, WHCF, Jimmy Carter Library.

50. I remind the reader that the majority of the seemingly unsubstantiated assertions throughout this section of the chapter derive from the author's interview with Gary Sick, National Security Staff member for Iran.

51. Recall that the rescue mission was the only option that offered the possibility of directly bringing about the release of the hostages. If successful, the administration need not worry about antagonizing the captors because the Iranians would no longer have control over the hostages.

52. Note that for the predictions of prospect theory to hold true, the option chosen need not be the riskiest one available. The theory is one of tendency. Therefore, if the chosen option is relatively risky, that is, if the actual choice decision is riskier than many alternatives of equal or greater expected value, the predictions of

the theory are borne out. To reiterate, if the choice made is risky *relative* to the other options that are available, or if a sure thing is taken over a gamble that presents equal or greater expected value, the predictions of prospect theory are supported.

53. Testimony, Carter to Congress, 12/5/79, "Hostages in US Embassy in Iran 11/79 Selected Congress [CF, O/A 749] [2], " Box 61, WHCF, Jimmy Carter Library.

54. Hamilton Jordan, *Crisis,* 248–49; and Jody Powell, *The Other Side of the Story,* 214–22.

55. The details of this exchange were recently released to the author under Freedom of Information Act requests. See drafts, "Possible Scenario," "Revised Scenario," "Final Scenario," and "Updated Scenarios"; and "[Iran], Scenario," Chief of Staff, Jordan, Jimmy Carter Library.

56. Executive Summary, Harold Brown/David Jones to Jody Powell, "Hostages in US Embassy in Iran 1980 No. 2 [CF O/A 749] [1]," Box 62, WHCF, Jimmy Carter Library.

57. The use of distinct historical analogies to inform arguments appeared to play an important role in this crisis. For more on the specifics of how these analogies informed predictions and biases in this case, see Rose McDermott, "Prospect Theory in International Relations: The Iranian Hostage Rescue Mission," *Political Psychology* 13 (1992): 237–63. For more general discussion concerning the use of analogies in decision-making processes, see Jervis, *Perception and Misperception in International Politics;* and Yuen Fung Khong, *Analogies at War* (Princeton, NJ: Princeton University Press, 1991). Jon Mercer has also pointed out to the author in personal communication that it seems likely that analogies are often chosen to fit the preferred decision, rather than the analogy driving the preference beforehand. To support this point, Mercer notes that hawks tend to pick hawkish analogies, just as doves prefer dovish ones. However, it is also possible that preferred analogies work through an availability heuristic for given decision makers and serve to bolster that person's predetermined beliefs. For more on belief perseverance, see Lord, Ross, and Lepper, "Biased Assimilation and Attitude Polarization: The Effects of Prior Theories on Subsequently Considered Evidence."

58. The previous account is found in both Brzezinski, *Power and Principle,* chapter 13; and Cyrus Vance, *Hard Choices,* chapter 19. A similar account is found in Jimmy Carter, *Keeping Faith* (New York: Bantam, 1982), chapter entitled "Almost Free."

59. Vance, *Hard Choices,* 410.

60. Letter, Vance to Carter, April 21, 1980, "Hostages in US Embassy in Iran, 1980 No. 2 [CF O/A 749] [3]," Box 62, WHCF, Jimmy Carter Library.

61. Author interviews with Sick and Saunders.

62. Author interviews with Sick and Saunders.

63. Vance, *Hard Choices,* 408–9.

64. Sick, *All Fall Down,* 341. Also Carter, *Keeping Faith,* 513.

65. Sick, *All Fall Down,* 358.

66. Sick notes this phenomenon in his book, *All Fall Down,* as well as in his interview with the author. Carter's descriptions of his perspectives in *Keeping Faith*

are consistent with this interpretation, although he doesn't make an explicit point of the power shift in the inner circle.

67. Sick, *All Fall Down,* 342–43.

68. Brzezinski, *Power and Principle,* 500.

69. Ibid., 484.

70. Harold Saunders, "Beginning of the End," in *American Hostages in Iran,* 282.

71. Zbigniew Brzezinski, "The Failed Rescue Mission," *New York Times Magazine,* April 18, 1982, 28.

72. Brzezinski, *Power and Principle,* 498.

73. Ibid., 499.

74. Ibid., 492.

75. Letter, John Kenneth Galbraith to Zbigniew Brzezinski, November 26, 1979, "CO-71 12/1/79–12/31/79," Box CO-33, WHCF, Jimmy Carter Library.

76. Brzezinski, *Power and Principle,* 493.

77. Zbigniew Brzezinski, "The Failed Mission," 29–30. Note the operation of the conjunction fallacy in this assessment. The conjunction fallacy demonstrates how events that require lots of sequences, each with a low probability of failure, will be judged to be more likely to succeed than is normatively warranted. This is because the probability of failure across many events of low probability is *higher* than the probability of failure of any one sequence in the event and people fail to take this factor into account in their judgments about the overall probability of success or failure. The classic example is the explosion of the space shuttle Challenger, where each component had a very low probability of failure. But, over time, the probability of failure rose sharply because of the combination of many components over many iterations. For more on the conjunction fallacy, see Tversky and Kahneman, "Extensional versus Intuitive Reasoning: The Conjunction Fallacy in Probability Judgment."

78. Jordan's memoirs are by far the most psychologically candid and sophisticated of the plethora of books written by Carter administration officials. In fact, Jordan is quite open about his anger at Vance for not believing early on in the likelihood of the rescue's success, and also for abandoning Carter in his time of greatest need after the mission failed. His book seems less affected by hindsight and impression management in this way than the others. See Jordan, *Crisis.*

79. Brzezinski, *Power and Principle,* 490.

80. Jordan, *Crisis.* For the best example of Carter's anger and frustration at the press about his decision to stay at the White House and not campaign across the country, see Press Conference No. 56 of the President of the United States, April 17, 1980, "Press 4–11/80," Box 92, Counsel, Jimmy Carter Library.

81. Jordan, *Crisis,* 229.

82. Note that this outcome assessment would have remained true even if the hostages had lost their lives.

83. Hearings, President to Congress, 12/5/79, "Hostages in US Embassy in Iran Selected Congress 11/79 [CF. O/A 749] [2]," Box 61, WHCF, Jimmy Carter Library. Again, for more on the role of affect in decision making, see that section in the concluding chapter.

84. For more on the groupthink effect, see Irving Janis, *Groupthink*. Janis describes the phenomenon of groupthink as a "quick and easy way to refer to a mode of thinking that people engage in when they are deeply involved in a cohesive ingroup, when the members' strivings for unanimity override their motivation to realistically appraise alternative courses of action" (9). This clearly *did not* happen in the Carter administration as evidenced by the drastic differences in opinions espoused by Vance and Brzezinski, among others. The reasons for this are no doubt many, but are certainly due in part to deeply held personal animosities between these participants, as well as the differing personal styles of some participants, such as Brzezinski, who did not shy away from confrontation.

85. Carter, *Keeping Faith*, 518.

86. It is interesting to note that the mission failed during the phase of the operation that was judged to be the most risky in advance. The planners were *most* confident of the phase of the plan that involved actually liberating the captives from the Embassy. See Briefing by Harold Brown, April 25, 1980, "Iran-Leg 4/24–30/80," Box 90, Counsel, Jimmy Carter Library.

87. U.S. Defense Department, "Rescue Mission Report," August 1980, typescript report, v.

88. Jordan, *Crisis*, 258.

89. Salinger, *America Held Hostage*, 237–38.

90. Powell, *The Other Side of the Story*, 256–57.

91. *Time*, May 12, 1980, 33.

92. As reported in Jordan, *Crisis*, 253–54.

93. Carter, *Keeping Faith*, 461.

94. The following account of the rescue mission is culled from a number of different sources. A good general source is Ryan, *The Iranian Rescue Mission*. The more detailed accounting is found in U.S. Defense Department, "Rescue Mission Report," August 1980 (typescript; this is the report issued under the direction of Admiral Holloway). Also see report, Special Operation Review Group to Joint Chiefs of Staff, "Iran-Rescue Mission 4–8/80," Box 92, Counsel, Jimmy Carter Library; and Report Harold Brown/David Jones to Jody Powell, "Hostages in US Embassy In Iran 1980 No. 2 [CF, O/A 749] [1]," Box 62, WHCF, Jimmy Carter Library.

95. Colonel Beckwith's assessment as noted in Jordan, *Crisis*, 260–61.

96. For a fascinating account of the technical reasons for the failure of the mission, see U.S. Defense Department, "Rescue Mission Report," August 1980 (typescript). Facts concerning the mission and its failure derive from this report and report, Special Operations Review Group to Joint Chiefs of Staff, "Iran-Rescue Mission 4–8/80," Box 92, Counsel, Jimmy Carter Library; and Report Harold Brown/David Jones to Jody Powell, "Hostages in US Embassy In Iran 1980 No. 2 [CF, O/A 749] [1]," Box 62, WHCF, Jimmy Carter Library.

97. It is easier to understand this incident if one imagines the scene at Desert One. It was pitch black, and there was total radio silence. Yet despite radio silence, there was tremendous noise coming from the engines of six helicopters and four C-130s (two others had already departed). This, combined with the sand kicked up from the engines, made visual and voice communication next to impossible. The

helicopter pilots were no doubt exhausted from flying for hours with heavy goggles, under difficult conditions and across unfamiliar terrain. Moreover, there was no central point of command, and no one really knew who was in charge of what, because there had never been a full dress rehearsal, and the obsession with secrecy had prevented many participants from meeting beforehand. Thus, the assumption that visual recognition was sufficient for command was incorrect. As a result, it was very difficult for anyone to know who to take orders from, where to get orders, or what exactly was going on. To make matters worse, central command, headed by General Vaught, head of the task force, was based in Qena, Egypt, and commands had to be made by satellite between Iran, Egypt, and Washington.

In addition, the mission location was near a traveled road, and Iranians who were passing through the desert during the mission were detained, providing a continual cause of concern for the leaders of the mission. Under these circumstances, it is easy to see why an accident of this nature might have taken place. Indeed, it is rather surprising that more casualties did not result. A couple of technical points help explain the outcome of the mission. First, helicopters are not designed to fly long missions under these conditions. All pilots were working off visual flight rules at low altitudes to avoid radar detection (scudrunning), using infrared night vision goggles to track terrain. Under this method of flight, navigation is often by dead reckoning, that is, the pilot uses heading, ground speed, adjustment for wind, and time to calculate where he is and where he is going. In the midst of dust clouds such as those encountered by the mission, it is virtually impossible for a pilot to see where he is going and to figure out how to get there. The helicopter crews did not have navigators and were not equipped with terrain following (TFR) or forward looking infrared (FLIR) navigation systems. Indeed, upon encountering the dust clouds, the pilots were forced to rely on passive navigational systems such as the PINS and OMEGA: the PINS is a self-contained inertial navigation system that provides up/down and right/left readings; the OMEGA is an automatic system that picks up readings from ten stations around the world and adjusts latitude and longitude, wind direction, and speed relative to these known posts. The pilots of the RH-53D helicopters had received little training in these systems and expressed low confidence in their ability to use them effectively.

Second, one of the difficulties with these helicopters is that once the engine is shut off, it is quite difficult to get it started again. More specifically, huge amounts of air must be sent into the turbines to get the blades started rotating, requiring the kind of jump start that a car gets by rolling it down a hill. In some recently made helicopters, auxiliary power units are used to provide this power. However, in most cases, lacking an external power source, cans of compressed air are used to start the engines. The problem is that these strategies don't always work. In the case of the Iranian rescue mission, the helicopters could only carry in something like two cans of compressed air per helicopter to restart the engines. As a result, it was necessary to have at least six operational helicopters at Desert One because the plan assumed that at least one of them would not start later in the mission due to this engine-starting problem.

While the proximal cause of the rescue mission failure was the inadequate number of helicopters, the more distal limitations imposed by such concerns as operational security were equally influential. For instance, the problem with dust clouds in the area was known to certain weather specialists but, because of the overriding security concerns, this information was not passed on to the actual pilots. In addition, the statistical information on failure rates of blade inspection method warning was known to those who serviced the craft, but again was not passed on in a usable fashion to those who flew the mission. Thus, when one of the warning lights went on in one helicopter, the pilot erroneously assumed it was accurate and turned back.

Indeed, part of the original difficulty with designing the mission had to do with finding the appropriate crews. The original squadron was a navy group tasked to minesweeping. These men were familiar with the plane, but not with the complex aspects of special operations missions. In fact, almost all the original pilots were replaced right before Christmas. Indeed, one of the JCS recommendations for future actions suggested the use of soldiers familiar with the mission who need only learn the relatively minor specifications of a new craft, rather than relying on those who knew the helicopter, but not the mission requirements. The JCS report mentioned experience gained in Project Jungle Jim (1961) that supported this contention. For more on this incident, see U.S. Defense Department, "Rescue Mission Report," August 1980 (typescript).

98. Transcript, "Issues and Answers," April 27, 1980, "American Hostages in Iran 4/27/80–10/22/80," Box 75, WHCF, Jimmy Carter Library.

99. Press Release, Carter, April 25, 1980, "Hostages in US Embassy In Iran, 1980 No. 2 [CF, O/A 749] [3]," Box 62, WHCF, Jimmy Carter Library.

100. Statement by the President, April 25, 1980, "Press 4–11/80," Box 92, Counsel, Jimmy Carter Library.

101. Letter, Jimmy Carter to Speaker of the U.S. House of Representatives and the President Pro Tempore of the Senate, April 27, 1980, "Iran 11/1/79–1/30/80," Box 13, Jimmy Carter Library.

102. Although the first telephone calls and telegrams ran about 80 percent positive and 15 percent negative on the rescue mission, within a matter of hours, support as directly expressed to the White House had dropped to about 60 percent positive. Report, Hugh Carter to Hamilton Jordan, April 25, 1980, 10:50 A.M., "Iran," Box 37, WHCF, Jimmy Carter Library. Also Reaction, April 25, 1980 7:40 P.M., "American Hostages in Iran 4/25/80," Box 75, WHCF, Jimmy Carter Library.

103. As mentioned previously, the explicit agreement exchanged the hostages for the unfreezing of Iranian assets and property that were being blocked by the United States. See Declaration of Algiers, 1/21/81, "CO 71 4/26/80–1/20/81," Box CO-32, WHCF, Jimmy Carter Library.

104. It is highly debatable whether *any* American action would have had a significant or determinate impact on Iranian policy. It is more likely that Iranian actions were dictated primarily by the *internal* political imperatives of Iran.

Chapter 4

1. Carter was aware that Americans in Iran were in danger and feared a replay of events that had taken place there the previous February 14. According to the

Congressional Research Service background document, the previous event unfolded as follows: "On February 14, 1979, an armed group of Iranian leftists attacked the U.S. embassy, which Ambassador Sullivan surrendered after some initial bloodshed. Some 70 Americans were taken captive, but were later released on orders from Khomeini's supporters. The decision to surrender the embassy was criticized in the U.S., although the positive intervention of pro-Khomeini groups might have been taken as a positive sign . . ." Issues definition, CRS-1, 2/20/80, "Iran-Regulations, Publications, 1–4/80, Box 79, Staff Office Files, Counsel's Office, Jimmy Carter Library.

2. The following general history is culled from a number of sources and draws heavily on archival material. Interested readers are directed to the following works: for the best general history of the Iranian hostage crisis, see Gary Sick, *All Fall Down.* The State Department's position is best represented by Cyrus Vance's *Hard Choices.* The National Security Advisor's position is characterized in Zbigniew Brzezinski's *Power and Principle.* Carter's reminiscences can be found in *Keeping Faith.* The most interesting and accurate retrospective can be found in Hamilton Jordan, *Crisis.* For something completely different, see the Shah's memoir, Mohammad Reza Pahlavi, *Answer to History* (New York: Stein and Day, 1980).

3. Issues Definition, Congressional Research Service, 2/20/80, "Iran-Regulations, Publications, 1–4/80," Counsel's Office, Jimmy Carter Library, 3–4.

4. It is interesting to note that this residence was not seen as acceptable by the Shah's ambassador to Washington, Ardeshir Zahedi, for security reasons, due to anti-Shah protests in California. Nelson Rockefeller's staff found an alternative site on the grounds of Callaway Gardens, a resort in Georgia. However, by that time, the administration had decided not to admit the Shah. Terence Smith, "Why Carter Admitted the Shah," *New York Times Magazine,* May 26, 1981.

5. There are several theories as to why the Shah chose not to come to America directly. The general consensus is that the Shah wanted to stay close to Iran in the event that the situation reversed itself, and the revolution was suppressed by the military or his other supporters. The Shah hoped to return to Iran in glory, much as he had in 1953, following a previous attempt on his crown by the nationalist then-premier, Mohammed Mossadegh (see Pahlavi, *Answer to History,* 13–14). At that time, with the help of the CIA and British intelligence, the Shah had returned to power relatively quickly and continued to rule for 26 more years (see Salinger, *America Held Hostage,* 20). During the interim period in 1953, the Shah had fled to Italy, and returned only after the coup had succeeded in restoring him to power (I am grateful to Robert Jervis for reminding me of the specifics of the Shah's flight in 1953). The experience in 1953 was no doubt a powerful anchor of experience for everyone involved, including the Iranian revolutionaries. This provides at least part of the explanation for why they were so insistent that the Shah be returned to stand trial once he had entered the United States. The Iranians believed that as long as the Shah remained alive and involved with U.S. leadership, the two forces might conspire together to engineer an overthrow of the new Iranian government and endanger the Islamic revolution, in much the same manner as the nationalists had been destroyed by these same powers in 1953.

The Shah, understanding these fears, no doubt wanted to be able to return to Iran from an Islamic country, rather than from the United States. This was especially true since the Shah had suffered much criticism for being a "puppet" of the American government in the months prior to his exile. The Shah provides the following explanation for why he did not go directly to the United States from Iran in his memoirs:

> I had intended to go to the United States soon after leaving Iran, but while in Morocco I began receiving strange and disturbing messages from friends in the U.S. who were in touch with the government and Carter administration. The messages although not unfriendly were very cautious: perhaps this is not a good time for you to come; perhaps you could come later; perhaps you should wait and see. About a month after my departure, the tone of the messages became warmer and they suggested that I could, of course, come to the United States if I were so inclined. But I was no longer so inclined. How could I go to a place that has undone me? (Pahlavi, *Answer to History*, 13–14).

Note that this comment does not explain why the Shah's initial move from Iran was to Egypt, not America.

6. Rockefeller and Kissinger had long-standing relationships with the Shah that dated back to at least 1951. Much of the Rockefeller fortune was from oil interests, and these interests helped exert pressure on the U.S. government in 1953 to help overthrow the coup attempt by National Premier Mossadegh, who had nationalized Iranian oil interests, among other things. After the Shah regained power in 1953, all of his business dealings went through Chase Manhattan Bank. David Rockefeller was chairman of Chase Manhattan Bank, which was principally responsible for Iran's Eurodollar deposits. In 1975, about two billion dollars in Iranian transactions were handled by Chase. Kissinger was also chairman of Chase's international advisory board (indeed, it was Nelson Rockefeller's recommendation to Richard Nixon that got Kissinger appointed as National Security Advisor). This information is distilled from Salinger, *American Held Hostage*, 19–20; and Smith, "Why Carter Admitted the Shah," May 26, 1981, 37, 40.

7. Carter, *Keeping Faith*, 452–53.

8. Sick, *All Fall Down*, 207.

9. William H. Sullivan, *Mission to Iran* (New York: Norton, 1981), 232–33.

10. Ibid., 276–77.

11. These dates are a matter of public record. However, somewhat differing ideological accounts of these events can be found in the various memoirs cited in note 2.

12. Carter, *Keeping Faith*, 452.

13. Ibid., 453–54.

14. Norman Ornstein et al., *Vital Statistics on Congress, 1984–5*, 178, 181.

15. It is actually not entirely surprising that the information about the Shah's medical treatment was not uncovered earlier. The Shah went to great lengths to conceal this information. Even French intelligence was not aware of his condition, though he was being treated by French doctors. As Sick, *All Fall Down*, notes in describing an article concerning the Shah's medical condition that appeared in the *New York Times Magazine* on May 26, 1981, under a byline by Lawrence K. Alt-

man, M.D., entitled, "The Shah's Health: A Political Gamble": "His account was fully consistent with (and considerably more comprehensive than) the information made available to the U.S. Government" (413).

16. Sick, *All Fall Down*, 208.

17. Terence Smith,"Why Carter Admitted the Shah," *New York Times Magazine*, May 16, 1981, 46.

18. Sick, *All Fall Down*, 205–6.

19. Vance, *Hard Choices*, 343–44.

20. Sick, *All Fall Down*, 212.

21. Salinger, *America Held Hostage*, 23–24.

22. Sick, *All Fall Down*, 212.

23. John McCloy had served as the U.S. military governor and high commander for Germany after World War II. He was also CEO of Chase Manhattan Bank at the time of the Shah's original overthrow in the 1950s. Although at the time he wrote this letter he worked as a lawyer for a New York law firm, he was nonetheless considered an influential high statesman of American foreign policy. For more on McCloy, see Sick, *All Fall Down*, 413.

24. Correspondence, Brzezinski to McCloy, McCloy to Vance, Vance to McCloy, 5/7/79, "CO 71," Box 31, WHCF, Jimmy Carter Library. It is also interesting to note that much of McCloy's argument rests on the importance of reputation for sustaining the credibility of American foreign policy. For a brilliant analysis of why this argument is fundamentally fallacious, see Jonathan Mercer, *Reputation and International Politics* (Ithaca, NY: Cornell University Press, 1996).

25. Ibid., "Correspondence."

26. Ibid., "Correspondence."

27. Brzezinski, *Power and Principle*, 472.

28. For more on how people search for evidence that supports their preexisting beliefs, while systematically discounting evidence that contradicts those beliefs and enhancing evidence that supports them, see Charles Lord, Lee Ross, and Mark Lepper, "Biased Assimilation and Attitude Polarization: The Effects of Prior Theories on Subsequently Considered Evidence," *Journal of Personality and Social Psychology*, 37 (1979), 2098–2109.

29. Sick, *All Fall Down*, 209.

30. Ibid., 210.

31. Ibid., 211.

32. Jordan, *Crisis*, 29.

33. Ibid., 29.

34. Brzezinski, *Power and Principle*, 474. Also see Smith, "Why Carter Admitted the Shah."

35. Carter, *Keeping Faith*, 452–53.

36. Ibid., 448.

37. Ibid., 453.

38. In spite of being unremitting in their opposition to the Shah's entrance into the United States, the Carter administration did make several concessions to the Shah's family concerning their ability to enter the United States. As Vance, *Hard Choices*, 344–45, recounts:

In response to an appeal by the Shah and after consulting with Naas (U.S. Chargé D'affaires in Tehran), we decided to allow the Shah's children to attend school in the United States. When Naas discussed this matter with Bazargan, the prime minister agreed that it should cause no problem, although he reiterated his warning about the dangers of admitting the Shah himself. The President determined that the empress could come to the United States for medical treatment, if necessary, but not to reside with the children. In permitting the empress to enter even temporarily for medical treatment, we would be skirting dangerously close to confirming suspicions in Iran that the United States still supported the Shah. Humanitarian concerns, however, demanded that we do whatever we could to help his family, as long as American lives and national interests were not subjected to unacceptable risks.

39. Sick, *All Fall Down,* 213.

40. The Shah had been diagnosed with a cancer of the lymph system called Waldenstrom's macroglobulinemia in 1974. He had been under the care of two French physicians, Drs. Flandrin and Bernard, since that time. He had been treated with chlorambucil, a drug that reduced the swelling in his lymph nodes and spleen. This illness resembles chronic lymphocytic leukemia, and the average lifespan after diagnosis is six to eight years.

The Shah's condition worsened after his exile, and a new form of cancer, Richter's syndrome, was diagnosed in March of 1979 in the Bahamas. The standard treatment for Richter's would have been to remove the spleen and thus prevent the further production of damaged cells. However, the Shah refused surgery and chose to be treated with chemotherapy, a remedy with limited effect, which often leads to secondary infections resulting from a weakened immune system. The specific treatment he chose was a combination of four drugs, known by its acronym, MOPP. MOPP is a standard treatment for Hodgkin's disease. In the Shah's case, the side effects of these drugs were too severe, and he was forced to stop treatment sooner than desired. An excellent overview of the specifics of the Shah's medical condition can be found in Lawrence K. Altman, "The Shah's Health: A Political Gamble," 48–52.

41. By the time the Shah reached Mexico in June, he was suffering from severe jaundice as a result of the Richter's syndrome, which Mexican doctors misdiagnosed as malaria. This incorrect diagnosis is what compelled the search for a tropical disease specialist to treat the Shah.

42. Carter, *Keeping Faith,* 452–56.

43. Ibid., 454.

44. Jordan, *Crisis,* 41–42. It is interesting to note Carter's aversion to being the sole dissenter in a crowd. Asch's famous conformity experiments elegantly demonstrate how difficult and unusual it is for an individual to resist the conformity of the crowd, even in the realm of "objective" measurements of reality, like the length of lines; see Solomon Asch, "Opinions and Social Pressure," *Scientific American* 193(5) (1955): 31–35. In this case, it is highly probable that Carter's ultimate agreement was influenced by the defection of Vance into the other coalition's camp. Even one other dissenter makes lack of conformity much more comfortable and

thus much more likely. Once Carter lost the confederate he had in Vance, it would have been much more difficult for him to remain the lone holdout against admitting the Shah.

45. Carter, *Keeping Faith,* 455. Note that this comment is very susceptible to retrospective hindsight bias. Whether Carter made this comment at the time, or how seriously he took it if he did make it, is suspect given the foresight it appears to give him. If he *really* thought that such an outcome would be virtually inevitable if he admitted the Shah, he would not have done so.

46. Vance, *Hard Choices,* 371–72.

47. It appears in retrospect, however, that this was not true. Although the equipment was not all available in one place in Mexico, adequate diagnostic equipment and adequately trained technicians did exist in that country. Moreover, no independent examination of the Shah was ever conducted by the U.S. government to confirm the severity of the Shah's condition while he was still in Mexico. The State Department medical officer, Dr. Eben Dustin, simply accepted Kean's recommendation for the Shah's transfer to New York. See Altman, "The Shah's Health: A Political Gamble."

48. Carter, *Keeping Faith,* 455.

49. Smith, "Why Carter Admitted the Shah," 36–37.

50. Sick, *All Fall Down,* 218.

51. Smith, "Why Carter Admitted the Shah," 42.

52. At that time, it was determined that the jaundice was caused by an obstruction in his gallbladder, and the Shah was operated on for its removal several days later.

53. Carter, *Keeping Faith,* 469.

54. Roper Reports, 12/11/79, "Iran, 11/79" folder, Box 34, WHCF, Jimmy Carter Library.

55. Telephone calls and mail summaries, 12/3/79, "American Hostages in Iran, 12/3/79–12/29/79," Box 75, WHCF, Jimmy Carter Library.

56. UPI press teletype, n.d., "Iran, 11/79," Box 34, WHCF, Jimmy Carter Library.

57. Ibid.

58. Report, Draft # 3,12/3/79, "Iran-Shah, 12/79," Counsel Files, Jimmy Carter Library (no box number—declassified for this study).

59. This was a costly decision for Panama. A $32 billion oil deal between Iran and Panama had just been signed at $2 a barrel below market price. This deal was instantly and unilaterally canceled by the Iranians upon learning of the Shah's asylum in Panama. In addition, rioting in Panama took place in response to the Shah's presence, and tourism declined significantly. Moreover, the Shah was not a gracious guest, and his American advisors made constant unsubstantiated charges against the Panamanians for everything from spying to overcharging. However, Torrijos in particular was very committed to helping the United States deal with the Shah out of his personal gratitude to Carter for pushing the Panama Canal treaties through Congress.

60. Report, Original understanding, 12/13/79, "Iran-Shah, 12/79," Counsel-Cutler, Jimmy Carter Library.

61. News Conference, 12/15/79, "Iran, Shah, 12/79," Box 93, Counsel Files-Cutler, Jimmy Carter Library.

62. Memo, A. Raphael to L. Cutler, 3/29/80, "Iran-Shah, 3/80," Counsel-Cutler, Jimmy Carter Library.

63. See Lawrence K. Altman, "The Shah's Health: A Political Gamble," 48–52. Also see Jordan, *Crisis,* and Sick, *All Fall Down.*

64. In attempting to stave off this extradition request, Panamanian officials became embroiled in the negotiation process between the American government and the Iranians concerning the release of the hostages. In a recently declassified, utterly fascinating report, Jordan describes his interaction with Panamanian officials concerning their discussions with Iranian leaders. Writing a memo directed to Carter, Vance, and Brzezinski, Jordan describes a Panamanian official's characterization of Iranian Foreign Minister Ghotbzadeh's reasoning for the American embassy takeover: "He [Ghotbzadeh] said that the plot to overthrow the American Embassy was an 'American conspiracy' involving Rockefeller, Kissinger, and others who had a dual purpose: First, to create an international crisis that would undermine the Ayatollah's efforts to establish an effective and strong Islamic republic; and second, to create a crisis of great magnitude for President Carter that would lead to his political defeat and would result in the election of a Republican that was controlled by Kissinger and Rockefeller who would work to have the Shah reinstated as the leader of the Iranian people . . . He said that President Carter was in danger of losing his Presidency if he did not successfully resolve the hostage situation. He said that the Ayatollah was in a very difficult position in Iran—he said that while he and Khomeini had no hope or desire to recover the Shah, that the students had become an increasingly powerful and difficult group with which to deal and that some way had to be found to resolve the crisis that did not make it appear that Khomeini had given in to U.S. pressure. He said that the Ayatollah had resorted to trying to substitute students totally loyal to him for the 'regulars' holding the hostages, but that once inside the compound they all behaved the same way." Note the power of conformity effects and groupthink that are implied in that statement about the actions of the students. Memo, Jordan to Carter, Vance and Brzezinski, n.d., "[Iran], Shah-Panama," Chief of Staff, Jordan, Jimmy Carter Library. Although this story sounds incredibly conspiratorial, it does not diverge drastically from Gary Sick's *New York Times* argument.

65. Letter, J. McCloy to C. Vance, 3/12/80, "Iran-Shah, 3/80," Counsel-Cutler, Jimmy Carter Library. Also see letter dated 3/11/80 for similar sentiments.

66. Letter, Family Liaison Action Group to Carter, 3/22/80, "Iran 3/80," Box 34, WHCF, Jimmy Carter Library. The mention of the U.S. military hospital no doubt refers to Gorgas, the U.S. military hospital in Panama that was considered as a possible site for the Shah's required splenectomy. This option was a possible alternative to Paitilla, the Panamanian hospital. The Shah was afraid of the possibility of sabotage at Paitilla, but the Panamanians refused to allow the operation to take place at Gorgas for political reasons and said that the Shah would not be allowed to remain in Panama after his operation if he were to have surgery at Gorgas. See Memo, Jordan and Raphael to Carter and Vance, 3/21/80, "Iran-Shah, 3/80," Counsel-Cutler, Jimmy Carter Library.

67. Memo, Jordan and Raphael to Carter and Vance, 3/21/80, "Iran-Shah, 3/80" Counsel-Cutler, Jimmy Carter Library.

68. Ibid.

69. Jordan, *Crisis,* 222.

Chapter 5

1. Dwight Eisenhower, *The White House Years: Waging Peace, 1956–1961* (Garden City, NY: Doubleday and Company, 1965), 546–47 (hereafter: *Waging Peace*).

2. Memo of Conversation, Special Assistant to the President with Eisenhower, 5/31/60, "1060-Meetings with the President-Vol 1 (3)," Box 4, OSANSA, Special Assistant to the President, Dwight D. Eisenhower Library.

3. This behavior is reminiscent of a self-fulfilling prophecy, whereby a person creates the very reality he expects to encounter. For the best review of the literature on this phenomenon, which can occur in both positive and negative contexts, see Mark Snyder, "When Belief Creates Reality," in *Advances in Experimental Social Psychology,* vol. 18, ed. Leonard Berkowitz (New York: Academic Press, 1984), 248–306.

4. It is interesting to note that when the administration first accepted partial responsibility for the overflights, without acknowledging Eisenhower's role in authorizing such activity, they blamed Soviet secrecy for America's need to conduct espionage. Soviet rejection of Eisenhower's 1955 Open Skies proposal was particularly emphasized as cause for extraordinary measures to ensure U.S. security interests. See Statement, Lincoln White to Press, May 7, 1960, "U-2 Incident [Vol. I] [May 1960] (1)" Box 25, OSS Alpha, Dwight D. Eisenhower Library.

5. The substance of the following discussion about the U-2 is culled from a variety of different sources, including extensive archival material. Two good general references on the subject can be found in the following works: For an account written shortly after the event that contains a bit of an apologist approach with a Pollyanna coating, see David Wise and Thomas B. Ross, *The U-2 Affair* (New York: Random House, 1962). For an exceptionally well-written and exhaustive account, see Michael Beschloss, *Mayday* (New York: Harper and Row, 1986).

6. Telegram, Willis to Herter, 6/29/60, "USSR-Vol.II of II (4) [June 1960], Box 15, OSS International, Dwight D. Eisenhower Library.

7. Concerning the downing of the plane itself, an editorial in the *New York Times* many years later revealed for the first time that there were three shots aimed at Powers's craft. The first was a near miss that disabled the craft, lowering its altitude. This is the point at which Powers apparently bailed out. The second shot hit the craft and damaged it. The third shot destroyed a Soviet fighter plane sent to intercept the U-2. This information is based on recent reports by Col. Gen. Georgi Mikhailov, who was deputy head of Soviet Air Command in 1960 (Stephen Ambrose, 27 December 1990, A19).

8. Telegram, Thompson to Herter, May 7, 1960, 4 P.M., "U-2 Incident [Vol.1] [May 1960] (3), OSS Alpha, Box 25, Dwight D. Eisenhower Library.

9. Document, May 6, 1960, "U-2 Incident, Vol. (1) July–Aug, 1960 (2)," Box 25, OSS Alpha, Dwight D. Eisenhower Library.

10. Diary, Ann Whitman for Dwight Eisenhower, Thursday, 5/5/1960, "DDE (ACW) Diary, May 1960," Box 11, Ann Whitman Diary, Whitman, Dwight D. Eisenhower Library.

11. Memo, Goodpaster for Record, 5/5/1960, "U-2 Incident [Vol. I] [May 1960] (3)," Box 25, OSS Alpha, Dwight D. Eisenhower Library.

12. "Events Relating to the Summit Conference," Report of the Committee on Foreign Relations, US Senate together with individual views, June 25, 1960, 86th Congress, 2d session, "U-2 Incident Vol. II May–June, 1960 (4)," Box 25, OSS Alpha, Dwight D. Eisenhower Library,

13. Department Statement, Lincoln White to Press, 5/5/1960, "U-2 Incident [Vol. 1] [May 1960] (1)," Box 25, OSS Alpha, Dwight D. Eisenhower Library.

14. Wise and Ross, *The U-2 Affair,* 93. See also "Events Relating to the Summit Conference," Report of the Committee on Foreign Relations, US Senate together with individual views, June 25, 1960, 86th Congress, 2d session, "U-2 Incident Vol. II May–June, 1960 (4)," Box 25, OSS Alpha, Dwight D. Eisenhower Library, 9.

15. Testimony before the Jackson Committee, June 10, 1960. Testimony hearings, Herter before the Jackson Committee, "U-2-References to NSC Machinery in Context w/[1960]," Box 18, OSANSA, NSC, Briefing Notes, Dwight D. Eisenhower Library, 31–32.

16. Press Release, NASA, 5/5/1960, "U-2 Incident [Vol. 1] [May 1960] (1)," Box 25, OSS Alpha, Dwight D. Eisenhower Library.

17. Beschloss, *Mayday,* 52. Emphasis in original.

18. For the importance of keeping the project secret, see Memo of Conversation, Special Assistant to the President with Eisenhower, 5/31/60, "1060-Meetings with the President-Vol 1 (3)," Box 4, OSANSA, Special Assistant to the President, Dwight D. Eisenhower Library.

19. Statement, Allen Dulles for Senate Foreign Relations Committee, 5/31/1060, "U-2 Incident Vol. II May 1060 (1)," Box 25, OSS Alpha, Dwight D. Eisenhower Library.

20. Statement, Allen Dulles for Senate Foreign Relations Committee, 5/31/1060, "U-2 Incident Vol. II May 1060 (1)," Box 25, OSS Alpha, Dwight D. Eisenhower Library.

21. Telegram, Thompson to Herter, 5/9/1960. "U-2 Incident [Vol. I] [May 1960] (3)," Box 25, OSS Alpha, Dwight D. Eisenhower Library.

22. Telegram, Freers to Herter, 5/10/1960, "U-2 Incident [Vol. I] [May 1960] (4)," Box 25, OSS Alpha, Dwight D. Eisenhower Library.

23. Memo, Discussion at the 444th Meeting of the National Security Council, Monday, May 9, 1960, "444 Meeting NSC, 5/9/60 NSC," Box 12, Whitman, Dwight D. Eisenhower Library.

24. The discussion in the preceding paragraph derives from Wise and Ross, *The U-2 Affair,* 101–2.

25. The discussion of this event is from "Events Relating to the Summit Conference, Report of the Committee on Foreign Relations, US Senate together with

individual views, June 25, 1960, 86th Congress, 2nd session," "U-2 Incident Vol. II May–June, 1960 (4)," Box 25, OSS Alpha, Dwight D. Eisenhower Library, 11.

26. Telegram, Thompson to Herter, 5/7/1960, "U-2 Incident [Vol. I] [may 1960] (3)," Box 25, OSS Alpha, Dwight D. Eisenhower Library.

27. Beschloss, *Mayday*, 246.

28. Ibid., 247.

29. Ibid., 248. Also Wise and Ross, *The U-2 Affair*, 105; and Eisenhower, *Waging Peace*, 550.

30. Eisenhower, *Waging Peace*, 558.

31. Statement, Lincoln White to Press, May 7, 1960, "U-2 Incident [Vol. I] [May 1960] (1)," Box 25, OSS Alpha, Dwight D. Eisenhower Library.

32. Beschloss, *Mayday*, 254.

33. Ibid., 252.

34. Memo, Bipartisan Leaders Breakfast, 5/26/1960, "Staff Notes May 1960 (1)," Box 50, DDE Diary, Whitman, Dwight D. Eisenhower Library.

35. Memo of Conversation, Lodge, Eisenhower, Persons, and Goodpaster, 5/26/1960, "Staff Notes May 1960 (1)," Box 50, DDE Diary, Whitman, Dwight D. Eisenhower Library.

36. "Events Relating to the Summit Conference, Report of the Committee on Foreign Relations, US Senate together with individual views, June 25, 1960, 86th Congress, 2nd session," "U-2 Incident Vol. II May–June, 1960 (4)," Box 25, OSS Alpha, Dwight D. Eisenhower Library, 12.

37. Telephone call, Nixon to Herter, "CAH telephone calls 3/28/60–6/30/60 (2)," Box 12, Herter, Dwight D. Eisenhower Library.

38. Apparently Eisenhower called off the U-2 flights in an informal conversation following a cabinet meeting on May 12. In the memo of conversation between General Goodpaster and Secretary Herter, "Goodpaster said he found what had happened was that the President and Gates stood up at the end of the Cabinet meeting that day and at that time the President told Gates to call off any provocative action by Defense in addition to cessation of the U-2 flights. Goodpaster said then the President and the Secretary (Herter) went into the President's office and the President told the Secretary and asked Goodpaster to inform Allen Dulles, which Goodpaster did." Memo, telephone call of Goodpaster to Herter, 6/1/1960, "Presidential Telephone Calls, 1–6/60 (1)," Box 10, Herter, Dwight D. Eisenhower Library.

39. George Kistiakowsky, *A Scientist at the White House* (Cambridge: Harvard University Press, 1976), 321.

40. Statement, Herter to the Press, May 9, 1960, "U-2 Incident [Vol I] [May 1960] (2)," Box 25, OSS Alpha, Dwight D. Eisenhower Library.

41. Statement, President to public, 5/11/60, "U-2 (1)," Box 20, Herter, Dwight D. Eisenhower Library.

42. Memo, 445th NSC Meeting, 5/24/1960, "445 Meeting NSC 5/24/60 NSC," Box 12, Whitman, Dwight D. Eisenhower Library.

43. Khrushchev's demands and Eisenhower's response in Memo, 445th Meeting of the NSC, 5/24/1960, "445th Meeting NSC 5/24/60," Box 12, Whitman, Dwight D. Eisenhower Library.

Most scholars agree that Khrushchev was under tremendous domestic political pressure at the time of the U-2 incident from hard-liners within his government who urged him to be "tougher" with the West. With the failure of his agrarian reforms, he was vulnerable to forces of opposition. See Beschloss, *Mayday,* on these points. From the perspective of prospect theory, Khrushchev's behavior at the summit occurred while he was operating in his own domain of losses. Thus, Khrushchev, like Eisenhower, may have been more willing to take greater risks with the "peace process" at the time of the U-2 incident and the Summit Meeting than he had been during his visit to the United States the previous September. This could certainly help account for his Berlin threats as well. However, there is not enough information available to speculate on all the factors that might have contributed to Khrushchev's behavior at the time of the Summit, and that analysis is certainly beyond the scope of this work. However, it is provocative to note that both leaders may have each been operating in a domain of losses without realizing that the other one was subject to those same considerations; in other words, each may have been more likely to accept risks himself, while simultaneously misunderstanding the motivations behind the gambles the other was taking. Regardless, the U-2 incident, and the controversy it caused, brought about the dissolution of the Summit little more than two weeks after the downing of Powers's plane.

44. Powers was released in Berlin, along with Frederick Pryor, another American, on February 10, 1962, in a prisoner exchange for the Soviet spy Rudolf Abel, the highest ranking agent that had been apprehended up to that point by the U.S. government. After quitting the CIA and being fired by Lockheed, Powers was killed on August 1, 1977, in a helicopter crash during a routine assignment reporting on traffic for a radio station in Los Angeles. Apparently, his craft ran out of fuel. His widow contended that he had been sabotaged by the CIA. It was upon the CIA's recommendation that President Jimmy Carter allowed Powers to be buried in Arlington National Cemetery. See Beschloss, *Mayday,* 400–401.

45. Careful review of the archival material makes evident that as much time as Eisenhower spent playing golf, however greatly exaggerated by the press, he never appeared to be either neglectful or disrespectful of the business of state. Anyone wishing independent confirmation of this contention is directed to a careful reading of the records from the National Security Council meetings in particular, 1952–1960, Dwight D. Eisenhower Library. For a concurring opinion, see Fred Greenstein, *The Hidden Hand Presidency* (New York: Basic Books, 1982).

46. James Reston,"How to Make Things Worse Than They Really Are," May 8, 1960, *New York Times,* Section 4, E 8. Reston's articles apparently received quite a lot of play in the Soviet press as well. In a telegram to Herter, Thompson notes that in the Soviet Union, "comment critical of US quoted in press stressed Reston article." Telegram, Thompson to Herter, 5/7/1960, "U-2 Incident [Vol. I] [May 1960] (3)," Box 25, OSS Alpha, Dwight D. Eisenhower Library.

47. James Reston, "President Sees Herter In Effort to Lessen Blow to Summit Talks; Soviet Exploits Plane Espionage/Flights Stopped/ Washington is Upset and Humiliated by Spy Developments," May 9, 1960, *New York Times,* 1.

48. James Reston,"What Kind of President Do you Want–III?," May 11, 1960, *New York Times,* 38.

49. The U-2 was a top secret project that was developed under the auspices of the CIA by Captain Kelly Johnson, who was at Lockheed at the time. Captain Johnson had a long history of success with designing aircraft: during World War I, he developed America's first tactical jet fighter, the F-80, in 141 days; by 1953, he had developed the nation's fastest plane, the Lockheed F-104 as well. The F-104 was transformed into the U-2. From the start, the goal of the U-2 was to fly higher and faster than any other aircraft. In 1954, the highest aircraft could reach 54,000 feet. The U-2 eventually flew at over 70,000 feet routinely. The final model was developed in 88 days at a cost of 19 million 1955 dollars. After the U-2 was shot down by the Soviet military in 1960, Richard Bissell commissioned Captain Johnson to develop a new plane capable of evading the Soviet military. In response to this request, Johnson produced the SR-71 "Blackbird" that flew at over 80,000 feet traveling at three times the speed of sound. By 1985, when a remote control version obviated the need for piloted flights, the SR-71 had survived over 1,000 attempts at interception by the Soviet military. For more on the development of the U-2, see Beschloss, *Mayday.*

50. Record of Action, Cabinet Meeting, 5/26/1960, "Cabinet Meeting of 5/26/1960," Box 16, Cabinet, Whitman, Dwight D. Eisenhower Library. Note how this characterization differs dramatically from the claim that such action was needed to prevent another "Pearl Harbor," the justification Eisenhower offered in his May 11 speech accepting responsibility. Statement, Eisenhower to public, 5/1/1960, "U-2 (1)," Box 20, Herter, Dwight D. Eisenhower Library.

51. Statement, Allen Dulles to Senate Foreign Relations Committee, 5/31/1960, "U-2 Incident [Vol. II] [May 1960] (1)" Box 25, OSS Alpha, Dwight D. Eisenhower Library.

52. Allen Dulles, *The Craft of Intelligence* (New York: Harper and Row, 1963), 67.

53. Eisenhower, *Waging Peace,* 546.

54. Beschloss, *Mayday,* 118. Emphasis in original.

55. Ibid., 118.

56. Stephen Ambrose, *Eisenhower: The President* (New York: Simon and Schuster, 1984), 568.

57. Eisenhower, *Waging Peace,* 551.

58. Wise and Ross, *The U-2 Affair,* 175.

59. Eisenhower, *Waging Peace,* 558.

60. Milton Eisenhower, *The President Is Calling* (Garden City, New York: Doubleday and Company, 1974), 335. Emphasis in original.

61. John Eisenhower, *Strictly Personal* (Garden City, New York: Doubleday and Company, 1974), 271.

62. Statement, Allen Dulles for Senate Foreign Relations Committee, 5/31/1960, "U-2 Incident Vol. II May 1960 (1)," Box 25, OSS Alpha, Dwight D. Eisenhower Library. Also note the pursuit of irrational consistency inherent in this belief structure. See Jervis, *Perception and Misperception in International Politics,* especially 128–43.

63. This process raises the issue of the role of motivational bias in decision making. For more on the effect of motivational bias in political decision making, see

Irving Janis and Leon Mann, *Decision Making.* For an overview of motivated bias in attribution, see Susan Fiske and Shelley Taylor, *Social Cognition* (New York: McGraw Hill, 1991).

Also note how the probability of success *and* secrecy was misjudged due to the conjunction fallacy. For more on that fallacy, see chapter 3, note 77. In this instance, a low probability was overweighted, and it was assumed that failure was next to impossible. This was true for both the success of the project militarily as well as the ability to keep it secret politically.

64. Beschloss, *Mayday,* 32–33.

65. Ibid., 118.

66. Ibid., 8.

67. Ibid., 404.

68. See Eisenhower–McCone conversation: Beschloss, *Mayday,* 404.

69. Litchenstein et al., "Judged Frequency of Lethal Events."

70. Kahneman and Tversky, "Prospect Theory: An Analysis of Decision under Risk."

71. It is ironic to note that the U-2 overflights would have soon become a moot issue anyway. In August, 1960, the United States launched its first reconnaissance satellite which was able to photograph Soviet targets more systematically and comprehensively than the U-2 had been able to do. More importantly, it was well beyond the Soviet military's ability to intercept.

72. Record of Action, Cabinet Meeting, 5/26/1960, "Cabinet Meeting, 5/26/1960," Box 16, Cabinet, Whitman, Dwight D. Eisenhower Library.

73. James Reston,"What Kind Of President Do You Want—III?, " May 11, 1960, *New York Times,* 38.

74. James Reston, "The Political Consequences Following the U-2," May 13, 1960, *New York Times,* 30. Emphasis deleted.

Chapter 6

1. Notes from NSC Meeting, August 31, 1956, "295th NSC Meeting, 8/30/56," Box 8, NSC-Whitman, Dwight D. Eisenhower Library.

2. This discussion of the Suez Canal and the crisis that its nationalization produced is culled from a complete and careful reading of all relevant archival sources in the Eisenhower Library. For more accessible and generally accurate reviews of the crisis see: for an account that is somewhat legalistic in nature, Robert Bowie, *Suez 1956* (London: Oxford University Press, 1974); the most engaging and informative memoirs on the subject can be found in Robert Murphy, *Diplomat Among Warriors* (New York: Doubleday and Company, 1964), chapter 26, "Suez" (1956); and Sherman Adams, *Firsthand Report* (New York: Harper and Brothers, 1961), chapter 13, "Showdown at Suez."

3. The Suez Canal concession had been given to France by Khedive Osmol of Egypt in 1866; the Sultan of Turkey agreed to the concession. The agreement was to last 99 years from the opening of the Canal to traffic, which meant that it was due to expire in 1967. The Suez Canal itself was designed by a French engineer, De Lessees, and built with international financial support. Construction of the Canal

was completed in 1869. In 1875, while Disraeli was Prime Minister of Great Britain, the British bought 44 percent of the Canal Company's holdings from Egypt. At the time of the crisis, the British owned about 400,000 shares in the Canal Company. See Diary, Dwight D. Eisenhower, August 8, 1956, "Diary," Box 17, DDE Diary-Whitman, Dwight D. Eisenhower Library. It later operated under the 1888 Constantinople Convention. Although the United States was not a party to this agreement, the treaty was signed by nine countries, including Britain, France, and Russia. The Company and the freedom of passage rights of the signatories were reaffirmed in the Anglo-Egyptian Treaty of 1954. Transcript of Television speech, John Foster Dulles to nation, August 3, 1956, "Suez Canal Report (Dulles) 8/3/56 Speech," Box 16, Whitman, Dwight D. Eisenhower Library.

4. Notes of Meeting, National Security Council, August 9, 1956, "292nd Meeting of the NSC," Box 8, NSC-Whitman, Dwight D. Eisenhower Library.

5. Notes from Bipartisan Leadership Meeting, August 12, 1956, "Leg Leaders Meetings 1956 (4) (July–Nov)," Leg 2, Whitman, Dwight D. Eisenhower Library, 3, 5.

6. "Points to be raised with Harold Macmillan and Roger Makins," September 25, 1956, "Suez Problem July–Nov 1956-Feb–Mar 1957 (6)," Box 7, Subject-Dulles, Dwight D. Eisenhower Library. This document also makes the point, however, that many other vessels that transitted the Canal were operated by Panamanian and Liberian subsidiaries of American companies and were registered under the flags of those nations.

7. Notes from Bipartisan Leadership Meeting, August 12, 1956, "Leg Leaders Meetings 1956 (4) (July–Nov)," Leg 2, Whitman, Dwight D. Eisenhower Library, 6.

8. Diary, August 8, 1956, "Aug 56 Diary," Box 17, DDE Diary-Whitman, Dwight D. Eisenhower Library.

9. Eisenhower, *Waging Peace*, 663.

10. Murphy, *Diplomat Among Warriors*, 418–21.

11. Diary, Dwight D. Eisenhower, August 8, 1956, "Diary," Box 17, DDE Diary-Whitman, Dwight D. Eisenhower Library.

12. Eisenhower, *Waging Peace*, 35.

13. Letter, Eden to Eisenhower, July 27, 1956, "Eden 7/18/56–11/7/56 (1)," Box 19, International-Whitman, Dwight D. Eisenhower Library.

14. Letter, Eden to Eisenhower, July 27, 1956, "Eden 7/18/56–11/7/56 (1)," Box 19, International-Whitman, Dwight D. Eisenhower Library.

15. Summary of Developments, September 6, 7, 19, 1956 (No. 3, 4, and 5), "Suez Summaries," Box 43, International-Whitman, Dwight D. Eisenhower Library.

16. Summary of Developments, September 19, 20, 21, 1956 (Nos. 12, 13, and 14), "Suez Summaries," Box 43, International-Whitman, Dwight D. Eisenhower Library.

17. Selwyn Lloyd, *Suez 1956* (London: Cape, 1978), 276.

18. Memo, President by Goodpaster, October 27, 1956, "Meetings with President Aug–Dec 56 (3)," Box 4, WH-Dulles, Dwight D. Eisenhower Library.

19. Transcript of the National Security Council Meeting, 11/1/56, "302nd NSC Meeting," Box 8, NSC-Whitman, Dwight D. Eisenhower Library.

20. Anthony Nutting, *No End of a Lesson: The Story of Suez* (London: Constable, 1967), 111.

21. Adams, *Firsthand Report,* 257.

22. Letter, Bulganin to Eisenhower, November 5, 1956," Bulganin 7/27/55–1/3/58 (2)," Box 56, International-Whitman, Dwight D. Eisenhower Library.

23. Ambrose, *Eisenhower: The President,* 368. While Eden and Mollet drew analogies between Nasser and Hitler, Eisenhower saw the Soviet leaders as being more like Hitler. Also note that Eisenhower's characterization of the Soviet leaders as "furious and scared" and thus dangerous represents an implicit acknowledgment of prospect theory's argument that those in a domain of loss ("scared") are more likely to take risks (and thus be "dangerous").

24. Notes from Bipartisan meeting, November 9, 1956, "Nov 56 Misc (3)," Box 20, DDE Diary-Whitman, Dwight D. Eisenhower Library.

25. Memo of Conversation, with President by Goodpaster, November 6, 1956, "Nov 56 Diary, Staff Memos," Box 19, DDE Diary-Whitman, Dwight D. Eisenhower Library.

26. Legislative Meeting, December 31, 1956, "Dec 56 Misc (1)," Box 20, DDE Diary-Whitman, Dwight D. Eisenhower Library.

27. Memo, Eisenhower by Goodpaster, November 21, 1956 of November 20, 1956, "Nov 56 Diary-Staff Memos," Box 19, DDE Diary-Whitman, Dwight D. Eisenhower Library.

28. For American efforts to press the Israelis for withdrawal, see Address by the President, February 21, 1957, "Suez Problem July–Nov 1956-Feb.–Mar 1957 (2)," Box 7, Subject-Dulles, Dwight D. Eisenhower Library.

29. Notes from NSC meeting, November 9, 1956, "303rd NSC Meeting 11/8/56," Box 8, NSC-Whitman, Dwight D. Eisenhower Library.

30. All statistics in the above paragraph are from Norman Ornstein et al., *Vital Statistics on Congress, 1984–5,* 177, 180–81.

31. State of the Union Speech, Eisenhower to Congress, January 5, 1956, "State of Union Jan 56 (1)," Box 14, Speech-Whitman, Dwight D. Eisenhower Library. Eisenhower's optimism arose from his belief that what he said about the positive state of America was not only true, but that much of it was a direct result of the success of his programs and policies.

32. Eisenhower, *Waging Peace,* 19.

33. Summary, "Dulles, Foster Feb 57 (1)," Box 8, Dulles-Herter-Whitman, Dwight D. Eisenhower Library.

34. Notes from NSC Meeting, November 1, 1956, "302nd NSC Meeting 11/1/56," Box 8, NSC-Whitman, Dwight D. Eisenhower Library.

35. Memo, Eisenhower by Goodpaster, October 30, 1956, "Oct 56 Diary-Staff Memos," Box 19, DDE Diary-Whitman, Dwight D. Eisenhower Library.

36. Notes from NSC Meeting, 11/8/56, "303rd NSC Meeting 11/8/56," Box 8, NSC-Whitman, Dwight D. Eisenhower Library. Quote on page 12.

37. I must note that in carefully reading through every one of the open docu-

ments concerning the Suez crisis in the Eisenhower archives (over 1000 pages), there are less than a handful of *private* mentions of the moral necessity of supporting an anticolonialist position. In almost all of these cases, the "moral" discussions were pragmatically manipulative in nature, as when all present recognized the need to frame a presentation to the United Nations or Nasser in such a way as to make it more acceptable. While there is no overt support of the allies' imperialist designs, neither is there an overriding *philosophical* emphasis on condemning it. Rather, as demonstrated by the great focus placed on such concerns in later memoirs, it is clear that this concern is emphasized as a more attractive retrospective explanation for behavior than the real one that clearly drove all policy discussions at the time. Such discussions were overwhelmingly preoccupied with doing whatever it took to maintain adequate access to oil supplies, including, but not limited to: accepting Egyptian sovereignty rights over the Canal territory, if not the Canal Company; condemning imperialist designs over former colonials; and so forth. While some of the statements in support of respect for Egyptian sovereignty and those expressing contempt for colonialist interests may appear to make the policy motivation moral in nature, the public nature of these sentiments belie their pragmatic intent. When I first glanced at the public documents and the memoirs, American foreign policy during the Suez crisis looked remarkably like a case of morality in action. (For a brilliant look at morality in American foreign policy, see Robert McElroy, *Morality in American Foreign Policy* [Princeton, NJ: Princeton University Press, 1992]. The Suez crisis is not specifically addressed in this work.) However, after carefully examining the private documents recorded at the time, which were not as biased by memory or impression management as the memoirs, I arrived at a different conclusion. These contemporary papers express overriding preoccupation, to the point of absolute obsession, with maintaining cheap and easy access to oil. The administration was, however, not stupid in pursuing their economic goals. Eisenhower officials knew that statements couched in politically correct anticolonial language was much more likely to achieve their goals, particularly within the United Nations and with Nasser himself, than pronouncements that neglected to mention the importance of sovereignty and anti-imperialism. This is not to say that the administration openly advocated deception, manipulation, or express racial prejudice among themselves; in private, morality was not consciously considered utilitarian, simply irrelevant. Only when the discussion turns to public statements do such moral concerns come into explicit focus. It must be noted, however, that a few administration officials were genuinely opposed to colonial motives. These moral arguments, however infrequent in spontaneous private discourse, were mostly pronounced by John Foster Dulles. A representative sample upon which to confirm this analysis can most efficiently be found in the NSC meetings, July 1956–Feb. 1957, NSC-Whitman collection, Dwight D. Eisenhower Library.

38. Eisenhower speaks of this fear numerous times in various NSC meetings, but nowhere more directly than in a letter to his friend Swede Hazlett: "But I can tell you one thing . . . the existence of this problem does not make sleeping any easier— . . . because of the opportunities that we have handed to the Russians." Letter, Eisenhower to Hazlett, November 2, 1956, "Nov 56 Misc (4)," Box 20, DDE Diary-Whitman, Dwight D. Eisenhower Library.

39. Supplementary Note, Eisenhower by Goodpaster, July 30, 1856 of July 28, 1956, "July 56 Diary-Staff Memos," Box 16, DDE Diary-Whitman, Dwight D. Eisenhower Library.

40. Ibid.

41. This included the First and Second User's Conferences in London. For a daily record of the events of these conferences, see "Suez Summaries," Box 43, International-Whitman, Dwight D. Eisenhower Library.

42. Memo of Conference, President by Goodpaster, October 29, 1956, "Oct 56 Diary-Staff Memos," Box 19, DDE Diary-Whitman, Dwight D. Eisenhower Library.

43. Memo, Eisenhower by Goodpaster, November 21, 1956, "Nov 56 Diary-Staff Memos," Box 19, DDE Diary-Whitman, Dwight D. Eisenhower Library.

44. The relationships between France, Britain, and Israel during the course of the crisis is beyond the scope of this work. However, interested parties are directed to Sylvia Crosbie, *Tacit Alliance* (Princeton, NJ: Princeton University Press, 1974), for an excellent examination of the French–Israeli link.

45. Peter Calvocaressi, *Suez: Ten Years After; Broadcasts from the British Broadcasting System* (London: British Broadcasting System, 1967), 7–10.

46. Anthony Eden, *Full Circle* (Boston: Houghton Mifflin, 1960).

47. This domino theory is pervasive in British and French communications with the United States concerning the Suez crisis. For a representative sample of this, see the Eisenhower–Eden correspondence, "Eden 7/18/56–11/7/56 (1)," Box 19, International-Whitman, Dwight D. Eisenhower Library.

48. Bowie, *Suez 1956,* 61.

49. Memo, Eisenhower by Dulles, August 30, 1956, "Meetings with President Aug–Dec 56 (6)," Box 4, WH-Dulles, Dwight D. Eisenhower Library.

50. Eden, *Full Circle,* 487.

51. Ibid., 518.

52. Letter, Anthony Eden to Eisenhower, September 6, 1956, "Eden 7/18/56–11/7/56 (2)," Box 19, International-Whitman, Dwight D. Eisenhower Library.

53. Ibid.

54. Intelligence Notes, August 10, 1956, "OCB 350.05 (File #3) (6) (Feb–Oct 56)," Box 111, NSC, OCB, Dwight D. Eisenhower Library.

55. Notes from NSC Meeting, August 31, 1956, "295th NSC Meeting, 8/30/56," Box 8, NSC-Whitman, Dwight D. Eisenhower Library.

56. Memo, Congressional Briefing with Secretary Dulles, October 31, 1956, " "Suez Prob. July–Nov 1956-Feb–Mar 1957(5)," Box 7, Dulles, Dwight D. Eisenhower Library.

57. Memo of Conversation, Eisenhower by Goodpaster, July 31, 1956, "July 56 Diary-Staff Memos," Box 16, DDE Diary-Whitman, Dwight D. Eisenhower Library. Emphasis added.

58. Memo of Conversation, Eisenhower by Goodpaster, July 31, 1956, "July 56 Diary-Staff Memos," Box 16, DDE Diary-Whitman, Dwight D. Eisenhower Library. Emphasis added.

59. Telegram, Barbour to Dulles, September 1, 1956, "Dulles, F Sept 56 (2),"

Box 7, D-H, Whitman, Dwight D. Eisenhower Library. Emphasis added. Note that the argument that operations could be narrow, successful, and relatively cost-less is reminiscent of Jervis's discussion of the pursuit of irrational consistency and the avoidance of value trade-offs in political decision making. See Jervis, *Perception and Misperception in International Politics,* esp. 128–143.

60. Roy Fullick, *Suez: The Double War* (London: H. Hamilton, 1979), 160. In the middle of the crisis, four weeks prior to his departure for Jamaica, Eden was running a fever of 106 degrees.

61. Telegram, Aldrich to Dulles, November 19, 1956, "Dulles, Foster Nov 56 (1)," Box 8, Dulles-Herter, Whitman, Dwight D. Eisenhower Library.

62. Telegram, Dillon to Dulles, July 31, 1956, "Dulles, John Foster, July 56," Box 17, Dulles-Herter-Whitman, Dwight D. Eisenhower Library.

63. Telegram, Dillon to Dulles, July 31, 1956, "Dulles, John Foster, July 56," Box 17, Dulles-Herter-Whitman, Dwight D. Eisenhower Library. Mollet went so far as to compare Nasser's book *The Philosophy of Revolution* to Hitler's *Mein Kampf,* arguing that "all leading officials in the Dept of State should read this book promptly." Throughout the crisis, Mollet never failed to invoke the Munich analogy consistently in his arguments about the necessity of containing Nasser's influence immediately before he was allowed to gain control over all of North Africa: "He [Mollet] said that Munich had cost the world dearly in lives and he only hoped that the present situation would not lead to even more dire results within the next 3 to 5 years." See Telegram, Dillon to Dulles, November 12, "Dulles, Foster Nov 56 (2)," Box 8, Dulles-Herter-Whitman, Dwight D. Eisenhower Library. Mollet apparently consistently failed to grasp that Nasser taking control of his own land in Suez from the *French* was not entirely analogous to Hitler's taking control of Czechoslovakia from the Czechs.

64. Standard interpretations of the Suez crisis often focus on the American desire to create and sustain the North Atlantic Treaty Organization. For standard examples of such interpretations see the following: For an example that notes the importance of NATO, see Alexander DeConde, *A History of American Foreign Policy,* 3d ed. (New York: Charles Scribner and Sons, 1978), 287–91. For an interpretation that mentions the moral imperatives, please see Walter LaFeber, *American, Russia, and the Cold War,* 4th ed. (New York: John Wiley and Sons, 1980), 190–95. The interpretation taken in this book argues for the central importance to the administration of open access to Middle Eastern oil for Western Europe. Please see note 37 in this chapter for the justification of that perspective.

65. Telegram, Dillon to Dulles, July 31, 1956, "Dulles, John Foster, July 56," Box 17, Dulles-Herter-Whitman, Dwight D. Eisenhower Library.

66. Diary, January 10, 1957, "Jan 57 Diary-acw (2)," Box 8, AW Diary-Whitman, Dwight D. Eisenhower Library.

67. Memo, Eisenhower and Dulles, November 17, 1956, "Meetings with Pres Aug-Dec 56 (3)," Box 4, Dulles-WH, Dwight D. Eisenhower Library.

68. Eisenhower, *Waging Peace,* 50.

69. Ibid., 122.

70. Ibid., 35.

71. Notes from NSC meeting, August 9, 1956, "292nd Meeting of NSC Aug 9 56," Box 8, NSC-Whitman, Dwight D. Eisenhower Library.

72. Telephone call, David Lawrence to Secretary Dulles, October 31, 1956, "Memoranda Tel Conv-Gen Oct 1 1956–Dec 29, 1956 (2)," Box 5, Telephone-Dulles, Dwight D. Eisenhower Library.

73. Telephone call, Lodge to Dulles, October 31, 1956, "Memoranda tel Conv-gen Oct 1 1956 to Dec 29, 1956," Box 5, Telephone-Dulles, Dwight D. Eisenhower Library.

74. Telegram, Bulganin to Eisenhower, November 5, 1956, "Bulganin 7/27/55–1/3/58 (2)," Box 56, International—Whitman, Dwight D. Eisenhower Library.

75. Memo, Eisenhower by Goodpaster, November 7, 1956, "Nov 56 Diary-Staff Memos," Box 19, DDE Diary-Whitman, Dwight D. Eisenhower Library.

76. Notes from NSC meeting, 11/8/56, "303rd NSC meeting 11/8/56," Box 8, NSC-Whitman, Dwight D. Eisenhower Library.

77. Notes from NSC, 11/30/56, "305th NSC meeting 11/30/56," Box 8, NSC-Whitman, Dwight D. Eisenhower Library.

78. Memo, Eisenhower by Goodpaster, November 21, 1956, "Nov 56 Diary-Staff Memos," Box 19, DDE Diary-Whitman, Dwight D. Eisenhower Library.

79. Report, Joint Chiefs of Staff for Secretary of Defense, August 3, 1956, "Suez Canal [July–Aug 56]," Box 11, OSANSA-NSC, Dwight D. Eisenhower Library.

80. Memo, Dulles Briefing Senate Foreign Relations Committee, September 27, 1956, "Suez Problem July–Nov 1956-Feb–Mar 1957 (6)," Box 7, Subject-Dulles, Dwight D. Eisenhower Library.

81. Eisenhower, *Waging Peace,* 80.

82. Adams, *Firsthand Report,* 246.

83. Pre-Press conference notes, September 11, 1956, "Sept 56 Diary-acw," Box 8, AW Diary-Whitman, Dwight D. Eisenhower Library.

84. Memo, Hagerty to Eisenhower, October 8, 1956, "Dulles, F Oct 56 (2)," Box 7, D-h-Whitman, Dwight D. Eisenhower Library.

85. Press Conference, Eisenhower, September 11, 1956, "Press 9/11/56," Box 5, Press-Whitman, Dwight D. Eisenhower Library.

86. Notes of Bipartisan Meeting, "Bipartisan Leaders Meetings 1956 (4) (July–Nov)," Box 2, Leg-Whitman, Dwight D. Eisenhower Library.

87. Memo, For the Record by Eisenhower, October 15, 1956, "Oct 56 Diary-acw (1)," Box 8, AW Diary-Whitman, Dwight D. Eisenhower Library.

88. Memo, Eisenhower by Goodpaster, July 31, 1956, "July 56 Diary Staff Memos," Box 16, DDE Diary-Whitman, Dwight D. Eisenhower Library.

89. Eisenhower, *Waging Peace,* 38–39.

90. Ibid., 40.

91. Memo, President and Ambassador Alphand, September 10, 1956, "Guy Mollet (4)," Box 12, International-Whitman, Dwight D. Eisenhower Library.

92. Letter, Eisenhower to Hazlett, "Aug 56 Misc (1)," Box 17, DDE Diary-Whitman, Dwight D. Eisenhower Library. Eisenhower's prescience of Carter's later imbroglio in Iran is interesting. In an ironic reversal of Suez, Carter tried to

entice the Western allies into supporting his position to engage in force to release the hostages, while the British and French advocated caution without reservation. In both cases, caution proved to be the better part of valor in the end.

93. Letter, Eisenhower to Hazlett, November 2, 1956, "Nov 56 Misc (4)," Box 20, DDE Diary, Whitman, Dwight D. Eisenhower Library.

94. Memo, Eisenhower by Goodpaster, November 21, 1956, "Nov 56 Diary-Staff Memos," Box 19, DDE Diary-Whitman, Dwight D. Eisenhower Library.

95. See, for example, LaFeber, *America, Russia and the Cold War,* 192; and DeConde, *A History of American Foreign Policy,* 291.

96. Memo, Eisenhower by Goodpaster, November 5, 1956, of November 2, 1956, "Nov 56 Diary-Staff Memos," Box 19, DDE Diary-Whitman, Dwight D. Eisenhower Library.

97. Notes, January 1, 1956, "Leg Leaders Mtgs 1957 (1) Jan–Feb," Box 2, Leg-Whitman, Dwight D. Eisenhower Library.

98. As noted, Eden spent 21 days in Jamaica in the middle of the crisis. See Roy Fullick, *Suez: The Double War.* Dulles was hospitalized on November 3 for emergency stomach cancer surgery and essentially spent most of the rest of the crisis in the hospital. Eisenhower himself was not in great physical shape either. He had had a heart attack barely a year before the start of the crisis and had surgery for ileitis on June 8, little more than a month before Nasser announced the nationalization of the Canal. See Letter, Howard to Persons, September 29, 1955, "The President-Illness," Box 1, L.Authur Minnich-OSS, Dwight D. Eisenhower Library.

Chapter 7

1. This characterization derives from Abraham Wadersman and William Hallman, "Are People Acting Irrationally: Understanding Public Concerns about Environmental Threats," *American Psychologist* 48 (June 1993): 681–86.

2. There is extensive literature on this topic, most of the best of which has been conducted by Paul Slovic, Sarah Litchenstein, and Baruch Fischhoff. The following discussion draws extensively on their work and constitutes an overly simplistic condensation and synthesis of much of it. For their seminal contributions to the field of risk perception, please begin with: Sarah Litchenstein, Paul Slovic, Baruch Fischhoff, Mark Layman, and Barbara Combs, "Judged Frequency of Lethal Events." Other major contributions include: Paul Slovic, Baruch Fischhoff, and Sarah Litchenstein, "Behavioral Decision Theory Perspectives on Risk and Safety," *Acta Psychologica* 56 (1984): 183–203; Baruch Fischhoff, Paul Slovic, Sarah Litchenstein, Stephen Read, and Barbara Combs, "How Safe is Safe Enough? A Psychometric Study of Attitudes toward Technological Risks and Benefits," *Policy Sciences* 9 (1978): 127–52; for the most comprehensive review of this literature, please see Paul Slovic, "Perception of Risk," *Science* 236 (1987): 280–85.

3. C. Starr, "Social Benefit versus Technological Risk," *Science* 165 (1969): 1232–38. Slovic's most succinct response is in Slovic, "Perception of Risk."

4. For an explication of the specifics of the psychometric approach, see Fischhoff et al., "How Safe is Safe Enough?"

5. Slovic, "Perception of Risk."

6. Litchenstein et al., "Judged Frequency of Lethal Events."

7. Fischhoff et al., "How Safe is Safe Enough?"

8. Slovic, "Perception of Risk."

9. A nice summary of these findings can be found in Daniel Goleman, "Hidden Rules Often Distort Ideas of Risk," *The New York Times,* February 1, 1994. In addition, it now appears that the use of chemical weapons extends to American soldiers stationed in the Middle East during the Gulf War, although no actual deaths have been officially attributed to that cause as yet.

10. Slovic, "Perception of Risk."

11. This notion is characterized in the paradigmatic biblical tale of John the Baptist, whose "repent now" message foretold the coming of the end of the world, when the chance for repentance would evaporate.

12. In fact, people often go to great comparative lengths to convince themselves of how they differ from the victim, so that they can convince themselves that a similar negative outcome will not befall them. This is not uncommon in the case of women responding to a rape victim, for example; the desire to distance is often quite strong because of the fear that it might happen to them as well. One of the protective aspects of the fundamental attribution error is that if we believe that something bad happened to someone because of what they are like as a person, and we can convince ourselves that we are not like the victim on the relevant criteria, we can use our positive illusions to perpetuate a false sense of security about all sorts of threats. For more on these biases, see Shelley Taylor, "Adjustment to Threatening Events: A Theory of Cognitive Adaptation," *American Psychologist* 38 (1983): 1161–73; and Shelley Taylor and J. D. Brown, "Illusion and Well-Being: A Social Psychological Perspective on Mental Health," *Psychological Bulletin* 103 (1988): 193–210.

13. This point is elegantly elaborated in Baruch Fischhoff, "Psychology and Public Policy: Tool or Toolmaker?" *American Psychologist* 45 (1990): 647–53.

14. Voluminous work on affect and emotion has been done in the field of psychology. A representative sample of this research might include the work of Robert Zajonc, C. E. Izard, and H. Leventhal. Some examples of Zajonc's work are "Feeling and Thinking: Preferences Need No Inferences," *American Psychologist* 35 (1980); "On the Primacy of Affect," *American Psychologist* 39 (1984); and, with Hazel Marcus, "Affect and Cognition: The Hard Interface," in *Emotions, Cognition, and Behavior,* eds. C. E. Izard, Jerome Kagan, and Robert Zajonc (Cambridge: Cambridge University Press, 1984); with P. Pietromonaco and J. Baugh, "Independence and Interaction of Affect and Cognition," in *Affect and Cognition,* eds. Michael Clark and Susan Fiske (Hillsdale, NJ: Erlbaum, 1982). Izard's work is best represented by *Human Emotions* (New York: Plenum, 1977). For a comprehensive overview of the subject, see H. Leventhal, "Toward a Comprehensive Theory of Emotion," in L. Berkowitz, ed., *Advances in Experimental Social Psychology,* vol. 13 (New York: Academic Press, 1980), 139–207. Also, with K. Scherer, "The Relationship of Emotion to Cognition," *Cognition and Emotion* 1 (1987); and

"The Integration of Emotion with Cognition," *Affect and Cognition.* For a more cognitive perspective on emotion, see Gordon Bower, "Emotion and Social Perception," paper given to the Western Psychological Association, San Francisco, April 27, 1991. The most widely recognized application of motivated biases to political decision making is Irving Janis and Leon Mann, *Decision Making.*

15. Richard Nisbett and Lee Ross, *Human Inference: Strategies and Shortcomings of Social Judgment* (Englewood Cliffs, NJ: Prentice Hall, 1980); and Kahneman, Slovic, and Tversky, *Judgment Under Uncertainty: Heuristics and Biases.*

16. As exemplified by Nisbett and Ross, *Human Inference: Strategies and Shortcomings of Social Judgment;* and Kahneman, Slovic, and Tversky, *Judgment Under Uncertainty: Heuristics and Biases.* See also Fiske and Taylor, *Social Cognition.*

17. For more on this interface, see Izard, Kagan, and Zajonc, *Emotions, Cognition, and Behavior.*

18. For evidence that more information merely polarizes preexisting biases, see Robert Vallone, Lee Ross, and Mark Lepper, "The Hostile Media Phenomenon: Biased Perception and Perceptions of Media Bias in Coverage of the Beirut Massacre," *Journal of Personality and Social Psychology,* 49 (1985): 577–85.

19. Richard Nisbett and T. Wilson, "Telling More Than We Can Know: Verbal Reports on Mental Processes." The classic example of this phenomenon involves people learning word pairs, like moon–ocean. Later, those same subjects are asked to name a detergent and subjects overwhelmingly respond by mentioning "Tide," even when they do not use that detergent. When asked if the word pairs influenced their later choices, the majority of subjects vehemently denied that one task had any impact on the other.

20. While some will argue that how people understand emotion has to do with how they feel, it is equally plausible to offer a social cognition explanation for the subjective importance that individuals place on their emotional states. How people think about their emotions tells us as much about how people think as it does about how they feel. A social cognition interpretation would argue that emotions are neither wholly essential nor totally constructed. Rather, the way individuals come to instill meaning into their various emotional states betrays a great deal about how stimulus is processed to arrive at meaning. For the most sophisticated example of this kind of social cognition argument applied to gender, see Lawrence Kohlberg, "A Cognitive Developmental Analysis of Children's Sex Role Concepts and Attitudes," in *The Development of Sex Differences,* ed. Eleanor Maccoby (Stanford, CA: Stanford University Press, 1966).

21. Eric Johnson and Amos Tversky, "Affect, Generalization, and the Perception of Risk," *Journal of Personality and Social Psychology* 45 (1983): 20–21.

22. Gordon Bower, "Mood and Memory," *American Psychologist* 36 (1981). As an aside, this provides an interesting explanation for why depressed people have such a hard time remembering positive events from their past. Mood-incongruent memories are indeed less cognitively accessible to them than mood-congruent events that function to remind depressives of the events that made them sad in the past, thus reinforcing their depressive mood.

23. The ideas in this section largely derive from an extended personal discus-

sion with Amos Tversky. I am deeply indebted to Tversky for the challenging and intriguing questions he posed about this issue, as well as for the wisdom and insight of his responses to my queries. While I of course remain wholly responsible for any faults, the structure and content of this section is largely influenced by Tversky's critical contribution to my thinking about this topic.

24. Eldar Shafir, I. Simonson, and Amos Tversky, "Reason-Based Choice," *Cognition* 49 (1993): 11–36. The following discussion is heavily based on this article. I am also indebted to Amos Tversky for personal communication and further insights on this topic.

25. For more on escalation in the face of sunk costs, see J. Schaubroeck and E. Davis, "Prospect Theory Predictions When Escalation Is Not the Only Chance to Recover Sunk Costs," *Organizational Behavior and Human Decision Processes* 57 (1994): 59–89; H. Garland and S. Newport, "Effects of Absolute and Relative Sunk Costs on the Decision to Persist with a Course of Action," *Organizational Behavior and Human Decision Processes* 48 (1991): 55–69; and Glen Whyte, "Escalating Commitment in Individual and Group Decision Making: A Prospect Theory Approach," *Organizational Behavior and Human Decision Processes* 54 (1993): 430–55.

26. Amos Tversky, "Contrasting Rational and Psychological Principles of Choice" (December 1994). Paper presented in "Wise Choices: Games, Decisions and Negotiations," a Colloquium in Honor of Howard Raiffa, 22–24.

27. Ross, "The Intuitive Psychologist and His Shortcomings: Distortions in the Attribution Process."

28. Kenneth Waltz, *Theory of International Politics* (Reading, MA: Addison-Wesley, 1979).

29. Nathan Leites, *A Study of Bolshevism* (New York: Free Press, 1953).

30. Kahneman, Knetsch, and Thaler, "Experimental Tests of the Endowment Effect and the Coase Theorem."

31. Fischhoff, "Predicting Frames," 103–16.

32. Robert Jervis, "Political Implications of Loss Aversion," in *Avoiding Losses/Taking Risks: Prospect Theory in International Conflict,* ed. Barbara Farnham (Ann Arbor: University of Michigan Press, 1994), 23–40.

33. This discussion draws heavily upon Shafir, Simonson, and Tversky, "Reason Based Choice."

34. D. Krantz, "From Indices to Mapping: The Representational Approach to Measurement," in *Frontiers of Mathematical Psychology,* eds. D. Brown and J. Smith (New York: Springer-Verlag, 1991), 1–52. This quote is from page 34.

Bibliography

In addition to the following publications, there is substantial use of archival materials from the Jimmy Carter Presidential Archives Library in Atlanta, Georgia, and the Dwight D. Eisenhower Presidential Archives Library in Abilene, Kansas. Interested readers are directed to specific citations in the relevant case chapters.

Adams, Sherman. *Firsthand Report.* New York: Harper and Brothers, 1961.

Adomeit, Hannes. *Soviet Risk-Taking and Crisis Behavior.* London: George, Allen and Unwin, 1982.

Altman, Lawrence K. "The Shah's Health: A Political Gamble." *New York Times Magazine,* May 26, 1981.

Ambrose, Stephen. *Eisenhower: The President.* New York: Simon and Schuster, 1984.

Ambrose, Stephen. "Secrets of The Cold War." *New York Times,* December 27, 1990.

Argyle, Michael, and J. Crossland. "The Dimensions of Positive Emotions." *British Journal of Social Psychology* 26 (1987): 127–87.

Asch, Solomon. "Opinions and Social Pressure." *Scientific American* 193 (1955): 31–35.

Beck, Aaron, John Rush, Brian F. Shaw, and Gary Emery. *Cognitive Therapy of Depression.* New York: Guilford Press, 1979.

Bem, Daryl. "Self Perception Theory." In *Advances in Experimental Social Psychology,* vol. 6, ed. Leonard Berkowitz, 1–62. New York: Academic Press, 1972.

Bernoulli, Daniel. "Exposition of a New Theory on the Measurement of Risk." *Econometrica* 22 (1954) (Original work published 1738).

Beschloss, Michael. *Mayday.* New York: Harper and Row, 1986.

Blacker, Coit D., and Gloria Duffy. *International Arms Control: Issues and Agreements.* Stanford, CA: Stanford University Press, 1984.

Bower, Gordon. "Mood and Memory." *American Psychologist* 36 (1981).

Bower, Gordon. "Emotion and Social Perception." Paper given to the Western Psychological Association, San Francisco, April 27, 1991.

Bowie, Robert. *Suez 1956.* London: Oxford University Press, 1974.

Brzezinski, Zbigniew. "The Failed Rescue Mission." *New York Times Magazine,* April 18, 1982.

Brzezinski, Zbigniew. *Power and Principle.* New York: Farrar, Straus, and Giroux, 1985.

Bueno de Mesquita, Bruce. *War and Reason.* New Haven: Yale University Press, 1992.

Calvocaressi, Peter. *Suez: Ten Years After; Broadcasts from the British Broadcasting System.* London: British Broadcasting System, 1967.

Carter, Jimmy. *Keeping Faith.* New York: Bantam, 1982.

Christensen-Szalanski, J. J., D. Beck, C. M. Christensen-Szalanski, and T. Koepsell. "Effects of Expertise and Experience on Risk Judgments." *Journal of Applied Psychology* 68 (1983): 278–84.

Christopher, Warren, et al. *American Hostages in Iran.* New Haven: Yale University Press, 1985.

Crosbie, Sylvia. *Tacit Alliance.* Princeton, NJ: Princeton University Press, 1974.

DeConde, Alexander. *A History of American Foreign Policy,* 3d ed. New York: Charles Scribner and Sons, 1978.

Dube-Rioux, L., and J. Russo. "An Availability Bias in Professional Judgment." *Journal of Behavioral Decision Making* 1 (1988): 223–37.

Dulles, Allen., *The Craft of Intelligence.* New York: Harper and Row, 1963.

Ebbeson, Ebbe, and Vladimir Konecni. "On the External Validity of Decision-Making Research: What Do We Know About Decisions in the Real World." In *Cognitive Processes in Choice and Decision Behavior,* ed. T. Wallsten, 21–45. Hillsdale, NJ: Erlbaum, 1980.

Eden, Anthony. *Full Circle.* Boston: Houghton Mifflin, 1960.

Eisenhower, Dwight D. *The White House Years: Waging Peace 1956–1961.* Garden City, NY: Doubleday and Company, 1965.

Eisenhower, John. *Strictly Personal.* Garden City, NY: Doubleday and Company, 1974.

Eisenhower, Milton. *The President Is Calling.* Garden City, NY: Doubleday and Company, 1974.

Elster, Jon. *Rational Choice.* New York: New York University Press, 1986.

Fischhoff, Baruch. "Predicting Frames." *Journal of Experimental Psychology: Learning, Memory, and Cognition* 9 (1983).

Fischhoff, Baruch. "Psychology and Public Policy: Tool or Toolmaker?" *American Psychologist* 45 (1990): 647–53.

Fischhoff, Baruch, Paul Slovic, Sarah Litchenstein, Stephen Read, and Barbara Combs. "How Safe is Safe Enough? A Psychometric Study of Attitudes toward Technological Risks and Benefits." *Policy Sciences* 9 (1978): 127–52.

Fiske, Susan, Donald Kinder, and W. M. Larter, "The Novice and the Expert: Knowledge-Based Strategies in Political Cognition." *Journal of Experimental Social Psycholgy* 19 (1983): 381–400

Fiske, Susan, and Shelley Taylor. *Social Cognition.* New York: McGraw Hill, 1991.

Fullick, Roy. *Suez: The Double War.* London: H. Hamilton, 1979.

Garland, H., and S. Newport. "Effects of Absolute and Relative Sunk Costs on the Decision to Persist with a Course of Action." *Organizational Behavior and Human Decision Processes* 48 (1991): 55–69.

George, Alexander. *Presidential Decisionmaking in Foreign Policy: The Effective Use of Information and Advice.* Boulder, CO: Westview Press, 1980.

Goleman, Daniel. "Hidden Rules Often Distort Ideas of Risk." *The New York Times,* February 1, 1994.

Greenstein, Fred. *The Hidden Hand Presidency.* New York: Basic Books, 1982.

Heidbreder, Edna. *Seven Psychologies.* New York: The Century Co., 1933.

Izard, Carol E. *Human Emotions.* New York: Plenum, 1977.

Izard, Carol, Jerome Kagan, and Robert Zajonc. *Emotions, Cognition, and Behavior.* Cambridge: Cambridge University Press, 1984.

Janis, Irving. *Groupthink.* Boston: Houghton Mifflin Company, 1972.

Janis, Irving, and Leon Mann. *Decision Making.* New York: Free Press, 1977.

Jervis, Robert. *Perception and Misperception in International Politics.* Princeton, NJ: Princeton University Press, 1976.

Jervis, Robert. "Political Implications of Loss Aversion." In *Avoiding Losses/Taking Risks: Prospect Theory in International Conflict,* ed. Barbara Farnham, 23–40. Ann Arbor: University of Michigan Press, 1994.

Johnson, Eric, and Amos Tversky. "Affect, Generalization, and the Perception of Risk." *Journal of Personality and Social Psychology* 45 (1983).

Jordan, Hamilton. *Crisis.* New York: Putnam, 1982.

Kahneman, Daniel, Jack Knetsch, and Richard Thaler. "Experimental Tests of the Endowment Effect and the Coase Theorem." *Journal of Political Economy* 98 (1990): 1325–48.

Kahneman, Daniel, Paul Slovic, and Amos Tversky. *Judgment Under Uncertainty: Heuristics and Biases.* New York: Cambridge University Press, 1982.

Kahneman, Daniel, and Amos Tversky. "Prospect Theory: An Analysis of Decision Under Risk." *Econometrica* 47 (1979).

Kahneman, Daniel, and Amos Tversky. "The Psychology of Preferences." *Scientific American* 246 (1982).

Kahneman, Daniel, and Amos Tversky. "Choices, Values and Frames." *American Psychologist* 39 (April 1984).

Kameda, Tatsuya, and James Davis. "The Function of the Reference Point in Individual and Group Risk Decision Making." *Organizational Behavior and Human Decision Processes* 46 (1990): 55–76.

Khong, Yuen Fung. *Analogies at War.* Princeton, NJ: Princeton University Press, 1991.

Kiesler, T., S. Kiesler, and J. Siegel. "Group and Computer-Mediated Discussion Effects in Risk Decision Making." *Journal of Personality and Social Psychology* 52 (1987).

Kistiakowsky, George. *A Scientist at the White House.* Cambridge: Harvard University Press, 1976.

Kohlberg, Lawrence. "A Cognitive Developmental Analysis of Children's Sex Role Concepts and Attitudes." In *The Development of Sex Differences,* ed. Eleanor Maccoby. Stanford, CA: Stanford University Press, 1966.

Koopman, Cheryl, Rose McDermott, Robert Jervis, Jack Snyder, and Joe Dioso. "Stability and Change in American Elite Beliefs about International Relations." *Peace and Conflict: Journal of Peace Psychology* 1 (1995): 365–82.

Koopman, Cheryl, Jack Snyder, and Robert Jervis. "Theory Driven versus Data Driven Assessment in Crisis: A Survey of *International Security* Readers." *Journal of Conflict Resolution* 34 (1990): 694–722.

Krantz, D. "From Indices to Mapping: The Representational Approach to Measurement." In *Frontiers of Mathematical Psychology*, eds. D. Brown and J. Smith, 1–52. New York: Springer-Verlag, 1991.

LaFeber, Walter. *American, Russia, and the Cold War*, 4th ed., 190–95. New York: John Wiley and Sons, 1980.

Lanir, Zvi, Baruch Fischhoff, and Stephen Johnson. "Military Risk-Taking: C3I and the Cognitive Functions of Boldness in War." *Journal of Strategic Studies* 11 (1988): 96–114.

Leites, Nathan. *A Study of Bolshevism.* New York: Free Press, 1953.

Leventhal, H. "Toward a Comprehensive Theory of Emotion." In *Advances in Experimental Social Psychology*, vol. 13, ed. Leonard Berkowitz, 139–207. New York: Academic Press, 1980.

Leventhal, H. "The Integration of Emotion with Cognition." In *Affect and Cognition*, eds. Michael Clarke and Susan Fiske. Hillsdale, NJ: Erlbaum, 1982.

Leventhal, H., and K. Scherer. "The Relationship of Emotion to Cognition." *Cognition and Emotion* 1 (1987).

Litchenstein, S., Paul Slovic, Baruch Fischhoff, Mark Layman, and Barbara Combs. "Judged Frequency of Lethal Events." *Journal of Experimental Psychology: Human Learning and Memory* 4 (1978): 551–78.

Lloyd, Selwyn. *Suez, 1956.* London: Cape, 1978.

Loke, W. H., and K. F. Tan. "Effects of Framing and Missing Information in Expert and Novice Judgment." *Bulletin of the Psychonomic Society* 30 (1992): 187–90.

Lord, Charles, Lee Ross, and Mark Lepper. "Biased Assimilation and Attitude Polarization: The Effects of Prior Theories on Subsequently Considered Evidence." *Journal of Personality and Social Psychology* 37 (1979): 2098–2109.

Lynn-Jones, Sean, Steven Miller, and Stephen Van Evera, eds. *Nuclear Diplomacy and Crisis Management.* Cambridge: MIT Press, 1990.

McDermott, Rose. "Prospect Theory in International Relations: The Iranian Hostage Rescue Mission." *Political Psychology* 13 (1992): 237–63.

McElroy, Robert. *Morality in American Foreign Policy.* Princeton, NJ: Princeton University Press, 1992.

McNeil, B., S. Parker, H. Sox Jr., and Amos Tversky. "On the Elicitation of Preferences for Alternative Therapies." *New England Journal of Medicine* 306 (1982).

Mercer, Jonathan. *Reputation and International Politics.* Ithaca, NY: Cornell University Press, 1996.

Murphy, Robert. *Diplomat Among Warriors.* New York: Doubleday and Company, 1964.

New York Times, 25 June 1979, 1.

Nisbett, Richard, and Lee Ross. *Human Inference: Strategies and Shortcomings of Social Judgment.* Englewood Cliffs, NJ: Prentice Hall, 1980.

Nisbett, Richard, and T. Wilson. "Telling More Than We Can Know: Verbal Reports on Mental Processes." *Psychological Review* 84 (1977).

Nutting, Anthony. *No End of a Lesson: The Story of Suez.* London: Constable, 1967.

Ornstein, Norman, et al. *Vital Statistics on Congress, 1984–5.* Washington, American Enterprise Institute for Public Policy Research 84.

Pahlavi, Mohammad Reza. *Answer to History.* New York: Stein and Day, 1980.

Paige, Jeffrey M. *Agrarian Revolution: Social Movements and Export Agriculture in the Underdeveloped World.* New York: Free Press, 1975.

Plous, Scott. *The Psychology of Judgment and Decisionmaking.* New York: McGraw-Hill, 1994.

Pollatsek, A., and Amos Tversky. "A Theory of Risk." *Journal of Mathematical Psychology* 7 (1970).

Powell, Jody. *The Other Side of the Story.* New York: William Morrow and Company, Inc., 1984.

Quattrone, George, and Amos Tversky. "Contrasting Rational and Psychological Analyses of Political Choice." *American Political Science Review* 82 (September 1988).

Reston, James. "How to Make Things Worse Than They Really Are." *New York Times,* May 8, 1960, section 4, E 8.

Reston, James. "President Sees Herter in Effort to Lessen Blow to Summit Talks; Soviet Exploits Plane Espionage/Flights Stopped/ Washington is Upset and Humiliated by Spy Developments." *New York Times,* May 9, 1960, 1.

Reston, James. "What Kind of President Do You Want—III?" *New York Times,* May 11, 1960, 38.

Reston, James. "The Political Consequences Following the U-2." *New York Times,* May 13, 1960, 30.

Ross, Lee. "The Intuitive Psychologist and His Shortcomings: Distortions in the Attribution Process." In *Advances in Experimental Social Psychology,* vol. 10, ed. Leonard Berkowitz. New York: Academic Press, 1977.

Ryan, Paul. *The Iranian Rescue Mission.* Annapolis, MD: Naval Institute Press, 1985.

Salinger, Pierre. *America Held Hostage.* Garden City, NY: Doubleday and Company, 1981.

Saunders, Harold. "Beginning of the End." In *American Hostages in Iran,* ed. Warren Christopher. New Haven: Yale University Press, 1985.

Schaubroeck, J., and E. Davis. "Prospect Theory Predictions When Escalation is Not the Only Chance to Recover Sunk Costs." *Organizational Behavior and Human Decision Processes* 57 (1994): 59–89.

Shafir, Eldar, I. Simonson, and Amos Tversky. "Reason-Based Choice." *Cognition* 49 (1993): 11–36.

Shilts, Randy. *And the Band Played On.* New York: Penguin Books, 1988.

Sick, Gary. *All Fall Down.* New York: Penguin Books, 1986.

Sick, Gary. "The Election Story of the Decade." *New York Times,* April 15, 1991.

Simon, Herbert. *Administrative Behavior: A Study of Decision-Making Processes in Administrative Organization,* 3d ed. New York: Free Press, 1976.

Simon, Herbert. "Information Processing Theory of Human Problem Solving." In *Handbook of Learning and Cognitive Processes,* vol. 5, ed. W. K. Estes. Hillsdale, NJ: Erlbaum, 1978.

Simon, Herbert, and James March. "Bounded Rationality, Ambiguity, and the Engineering of Choice." *The Bell Journal of Economics* 9 (1978): 587–608.

Skocpol, Theda, and Margaret Somers. "The Use of Comparative History in Macro-Social Inquiry." *Comparative Studies in Society and History* 22 (April 1980): 174–97.

Slovic, Paul. "Assessment of Risk-Taking Behavior." *Psychological Bulletin,* 61 (1964).

Slovic, Paul. "Perception of Risk." *Science* 236 (1987): 280–85.

Slovic, Paul, Baruch Fischhoff, and Sarah Litchenstein. "Facts vs. Fears: Understanding Perceived Risk." In *Societal Risk Management: How Safe Is Safe Enough?,* eds. R. Schwing and W. A. Albers, Jr. New York: Plenum, 1980.

Slovic, Paul, Baruch Fischhoff, and Sarah Litchenstein. "Response Mode, Framing, and Information Processing Effects in Risk Assessment." In *New Directions for Methodology of Social and Behavioral Science: Question Framing and Response Contingency,* vol. 11, ed. R. Hogarth. San Francisco: Jossey-Bass, March 1982.

Slovic, Paul, Baruch Fischhoff, and Sarah Litchenstein. "Behavioral Decision Theory Perspectives on Risk and Safety." *Acta Pscyhologica* 56 (1984): 183–203.

Slovic, Paul, and Sarah Litchenstein. "Preference Reversals: A Broader Perspective." *American Economic Review* 73 (September 1983).

Slovic, Paul, Shmuel Sattath, and Amos Tversky. "Contingent Weighting in Judgment and Choice." *Psychological Review* 95 (July 1988).

Smith, Terence. "Why Carter Admitted the Shah." *New York Times Magazine,* May 26, 1981.

Smith, Terence. "Putting the Hostages' Lives First." *New York Times Magazine,* May 26, 1981, 93.

Snyder, Mark. "When Belief Creates Reality." In *Advances in Experimental Social Psychology* vol. 18, ed. Leonard Berkowitz, 248–306. New York: Academic Press, 1984.

Starr, Chauncey. "Social Benefit versus Technological Risk." *Science* 165 (1969): 1232–38.

Sullivan, William H. *Mission to Iran.* New York: Norton, 1981.

Taylor, Shelley. "Adjustment to Threatening Events: A Theory of Cognitive Adaptation." *American Psychologist* 38 (1983): 1161–73.

Taylor, Shelley, and Jon Brown. "Illusion and Well-Being: A Social Psychological Perspective on Mental Health." *Psychological Bulletin* 103 (1988): 193–210.

Tetlock, Phil, and Aaron Belkin. *Counterfactual Thought Experiments in World Politics: Political, Methodological and Psychological Perspectives.* Princeton, NJ: Princeton University Press, 1996.

Time, April 14, 1980.

Time, May 5, 1980.

Time, May 12, 1980.

Triska, Jan, and David Finley. *Soviet Foreign Policy.* New York: Macmillan, 1968.

Tversky, Amos. "Elimination by Aspects: A Theory of Choice." *Psychological Review* 79 (1972).

Tversky, Amos. "Contrasting Rational and Psychological Principles of Choice." Paper presented in "Wise Choices: Games, Decisions and Negotiations," a colloquium in honor of Howard Raiffa (December 1994).

Tversky, Amos, and Dale Griffin. "Endowment and Contrast in Judgments of Well-Being." In *Strategy and Choice,* ed. Richard Zeckhauser. Cambridge: MIT Press, 1991.

Tversky, Amos, and Daniel Kahneman. "The Framing of Decisions and the Psychology of Choice." *Science* 211 (January 30, 1981).

Tversky, Amos, and Daniel Kahneman. "Extensional versus Intuitive Reasoning: The Conjunction Fallacy in Probability Judgment." *Psychological Review* 90 (October 1983): 293–315.

Tversky, Amos, and Daniel Kahneman. "Rational Choice and the Framing of Decisions." *Journal of Business* 59 (1986).

Tversky, Amos, and Daniel Kahneman. "Loss Aversion in Choice and Exchange." Unpublished manuscript, Stanford University and University of California, Berkeley, 1990.

Tversky, Amos, and Daniel Kahneman. "Advances in Prospect Theory: Cumulative Representation of Uncertainty." *Journal of Risk and Uncertainty* 5 (1992): 297–323.

Tversky, Amos, Paul Slovic, and Daniel Kahneman. "The Causes of Preference Reversal." *American Economic Review* 80 (March 1990).

U.S. Defense Department, "Rescue Mission Report," August 1980 (typescript). [This is the report issued under the direction of Admiral Holloway.]

Vallone, Robert, Lee Ross, and Mark Lepper. "The Hostile Media Phenomenon: Biased Perception and Perceptions of Media Bias in Coverage of the Beirut Massacre." *Journal of Personality and Social Psychology* 49 (1985): 577–85.

Vance, Cyrus. *Hard Choices.* New York: Simon and Schuster, 1983.

Von Neumann, J., and O. Morgenstern. *Theory of Games and Economic Behavior,* 2d ed. Princeton, NJ: Princeton University Press, 1947.

Wadersman, Abraham, and William Hallman. "Are People Acting Irrationally: Understanding Public Concerns about Environmental Threats." *American Psychologist* 48 (June 1993): 681–86.

Waltz, Kenneth. *Theory of International Relations.* Reading, MA: Addison-Wesley, 1979.

Whyte, Glen. "Escalating Commitment in Individual and Group Decision Making: A Prospect Theory Approach." *Organizational Behavior and Human Decision Processes* 54 (1993): 430–55.

Wise, David, and Thomas B. Ross. *The U-2 Affair.* New York: Random House, 1962.

Zajonc, Robert. "Feeling and Thinking: Preferences Need No Inferences." *American Psychologist* 35 (1980).

Zajonc, Robert. "On the Primacy of Affect." *American Psychologist* 39 (1984).

Zajonc, Robert, and Hazel Marcus. "Affect and Cognition: The Hard Interface."

In *Emotions, Cognition, and Behavior,* eds. C. E. Izard, Jerome Kagan, and Robert Zajonc. Cambridge: Cambridge University Press, 1984.

Zajonc, Robert, P. Pietromonaco, and J. Baugh. "Independence and Interaction of Affect and Cognition." In *Affect and Cognition,* eds. Michael Clarke and Susan Fiske. Hillsdale, NJ: Erlbaum, 1982.

Index

Aaron, David, 91
Acceptance in framing, 22–23
Affect, role of, 170–75, 222–23n. 14
Afghanistan, Soviet invasion of, 61
Algeria and French framing of Suez
  crisis, 135, 147, 153
Anchoring as judgmental heuristic, 6, 7
Anderson, Jack, 70
Aswan Dam, 135
  funding of, 137–38
Availability as judgmental heuristic, 6,
  7, 194–95n. 8

Bani-Sadr, Abolhassan, 46, 57
Base rate, judgmental heuristic of
  representativeness and, 7
Bay of Pigs as historical analogy for
  Iranian hostage rescue mission,
  51–52
Beckel, Bob, 47, 48
Beckwith, Charles, 69
Bernoulli, Daniel, 15–16, 17, 18
Bissell, Richard, 108, 113, 115
  and U-2 incident cover-up, 128
Bohlen, Charles, 116, 117
  and Eisenhower's admission of
    espionage, 119–20
Bonney, Walter, 113
Bowie, Robert, on Suez crisis, 147–48
Brown, Harold, 57, 99
Brzezinski, Zbigniew, 51, 54, 58, 67,
  72–73, 80
  and decision making in denial of
    asylum for the Shah, 92–94
  domain of, in Iranian hostage rescue
    mission, 68

framing of denial of asylum for the
  Shah by, 88–91, 103
framing of Iranian hostage rescue
  mission by, 60–64, 195n. 31
Bulganin, Nikolai, 141, 156, 164

Cabell, Charles, 115
Camp David accords. *See* Middle East
  peace treaty
Cancellation in framing, 22, 23
Carlucci, Frank, 70, 91
Carter, Jimmy, 2, 11, 73–75
  and Brzezinski's framing of Iranian
    hostage rescue mission, 60–64
  decision making of, in Iranian
    hostage rescue mission, 67–73
  decision making of, regarding asy-
    lum for the Shah, 77–81, 91–94,
    97–98
  domain of, in denial of asylum for
    the Shah, 81–83
  domain of, in Iranian hostage rescue
    mission, 47–51
  framing of options by, in Iranian
    hostage rescue mission, 51–
    57
  framing of options by, regarding
    asylum for the Shah, 83–91,
    95–97
  and Jordan's framing of Iranian
    hostage rescue mission, 64–65
  and outcomes of granting asylum to
    the Shah, 98–105
  and Vance's framing of Iranian
    hostage rescue mission, 58–
    60

233